Liberating News

Liberating News

A Theology of
Contextual Evangelization

by

ORLANDO E. COSTAS

WILLIAM B. EERDMANS PUBLISHING COMPANY
GRAND RAPIDS, MICHIGAN

255 Jefferson Ave. S.E., Grand Rapids, Mich. 49503

Printed in the United States of America

Library of Congress Cataloging-in-Publication Data

Costas, Orlando E.
Liberating news: a theology of contextual evangelization /
by Orlando E. Costas.
p. cm.
ISBN 0-8028-0364-4
1. Evangelistic work. 2. Missions—Theory. 3. Christianity and culture.
4. Liberation theology. I. Title.
BV3793.C65 1989
269'.2—dc19 89-1590
CIP

A
Rosalina Rivera
y
Ventura Enrique Costas

Mis padres,

a quienes les debo el conocimiento
del evangelio, por su apoyo moral y
espiritual para su transmisión
a los pueblos de la tierra.

Con afecto,

Orlando E. Costas

Contents

Preface

"The practice of evangelization has been the passion of my ministerial career . . ." I found these words scribbled on a piece of paper on which Orlando had begun writing a preface to this book while still in the hospital. But he did not have the strength to continue; instead, unspoken thoughts trailed without a clue of what he wanted to say. What he did leave me was an inspiring testimony that, during twenty-five years of sharing in life and ministry, revealed a mind, heart, and life transformed by a powerful faith in Jesus Christ, a commitment to put into practice the teachings received as a child from devoted Christian parents, and a passion to communicate the gospel message in all its integrity.

The pilgrimage that took us across various continents to study and work is a narrative packed with stumblings and successes, dreams and visions come true, challenges for growth and maturity, demands and expectations fulfilled, and much more. Orlando's zeal to write at different stages of his missiological development was part of his desire to share—especially with the Latin American world—the research and insights of his own journey of faith as a pastor, evangelist, and missiologist. "One must put things in writing because time is running out," he would often say to me. His mind was never at rest. Daily experiences with and challenges from laity, pastors, and theological peers spawned ideas for new writing projects. Old ideas took new forms; new ones were revised. Indeed, the driving force of the last decade of my husband's life was to piece these ideas together in a book on a contextual theology of evangelization.

For years he struggled with this project, which would encompass his years of involvement in evangelistic programs, his seminars for pastors, and the courses he taught and the lectures he delivered in the Americas and Europe. He envisioned the book as a three-volume project, to be available in both English and Spanish editions, that would provide a theoretical framework of contextual evangelization, intercultural case studies of evangelistic contextualization, and a focus on the method and strategy of contextual evangelization.

When we left for a three-month sabbatical in Israel in February of 1987, Orlando took with him an unfinished manuscript of the first volume. His goal was to complete it and then test parts of it, along with materials for his other volumes. He wanted to undertake this assessment with pastors and theological students at the Free University of Amsterdam, which he planned on doing at the end of his sabbatical, when he was scheduled to teach two intensive one-week courses in Holland. This interaction, he projected, would afford feedback from people in different cultural situations. But the devastating news of the disease that was already ravaging his body terminated his plans for further travel and future writings.

Orlando's hope for this project — which he shared with his sabbatical committee before leaving for Europe — was that it would provide a cross-cultural bridge between the social and personal dimensions of the gospel, the communal and institutional aspects of the church-in-mission, the confessional and ideological boundaries of the ecumenical and missionary church, and the theoretical and practical functions of theology. He wanted the material to enrich the teaching of evangelization in theological seminaries in both of the Americas. His vision was that readers would be led to practice a renewed evangelization, faithful to the Word of God and incarnated in their respective contexts.

If some of these goals can be met through the pages that follow, then the soul and body-wrenching pain of Orlando's last months of life, spent to give final witness to the liberating message of the cross, will not be in vain. To God be the glory and the honor!

Rose L. Feliciano Costas
November 1988

Introduction

Orlando Costas did what he said. He taught us about the fullness of the gospel, and he lived it. Behind this work about an evangelism that is Good News for both the sinner and the sufferer is an evangelist who embodied the *integrity* of mission (so the title of one of his works, *The Integrity of Mission*).

I first became aware of this pioneer of "holistic evangelism" when reading his ground-breaking work on missiology entitled *The Church and Its Mission,* published in 1974. Yes, it *was* "a shattering critique from the Third World," as the subtitle proclaimed! Criticizing both church-growth theory and liberation theology as half-truths? Holding out for both a radical Word and a radical deed? This was news — liberating news, because evangelism in the 1970s was regularly polarized between the tellers and the doers. So began the long friendship between Orlando and me, one that went from association in the Word-in- deed evangelism movement of the United Church of Christ to comradeship on picket lines and colleagueship in academia.

Along the way I could see the ideas in *Liberating News* taking shape, crystallizing in an outline that Orlando developed in 1983 called "Out of the Depths: A Contextual Theology of Evangelism." Several years later, in 1987, Orlando expressed satisfaction with the near-finished project in a letter he wrote to me during his Jerusalem sabbatical: "I have now completed six of the eight chapters, am in the midst of the seventh, and have done some research for the eighth. . . . One more to go!" These were weighty words, because Orlando had just learned about the dangers of his physical condition. In those closing months, with the indispensable help of his life partner, Rose, he finished the book, and the race (2 Tim. 4:7). We now have in our hands a theology of evangelization that is destined to become a classic in the field.

Remembering the time of tribulation in which these pages were written opens up their deep meaning:

> To live in the Spirit is to experience joy when all around seem so sad, to hope even where there seems to be so little to be so little to be hoped for. . . . That is what the message of the cross is all about: life through death and hope beyond it. . . . Where there is hope there is the certainty of love, because there is God —the Alpha and Omega, the great One from whom no one, nor anything, can separate us (Rom. 8:31ff.).*

Orlando's life and work are marked by the same unswervingness of purpose that saw this volume through to the end. Implacable, passionate determination—what else would we expect from an evangelist? Here is a gift from God, a charism given to some in the church, without which the Body would wither and die. It accounts for Orlando's wide personal influence and remarkable institutional achievements: his founding of CELEP, his formative role in ABC (American Baptist Churches) and UCC (United Church of Christ) mission strategies and actions, his mentoring of countless students and pastors, his impact on the North American Hispanic community, his leadership role in both evangelical and ecumenical circles, the changes he effected in the educational institutions in which he worked (for example, the vision of global Christianity, international mission, and multicultural richness that he as dean, together with George Peck as president, brought to Andover Newton), and much more. Colleagues who held vigil with Orlando's family by his bedside in his last pain-wracked months were amazed by the phone calls and correspondence that came from around the world, testifying to this legacy.

Of course, vision and determination can invite resistance as well as effect change. Implacability can be viewed as inflexibility! What prophet has not been so accused of—and indeed been subject to—just those temptations? But in the end we thank you, Lord, for stubborn visionaries, and especially for this one.

*This and subsequent quotations were taken from an early typescript of this book.

An outstanding aspect of Orlando's *theoria* and *praxis* is, of course, contextuality. "The gospel cannot be shared in a sociocultural vacuum," he declares in this book. And the gospel should be shared from a particular sociocultural context: "Evangelization is to be undertaken . . . from below . . . from the depth of human suffering," with a view to the "transformation of a world of fears and tears into a new order of peace and justice, laughter and joy." The Good News is *liberating* for "both sinners and the victims of sin." Traditional evangelism stresses the former but often forgets the latter. But Orlando ever and again reminded us of the wholeness of mission. The plight of the poor in the barrios of Montevideo and the tenements of East Harlem must be at the heart of holistic evangelism.

Further, the contextual act of solidarity with the sufferer is *more* than social-service ministries that care for the hurt and the helpless after the damage is done, important as these ministries are. Contextual evangelism means a social action that seeks to remove the systemic causes of human misery. This is no Dale Carnegie approach calculated only to "win friends and influence people." If our chief Evangelist admonished us to love our enemies, then we must be ready to make some. This costly obedience to the reign of God is the subject of a Nicaraguan song that Orlando loved and that he and Rose translated:

> Sent by the Lord am I.
> My hands are ready now
> to help construct a just
> and peaceful loving world.
> The angels cannot change
> a world of pain and hurt
> into a world of love,
> of justice and of peace.
> The task is mine to do.
> Make it reality—
> O help me, God, obey,
> help me to do your will.

Orlando has hard words for all kinds of culturally domesticated evangelism: "The problem with a lot of activities that pass for evangelization is that they fail to meet the test of the cross. The gospel they proclaim has been made such a marketable message with a plastic Jesus and an inoffensive call . . . carbon copies of a consumerist society."

Contextual evangelization means "no cross, no crown," no reconciliation without liberation.

Liberation, yes—but *news* too. This is a gospel for sinners as well as for victims of sin, Orlando points out: "The communication of God's liberating news is centered on the cross of Jesus Christ and leads to a call to conversion. The gospel issues an invitation to experience a new life in the Holy Spirit through repentance and faith in Christ." Social action without the proclamation of the gospel and the call to conversion is a half-executed mission. The evangelical Word is inseparable from the liberating deed.

On the day I write this—the first anniversary of Orlando's death—some words of his carry special power for me. They speak of the full gospel—of faith, hope, and love. To this evangel his whole life and ministry bore witness. Trusting in this gospel, Orlando met the last enemy.

> The proclamation of the cross is, therefore, the communication of liberating news—the message of life, of hope and love through faith in the one who suffered death and shame for all, that all might live, look to the future with hope, and be assured of God's love, which surpasses all odds. We live, accordingly, hoping and loving.

Gabriel Fackre
5 November 1988

CHAPTER I

Theology, Context, and Evangelization

The Theoretical Framework

Theology and evangelization are two interrelated aspects of the life and mission of the Christian faith. Theology studies the faith; evangelization is the process by which it is communicated. Theology plumbs the depth of the Christian faith; evangelization enables the church to extend it to the ends of the earth and the depth of human life. Theology reflects critically on the church's practice of the faith; evangelization keeps the faith from becoming the practice of an exclusive social group. Theology enables evangelization to transmit the faith with integrity by clarifying and organizing its content, analyzing its context, and critically evaluating its communication. Evangelization enables theology to be an effective servant of the faith by relating its message to the deepest spiritual needs of humankind.

It is unfortunate that too often these two complementary ministries have been viewed as adversaries rather than partners. Theologians say relatively little about evangelization, and missionaries and evangelists have a hard time seeing the relevance of theology for their task. Theologians need to be reminded that mission (as primary evangelization) "is the mother of theology" (Kaehler) because it is the process by which the church comes into being. Missionaries and evangelists need to be made aware of the fact that theology is the spinal cord of the church: it strengthens it and helps it to stand tall. Without theology, the church runs the risk of collapsing, unable to understand itself or its message and mission in the world, ill-equipped both intellectually and spiritually to deal with the challenges of its social context. Without evangelization, theology is reduced to an academic, abstract, and exclusive intellectual exercise of little service to a faith that is inherently open and oriented to the world.

Theology and evangelization not only have complementary roles in the Christian faith but need each other to fulfill these roles. It is necessary, therefore, to understand the nature and function of theology in the context of evangelization and to reflect on evangelization in a theological context.

All religious communities have their theologies, be they explicit or implicit. They have their own way of thinking and explicating their convictions and teachings. Christian theology is the reflective process by which the Christian community seeks to understand and articulate the meaning and implications of its faith.

A Constructive Discourse

The term "theology" means literally a rational discourse about God (Gr. *theos* = God, *logos* = reasoned discourse). To say that theology is a rational, or reasoned, discourse is not to locate it in the domain of pure reason. Christian theology is not an abstract, speculative, or purely rational reflection—although, to be sure, it is philosophical in the sense that it is a theoretical, intellectual, ordered reflection on the structure, categories, and concepts of reality as a whole and their meaning for the people of God.[1] But Christian theology cannot be simply a philosophy—a discourse on human wisdom that stands on pure reason—because it stands on revelation, or the process by which God (ultimate reality) is known in the community of faith.

For Christians, theology is the intelligence of faith. It is that reflection which seeks to understand the content of faith and its implications for life. Christian faith derives its content from God's self-revelation. In this process God is disclosed as love, as the one who is holy and just; as creator, redeemer, sanctifier, and sovereign; as father and mother, brother and sister, and friend—in short, as transcendent and immanent.

God's self-disclosure also mirrors our own human reality; in it we are able to see reflected who we really are, where we come from, and what our destiny is. In this sense, theology is theological anthropology (a reflection on humanity from the perspective of divine revelation).

The purpose of revelation is the true knowledge of God and ourselves. This knowledge is made available in the communion of faith. The church is the community that has appropriated this knowledge and bears witness to it in the world.

Revelation is divine speech—God's Word. This is not to be understood simply as a codification of concepts or propositions, but as history-making creative events, pregnant with meaning. God's Word comes to us "in many and various ways" (Heb. 1:1; cf. Ps. 19:1; Rom. 1:19-20; 2:15). For Christians, the clearest, most concrete and definitive expression of God's Word is Jesus of Nazareth in his life and work (Heb. 1:2; John 1:1-3, 14). The meaning and significance of Jesus, God's Incarnate Word, continue to make themselves known to us. For as the Book of Revelation tells us, "he has a name . . . which no one knows but himself" (Rev. 19:12). It can be argued that the self-disclosure that comes through God's Word has not yet concluded, although we have sufficient "light" to come to a certain (though open) saving knowledge of God through the revelation that has already been made available in Jesus of Nazareth. He is, therefore, the norm of Christian theology.

This revelation that has come to us and continues to shed light on our path is witnessed to in various sources. The term "source" brings to mind several images. It is used to designate the fountainhead, or origin, of a river or stream, a spring or the place where a flow of water begins. It is also used in reference to generating power. It may further be understood as a starting point, an initiator (author), or a work that supplies information. All these images help us understand what is meant by the sources of Christian theology.

First, a theological source is a revelatory spring. It is a fountainhead of faith. It is a place where we find the foundational content of Christian faith. Second, a theological source is a generating nucleus of faith—in other words, a location where theological reflection is stimulated, a pivot around which theology revolves. Third, a theological source is an information center. As a point of departure for and foundational witness to the faith, it is a referent that confronts us with its truth over against which we may judge the truth of our articulation of the faith.

There are three basic sources of Christian theology: Scripture, tradition, and experience.[2] Of these, the primary source is *Scripture,* which for Christians is made up of the Hebrew Scriptures, otherwise known as the Old Testament, and the New Testament. This is the faithful record of God's saving deeds in ancient Israel and the early Christian community. It testifies to God's self-disclosure as witnessed to and interpreted by the people of God through music and poetry, prayers and liturgies, historical narratives, religious instruction, and preaching —materials recorded, edited, and integrated into a library (Bible) of authorized writings (canon). Christians recognize the Bible as God's Word insofar as it is the written record of God's revelation and the product of the inspirational activity of the Holy Spirit (who "breathed" inspiration into its complex list of collaborators), God's saving word amidst the frail and fallible reality of human history.[3] As God's written Word, it finds its foundational reference in Jesus Christ, the Incarnate Word, and is confirmed by the power of the Holy Spirit, manifested in the proclamation and teaching of the gospel and its saving effect in the life and mission of the community of faith. This explains why many Christians consider the Bible to be a rule of faith and practice: it instructs, reproves, corrects, and guides in the practice of faith (cf. 2 Tim. 3:16-17).

The second source, *tradition,* is the process through which the Christian community transmits the legacy of the faith to new generations. This includes the canonical Scriptures and their central message —namely, the gospel of God revealed in Jesus Christ. It also includes the diverse Christian communities that have sprung up over time and space, with their divergent interpretations of the faith and the universality of their essential message expressed in the various ecumenical creeds, ecclesiastical confessions, and covenants of faith. Through tradition the church preserves its legacy. Thus the biblical canon set boundaries for the body of recognized writings in accordance with broad guidelines mutually accepted by the church at large over a period of nearly five centuries. The same principle applies to the apostolic rule of faith—namely, the *kerygma,* or proclamation of the gospel. It is by the transmission of the gospel that faithfulness to the apostolicity (sent-forth, or missionary character) of the church is maintained. The transmission of the faith is the product and verification of its apostolic legacy.

Tradition, however, is not only a process of transmission and preservation of the church's faith; it is also a process of the reformulation and reconstruction of the church's mission. It is not static but dynamic, moving from generation to generation across many boundaries and becoming part of the life and thought of many people. Tradition makes possible new images and concepts. Indeed, it serves as witness to and filter for the new "light" that breaks through with fresh theological insights as the Christian community confronts new challenges and transmits the gospel across time and space. Tradition is, therefore, a source of theological reflection because it receives, filters, and yields new insights concerning God's mystery and mighty deeds in the world.[4] These insights, of course, cannot contradict the *explicit* teachings of the Scriptures; if they did, they would be in direct opposition to the primary witness of the faith. However, they do clarify, expand, and deepen the explicit teaching of the Scriptures and the corroborated witness of tradition. Consequently, they instruct and edify God's people, stimulating and encouraging them in their pilgrimage toward the kingdom of God.

As for *experience,* it is the peculiar manner by which persons and communities enter into contact with the faith and interpret and incorporate it into their own history. This view is based on an understanding of experience as a learning process that occurs through direct contact with persons and things. All experiences employ an "encounter" with someone or something, the assimilation of perceptions and their interpretations. All experiences are part of events which integrate the person and the collective, culture and history. *Christian* experience is the process by which women and men encounter God-in-Christ, assimilate the perception of that event, and begin a long pilgrimage of exploration into the meaning and implications of that encounter. It is a subjective (internal) event because it involves direct communion with God. It also has an objective dimension because it originates externally and is informed and confirmed externally. Such an encounter appears as God-initiated, yet its perception is informed by the written Word transmitted by tradition.

Christian experience is holistic insofar as it involves an event both personal and communal. It also involves experience both cultural and religious. It is important to properly stress these multiple factors in Christian experience. If the intimate and personal (existential and mystical) are overstressed, one ends up reducing God to the realm of the private. If the sociocultural element is overstressed, God and culture become indistinguishable—or, worst yet, God ends up being absorbed into history itself. There is, therefore, a dialectical tension in the all-encompassing wholeness of Christian experience between the personal and the communal, between the historico-socio-cultural and the religious.

Experience may open up previously undiscovered dimensions of the faith through varied and dynamic events. This explains the importance of world evangelization: it enables the faith to spread across new frontiers and thereby acquire richer images, brighter concepts, and deeper insights into the meaning of the faith. Such Christian experience needs to be verified externally through a process of critical evaluation. Its contribution to Christian knowledge is determined by Scripture and tradition. Thus it cannot substitute for or contradict the clear teaching of Scripture, or stand over against the confirmed witness of tradition. Its function as a source of Christian knowledge is to be understood in the context of Scripture and tradition. This means that not all the sources of theology have equal value, although each has a role to play.

Theology clarifies in an ordered and coherent manner the faith that the Christian church has received, lives, professes, and proclaims to the world. It studies and organizes what Christians believe and practice in light of the three sources just mentioned, and it does so in relation to the challenges that the church faces in its life and mission.

A Critical Reflection

Because theology seeks to plumb the depths of faith and respond to the challenges of history, it engages in a rigorous quest for truth. This search is unlike the insatiable quest that marked the Enlightenment, which discarded the possibility of truth in any discourse that did not submit itself to pure reason. Theology incorporates the critical (scientific) method of inquiry into the truth, treating that method as a discipline at the service of faith, not as a field of learning which disregards the reality of faith. Thus theology is a critical discipline that seeks to understand the mystery of faith, which points to a reality whose disclosure is not readily available to the inquiring mind. Indeed, the knowledge of God does not come merely or even primarily as the result of intellectual effort. For God is not an object that can be analyzed and dissected like a plant or a body. Nor, as we have noted, is God a pure concept that can be studied abstractly. The knowledge of God is, above all else, communion with God, the experience of God's presence, the fulfillment of God's will, and participation in God's mission. It is a holistic knowledge because it is relational, experiential, ethical, and missional.

Such knowledge is made possible by the gift of faith. This is the grace God gives us to move beyond reliance on ourselves and to trust in him and commit our lives to his care and service. Faith presupposes understanding and praxis as well as trust and commitment. To know God is to engage in a quest for an intellectual apprehension of all that God has made known in revelation. Faith seeks understanding (Anselm), and therefore probes into the depths of God's mystery. It also requires *praxis*—that is, hearing and doing God's Word, reflecting on God's path and following it. Faith means, then, obedience to God's will, and leads to a holistic knowledge of God.

In Christian theology, the knowledge of God is mediated by Jesus Christ, the eternal Son of God. It is through him that we are able to enter into communion with God. In the words of John's Gospel, we know "the only true God" through Jesus Christ, "who . . . has made him known" (John 17:3; 1:18). The gift of faith is made available by the power of the Holy Spirit. The Spirit is the divine agent who animates or energizes faith, and thereby facilitates the experience of God in Christ. The Spirit makes it possible for us to move beyond our close circles, making us conscious of God's eternal love and helping us to trust in and commit ourselves to Jesus Christ as the sole guarantee of that love. In other words, the Spirit reveals God's love in Christ and makes possible an obedient response through Christian praxis.

A Contextual Endeavor

Christian theology is not only a constructive and critical discourse on the God of revelation whom we know through Jesus Christ by the power of the Holy Spirit. It is also a contextual endeavor to interpret the faith. The context of theology is not just the concrete historical, social, cultural, and religious reality in which the Christian community lives, confesses the faith, and reflects upon it. It is also the web of relationships that shape its theological sources. Theology is concerned with the complex dynamics in which the faith originates and is transmitted and experienced, and how such complexity informs and shapes its understanding and communication in particular situations.[5] Theology is further concerned with the questions that these situations pose to the faith—how they affect the interpretation of Scripture, tradition, and Christian experience and lead to a renewed articulation of the faith. For, as Juan Luis Segundo has stated, "Each new reality obliges us to interpret the Word of God afresh, to change reality accordingly, and then go back and re-interpret the Word of God again."[6]

Christian theology is by its very nature contextual. It passes through a hermeneutical "circulation," a process that aims at a new understanding of the past and present of the faith in the hope of transforming its future practice. According to Segundo, such a process imposes a double condition. First, it requires that the questions rising out of the present be "rich enough, general enough and basic enough to force the theological community to change its customary conception of life, death, knowledge, society, politics and the world in general."[7] If the outlook remains the same, it is because the questions that are being asked are superficial. A second condition is that the responses to the new questions change the customary way of interpreting Scripture. Even if the questions are rich enough to change the theologian's outlook on life, the hermeneutical process is truncated if these questions do not lead to a new way of interpreting the primary source of the faith.

C. René Padilla, closely paralleling Segundo's four-step "hermeneutical circulation,"[8] has suggested that a contextual hermeneutical approach involves a dialogue between the interpreter's historical context and Scripture, between the interpreter's particular perspective (world-and-life view) and Scripture, and between the situation and the interpreter's particular understanding of Scripture (theology). He points out that inadequate understandings of issues can produce inadequate questions:

> We begin . . . by analyzing our situation, listening to the questions raised within it. Then we come to Scripture asking, "What does God say through Scripture regarding this particular problem?" The way we formulate our questions will depend, of

> course, on our world-and-life view; that is, the historical situation can only approach Scripture through the current world-and-life view of the interpreters. Lack of a good understanding of the real issues involved in living in a particular situation will be reflected in inadequate or misdirected questions, and this will hinder our understanding of the relevance of the biblical message to that situation.
>
> On the other hand, the better our understanding of the real issues in our context, the better will be the questions which we address to Scripture. This makes possible new readings of Scripture in which the implication of its message for our situation will be more fully uncovered. If it is true that Scripture illuminates life, it is also true that life illuminates Scripture.
>
> As the answers of Scripture come to light, the initial questions which arose in our concrete situation may have to be reformulated to reflect the biblical perspective more adequately. The content of theology, therefore, includes not only answers to specific questions raised by the situation but also questions which the text itself poses to the situation. . . .
>
> The deeper and richer our comprehension of the biblical text, the deeper and richer will be our understanding of the historical context (including the issues that yet have to be faced) and of the meaning of Christian obedience in that particular context.[9]

This model is helpful insofar as it takes Scripture seriously as a primary source of revelation and yet is open to the questions raised by the interpreter's historical situation. It also recognizes the need to analyze the interpreting context and acknowledges the influential role of the particular perspective of the interpreter. However, it does not take into account the influential role of tradition in delivering Scripture to the interpreting community. Nor does it consider the fact that Scripture itself has its own hermeneutical circulation. It takes more than grammatical and historical analysis to recover the biblical text and its original intent and canonical function, as recent biblical scholars and theologians have pointed out.[10] Nevertheless, the fact that the end product (theology) is brought to bear upon the historical situation with new questions posed by Scripture and a clearer and deeper Christian obedience gives "a spiral structure" to the hermeneutical process. This enables theology to be ever more relevant and renovating, and leads to a more faithful contextual witness to the gospel.

Theology as a contextual endeavor takes seriously into account the experience and sociohistorical location of the hermeneutical community. It is also conscious of the role of tradition in the hermeneutical community's reading of the biblical text. The role of tradition is in turn mediated by the experience of the community. Experience shapes the community's appropriation of tradition, and vice versa. Thus, for instance, a Protestant or Catholic experience of faith undoubtedly affects the way tradition is read and handled. Similarly, the Christian experience of racial minorities, women, and the poor in general affects their analysis of Scripture and tradition. In each of these cases, text and tradition will be seen through the spectacles of particular experience.

A Particular Sociohistorical Location and Theological Tradition

This book is informed by the experience of oppressed racial-minority Christians in North America in solidarity with other oppressed groups and the poor majorities of the Two Thirds World.[11] More specifically, it is rooted in the experience of North American Hispanic Christians and their Latin American brothers and sisters. Elsewhere I have described both the historical context of these sociological blocks and the nature of their Christian experience.[12] Here I should like to add that this experience is informed and confirmed by a "radical evangelical tradition." This particular tradition represents a stream of evangelical theology and spirituality with a burning passion for world evangelization, and it is undergirded by four theological principles: Scripture as a rule of faith and practice, salvation by grace through faith, conversion as a distinct experience of faith and a landmark of Christian identity, and the demonstration of the "new life" through piety and moral discipline. The distinctiveness of the radical evangelical tradition is particularly evident in its insistence on taking its missiological concern and theological principles to their roots and ultimate consequences. As a result, it has been influential in such "world formative"[13] movements as the Wesleyan movement in Great Britain, the early Baptist mission of William Carey in Bengal (India), the Moravian missions during the eighteenth century, the antislavery movement in Britain and the United States, the early feminist and Social Gospel movements in nineteenth-century North America, and, more recently, the civil rights movement and the Witness for Peace movement.[14] We might further argue that in terms of its spiritual roots and social impact, the radical evangelical tradition has links with the twelfth-century Waldensian movement, the thirteenth-century Franciscan and Dominican friars, the sixteenth-century Spanish mystics, the apostolate of Bartolomé de las Casas in New Spain (seventeenth century), and the Basic Ecclesial Community movement in contemporary Latin America.

To be sure, radical evangelicals stand in the larger tradition of the sixteenth-century Protestant Reformation. As such, they look to the authority of the Bible as a rule of faith and practice. Radical evangelicals have been basically concerned not with a theoretical view of the Bible (the doctrine of inspiration) but with its content and implication for life.[15] This has been reinforced by spiritual and theological ties with early Calvinistic "social piety,"[16] the Anabaptist emphasis on "evangelical ethics,"[17] and the so-called Second Reformation (the Pietist movement of the seventeenth and eighteenth centuries, including the evangelical awakening in the British Isles, which sought to complete the first theological Reformation by advocating the reformation of life).[18] These and subsequent movements (e.g., North American revivalism, the Holiness movement, and the Afro-American religious movement[19]) have kept alive, in various and sundry ways, the biblical emphasis on the praxis of faith. Thus radical evangelicals approach Scripture as a rule of practical faith—that is, a faith that becomes flesh, that is spiritually energizing and, therefore, historically transformative.

The experience of North American racial-minority Christians in general and of Hispanics and Latin Americans in particular can be described as unique expressions of, or closely related to, the radical evangelical tradition. Their songs and prayers, sermons and testimonies, festivities and dramatizations—all reflect a biblical faith with a transformative, liberating thrust. Because they find themselves in a marginal and oppressive situation, they often articulate this practical dynamic in terms of survival and hope. Thus James H. Cone describes the Christian experience of his childhood congregation in Bearden, Arkansas: At Macedonia African Methodist Episcopal Church (A.M.S.) he and fellow church members "encountered the presence of the divine Spirit, and their souls were moved and filled with an aspiration for freedom." He adds, "Through prayer, song, and sermon, God made frequent visits to the black community in Bearden and reassured the people of his concern for their well-being and his will to bring them safely home."[20]

The experience of black Christians has been duplicated over and over in the life struggles of other North American minority Christians. Paul Nagano, for example, is a Japanese-American Baptist minister who as a young man had to spend two years in a North American concentration camp during World War II. When I visited him at his home in Seattle, Washington, he shared with me how he and other Japanese Christians were able, through their faith in Jesus Christ, to survive and overcome such a humiliating ordeal. After he left the concentration camp, he attended Bethel Seminary in St. Paul, Minnesota.

Like Black-American and Asian-American Christians, Hispanic Americans have learned to survive and hope through their faith in Christ and the living out of that faith in the ecclesial community. When Piri Thomas, a Puerto Rican ex-convict in New York City, returned to his aunt's apartment in East Harlem after serving six years in Sing Sing Prison on a fifteen-year sentence for armed robbery, he was captivated by the spirituality of her Pentecostal Christian faith. He asked her about the meaning of her faith, and she answered, "'It's what gives us poor people strength to live in these conditions. It's like being part of a familia that is together in Cristo and we help each other with the little materials we may possess.'"[21] A few weeks later Piri visited his aunt's storefront church and was deeply moved by the sermon and the call to confess Jesus Christ as personal savior. He describes the nature of his walk to the altar in response to the gospel call:

> This walk was nothing like I ever took. It was different. There wasn't anybody waiting at the end to hurt me. It wasn't like the long walk down El Barrio's streets on the way to a bop, or to pull a job—or holding my bloody side, stumbling and walking down that long cold street. It wasn't nothing like the long walks through the echoing Tombs—or the way to Courts—or the walk before the Big Judge. Oh, God, it wasn't like the long walk through the long years in prison through cell hall blocks and green-barred cell tiers—or the long wait and long walk to see the Wise Men, the Parole Board, and going back again after two years. It wasn't like the long walk from one prison to another,

> from one court to another—or the long walk to freedom with the long invisible rope around my neck held by a probation officer and a parole officer. It was unlike any of my long walks. This one hadda be for something better. This one couldn't be a blank —it hadda be for real. I was gonna be somebody after this long walk. I was gonna be a positive power—like I said—like the Big Man said—like on the kick of "Suffer the little children to come unto me."[22]

The kind of personal liberating experience Piri Thomas had is common among Hispanic Christians in urban North America. For many Mexican-Americans in the Southwest, however, Christian faith is part of a long cultural experience, the fruit of the inculturation of the gospel in "the Mexican-American way of life," which has begun to be reappropriated through the rediscovery of the gospel. According to Virgilio Elizondo,

> The ensemble of the yearly celebrations of the people is . . . the *living Christian creed* of the Mexican-American ecclesial community. It does not so much *recite* the creed in an abstract way as *live* it out, celebrate it, and transmit it in real life and a life-filled celebration. Our confession of faith is lived out in the language, songs, gestures, dramatizations, and symbols of the people. It is our Christian tradition. It is our creed as received, interiorized, and expressed collectively by our faith community.[23]

During the last several decades, Catholic and Protestant Christians in Latin America, like their Hispanic counterparts in North America, have experienced an authentic spiritual awakening. This experience can be described as a rediscovery of the personal and social dimensions of the gospel. Protestants, who have experienced Christ as their personal savior from sin and death, have increasingly been coming to terms with the fact that Jesus is also concerned with the sociopolitical aspirations of people. Catholics, who in the past found it easier to relate Christ to culture, have come to realize the need for the personal appropriation of the faith and the need in Latin America for a re-evangelization of a culture that has become increasingly secular.[24] What has led to this experience of spiritual renewal is what Esther and Mortimer Arias have described as "the discovery of the poor" and the concomitant rediscovery of "the gospel."[25] The Third Catholic Bishop's Conference, which met in Puebla, Mexico, in 1979, evidenced this two-pronged renewal. It acknowledged that the poor are a key to an adequate understanding of the gospel and its proclamation in the world:

> The poor are the first addressees of mission—in Jesus and in His Church. And the poor have also a potential for evangelization, because they question the Church constantly, calling her to conversion, and because many of them carry out in their lives the evangelical values of solidarity, service, simplicity and availability to receive God's gift.
>
> In coming near to the poor to accompany and serve him or her, we are doing what Jesus taught us, when he became our brother, poor as we are. Consequently, our service to the poor is the privileged criterion, though not exclusive, of our following Christ. The best service to our brother or sister is evangelization which prepares him or her to become children of God, to liberate them from injustices and promote their whole human life.[26]

A few months after the Puebla meeting, Latin American Protestants meeting in a continental assembly at Oaxtepec, Mexico, also acknowledged the importance of the poor and oppressed in evangelization:

> We have heard . . . the urgent call to integral holistic proclamation of the Gospel. We have recognized that the Church is inserted in a reality which shows the consequences of sin and that it participates in this reality. We have been challenged to look for the . . . Kingdom in the midst of great contradictions and the poignant needs of our peoples. . . .
>
> We confess that our indifference to the cry of the most forgotten, most oppressed and most needy sectors of our countries is a contradiction to the demands of the Gospel. We confess that we have not always been listening to the voice of our Lord, claiming us to take solidaristic and efficacious actions in favor of those who suffer.
>
> We make a joint call to Christians in Latin America to respond to the demands of the justice of the Kingdom in an obedient and radical discipleship.[27]

The remarkable convergence between Catholics and Protestants in Latin America and Hispanic North America concerning the cry of the poor and the promise of the gospel reflects the ecumenical nature of a spiritual experience that can only be described as an authentic spiritual and theological awakening.[28] For in discovering the poor, the powerless, and the oppressed (i.e., those who have been locked out of history or treated as outsiders and considered nonpersons) as the privileged addressees of the gospel, Latin American Christians have also experienced the gospel as life and joy in an environment of death and misery.[29] Indeed, it is among the poor and disenfranchised of the world that by and large (though by no means exclusively) we find the signs of the presence of the new world promised in the gospel (the personal and social experience of love and freedom, justice and peace) in ways that, if small and provisional, are historically concrete.

It should come as no surprise that at the heart of this spiritual awakening of Christ's church among the poor, powerless, and oppressed lies the awareness of evangelization as a privilege, a responsibility, and an opportunity "in an age of deadly illusions, false dreams, and alienating ideologies."[30] Sharing the vision of evangelization from the "under" and "outerside" of life, where singing "the Lord's song in a foreign land" (Ps. 137:4) has become a gift of the Spirit, is the privilege, responsibility, and opportunity of Hispanics and other North American racial-minority Christians and their Latin American sisters and brothers.

This book is inspired by that vision. It is written, in fact, for and on behalf of those who have been witnesses of such an experience, as a theological contribution to their own praxis and the evangelizing vocation of the Christian church at large. It is also written against the backdrop of the radical evangelical tradition in dialogue with other streams of the larger ecumenical church, even as the experience of Hispanics and other North American racial minorities is linked to that of Latin American Christians—and, we might add, to the corresponding experiences of Christians elsewhere in the Two Thirds World. From this experiential vantage point, situated, as it were, on the periphery of the Americas, and filtered through the radical evangelical tradition and the ecumenical process of traditioning, I propose to engage in a constructive, critical, and contextual theological reflection on evangelization as a prophetic and apostolic task in light of Scripture as a prophetic and apostolic text.

A Prophetic and Apostolic Foundation

It is readily acknowledged that God's written Word passed through human hands. Everything that is found in Scripture was written by human beings, as we have noted, "to instruct" us "for salvation" (2 Tim. 3:15). And in the process of instructing for salvation, in the fulfillment of the prophetic and apostolic tasks (1 Pet. 2:9-10; 2 Cor. 5:20), the human authors of Scripture were "moved by the Holy Spirit" (2 Pet. 1:21). Their teaching, witness, and proclamation were instrumental in conveying God's Word. God uses the fulfillment of the prophetic and apostolic mission, the oral word, the word of the gospel (Rom. 10:14-18) to "breathe" (Gr. *theopneustos*—2 Tim. 3:15) God's own Word. The word of the prophets and the apostles is thus "truly God's Word addressed" to humanity.[31] The church is "built upon the foundation of the apostles and prophets, Christ Jesus himself being the cornerstone" (Eph. 2:20). Their word, being the initial proclamation of the gospel, becomes the ground upon which the church's mission is built. The church is the successor of the prophets and the apostles. Its evangelizing mission is a prophetic and apostolic task. What makes this succession possible is the written text, wherein God's Word, revealed through the prophetic and apostolic word, is faithfully transmitted. As Karl Barth has also pointed out,

> Everything depends for the idea of a living succession upon the *antecessor* being thought of as still alive and possessed of free power as compared with the *successor.* But if, as is the case here, the *antecessor* is one who has long been dead, this can only happen when his proclamation is fixed in writing and when it is recognized that he still has life and free power today over the Church in this very written Word of his. It is upon the written nature of the canon, upon its character as *scriptura sacra,* that its autonomy and independence hang, and therefore its free power towards the Church, and therefore the living nature of the succession. Of course it might also have pleased God to give His Church the canon in the form of an unwritten prophetic and apostolic tradition. . . . [But this would leave the canon] as faintly distinguishable from the life of the Church, as we can distinguish the blood of our fathers which flows in our veins from our own blood; in other words, the Church is once more left to her soli-

> tary self and concentrated upon herself, upon her own aliveness. Whatever such spiritual-oral tradition there may be in the Church, obviously it cannot possess the character of an authority irremovably confronting the Church, because it lacks the written form. In the unwritten tradition the Church is not addressed, but is engaged in a dialogue with herself.[32]

The biblical text is, still, a *human* word, even though God breathed it. The fact that the words of the prophets and the apostles are used to transmit God's Word does not exempt Scripture from historical conditioning. Indeed, the fact that these words are human makes them unique as vehicles of God's revelation. God has chosen to be known in and through human words. God's written revelation comes to us, therefore, as part of human history.

This means, as we have already noted, that in order to understand, proclaim, and teach Scripture, we need to give it the same scrutiny we give any human document. We must critically analyze the historical conditions in which the Bible arose in order to adequately interpret and communicate its message. Such a critical scrutiny, as we have also seen, affects not only Scripture as such but also our own interpretation and use of it, which suffer from our own historical conditioning. The truth of faith is thus mediated by our respective sociohistorical contexts.

Precisely because the Bible is a prophetic and apostolic book of faith, however, it must also be interpreted in faith. It not only represents the historical witness of the community of faith but also presupposes an attitude of faith on the part of its readers. As has been observed, faith is neither an abstract body of truths nor a theoretical exercise. Faith is trust and commitment as well as understanding and praxis; in a word, it means obedience (Rom. 1:5). To read Scripture in faith as a prophetic and apostolic text is consequently to interpret it in obedience, in meditation and in engagement; it is not only to hear but also to do the Word (James 1:22). Obedience, therefore, is the place from which the Word can be understood and transmitted, and where its truth can be verified.[33]

Theology and Evangelization in Context

To write a theology of evangelization informed by a prophetic and apostolic biblical text and patterned after the evangelizing mission of the prophets and the apostles is to reflect critically and constructively on the *evange*lical content and evangelistic context of the Christian faith for a more faithful, holistic, and liberating engagement in and through the church's mission. This means clarifying the content of the gospel and the context of its communication for a more historically efficacious transmission. It implies, further, enabling the church as a prophetic and apostolic community and institution to understand evangelization as the transmission of the gospel to those who have yet to hear or receive its message for the first time, as well as to those who, although they are part of a sociocultural situation where the gospel has been proclaimed and collectively received, have not had the joy of adequately appropriating it in their personal lives and social relations.

To reflect on evangelization in a theological context is to approach it as a divine calling rather than a humanly initiated activity. One does not participate in evangelization because one so chooses but rather because one is part of a faith community that has been summoned by God out of the darkness of alienation and unbelief into the marvelous light of God's liberating grace and covenantal fellowship, and sent forth to declare God's wonderful deeds (1 Pet. 2:9-10). Therefore, evangelization is a labor of love rather than a proselytistic crusade. To proselytize is to try to get people to change from one religious belief system, ideology, or political party to another, usually through the offer of psychological, social, cultural, political, or economic incentives or through the application of pressure. In contrast, to evangelize is to share with others lovingly and respectfully the joyful news and liberating grace of the gospel, to extend its invitation to faith in Christ and participation in his fellowship, and to commit the person or community's response to the Holy Spirit. Authentic evangelization refuses to be coercive and is always respectful of human dignity and freedom because it is an act of love. It is, therefore, against proselytism.[34]

To reflect on evangelization in a theological perspective is to underscore its role as a witness of faith. To evangelize is to bear witness to the God in whom we have put our trust and to whose service we have committed our lives. It is a personal testimony dependent on God's mercy and power. It is not, therefore, a consumeristic technique to attract people to the Christian faith and recruit them for the church. While there are those who respond in faith to the witness of faith and end up becoming part of the community of faith, such a decision cannot be authentic if it is induced externally by the art of human persuasion or marketing technique. Theologically, an evangelistic decision can be authentic only if it is the result of the Spirit's inner witness corroborating the church's external witness of faith. Similarly, evangelization is an act of hope rather than a manipulation of the future. To evangelize is to hope in the power of God's Spirit to enable those who hear the gospel and see it in action to understand its relevance for their lives, embrace it in faith, and follow in its path. Even though one may toil in tears without seeing much result, one may be assured that sooner or later God will honor one's witness and there will be those who will respond in faith to the gospel's invitation. For, as the psalmist reminds us, the evangelizer who "goes forth weeping, bearing the seed for sowing, shall come home with shouts of joy, bringing his sheaves with him" (Ps. 126:6).

CHAPTER II

Contextual Evangelization

A Personal and Social Witness

It was the late D. T. Niles who described evangelization as "one beggar telling another where to find bread." This vivid imagery (especially if it is pluralized) puts evangelization in a personal yet social context: a beggar sharing a great discovery with other beggars.

On the one hand, this analogy implies that the communication of the gospel presupposes a personal experience: finding bread as a beggar. For the well-to-do, bread hardly means anything. They have access to all they want. But for a hungry beggar, bread may be the difference between life and death. On the other hand, this analogy implies that evangelization is a social event, an act of genuine concern for people who find themselves in the same situation. People who need bread. It is a selfless act, sharing the bread of life with others. Most poor folks—of which beggars are the most indigent representatives—are, by and large, not selfish. They gladly share: they may not have much, but if one goes into their homes, they will bend over backward to try to share the little they do have. One of the problems of affluence is that it tends to harden one's heart. Generally speaking, the affluent, especially if they happen to have earned their wealth the hard way, find it difficult to share what they have without some kind of external incentive—a tax break, for example. How hard it is for those of us who live in affluent lands and situations to give when there is not that kind of incentive. Jesus said, "How hard it is for those who have riches to enter the kingdom of God! For it is easier for a camel to go through the eye of a needle than for a rich [person] to enter the kingdom of God" (Luke 18:24-25).

The problem with being affluent is not simply that one finds it hard to trust in God but especially that one finds it difficult to share what one has worked so hard for. This is typical not just of the very affluent but of all of us who have acquired any goods in life—a house, a car, or some other commodity. Whatever it is, giving up what we have is simply not easy. That is why, for the rich, entering into the kingdom implies a radical transformation—what the Epistle to the Philippians calls *kenosis,* an emptying of oneself, becoming poor or vulnerable like the poor, totally dependent on God.

It is at that point and only at that point—where possessions are of no avail, where one cannot buy one's way into the presence of God, where one becomes in God's sight a literal beggar—that one is spiritually equipped to be a witness for Christ and the gospel. When one becomes vulnerable, completely naked before God, totally dependent on God's grace, one's faith ceases to be merely personal and becomes social. For it is at the point where one's faith is put out there, as it were, in the public square, nakedly before God—which is to say before the whole world, since God is never a private deity—that faith ceases to be a purely personal possession and becomes a social matter.

Evangelization implies bearing witness to the God who saves us from the misery of the human condition. It is an intensely personal and extensively social witness that requires immersion in a particular sociohistorical context and participation in the struggles of humanity. An evangelistic witness is a person who is not ashamed to let everyone see and hear about his or her experience of God, who identifies with and appropriates the fears and hopes of others, and who from that vantage point shares lovingly, even passionately, the gospel in word and deed.

In this chapter we shall analyze the personal and social dimensions of evangelization in three propositions. The first addresses the contextual nature of evangelization, the second focuses on the divine initiative, and the third deals with the praxis that must accompany every evangelistic witness.

Evangelization and the Human Situation

First of all, *evangelization is a witness that takes place in a given social and historical context.* It is part of a living space with its own cultural, geographic, economic, social, and political characteristics, and it is carried out in a temporal moment, be it a generation or an epoch.[1] In such a situation there is a continuous interaction between persons and groups and between ideas, attitudes, values, and feelings, which are woven together and mutually influence behavior.[2]

Evangelization involves, therefore, social and historically situated human beings. It has nothing to do with abstract people, with women and men who exist only in theoretical schemes. Phrases like "contemporary men and women" so universalize a particular type of person that few people can recognize themselves in the description. Humanity does not exist in the abstract. Thus there is no such thing as a contemporary man or woman. There are women and men in concrete contemporary situations.

Evangelization is geared to real people, people of "flesh and bone" (Unamuno), conditioned by their time and space. Such people are surrounded by specific circumstances that demonstrate their human vulnerability. They are besieged by a deep feeling of insecurity because they have no control over tomorrow. They know that sooner or later they will have to face death alone and empty. As the psalmist states, "The years of our life are threescore and ten, or even by reason of strength fourscore; yet their span is but toil and trouble; they are soon gone, and we fly away" (Ps. 90:10).

Evangelization always deals with people who have both sinned and been sinned against. As Raymond Fung has well noted,

> A person is not only a sinner, a person is also the sinned against. . . . Men and women are not only willful violators of God's law, they are also the violated. This is not to be understood in a behavioristic sense, but in a theological sense, in terms of sin, the domination of sin, and of our "struggle against sin . . . to the point of shedding our blood" (Heb. 12:4). . . . [Humankind] is lost, lost not only in the sins [of its] own heart but also in the sinning grasp of principalities and powers of the world, demonic forces which cast a bondage over human lives and human institutions and infiltrate their very textures.[3]

Therefore, "the context . . . of the sinned-against struggling against the forces of sin" should be seen as "an evangelizing context."[4] It is in such a context that evangelization often takes place, and out of which the victims of sin realize that they are also sinners "in such a way that [they] cannot respond with a 'So what?'. Together with the fact of being sinned against, soon comes the stark naked fact of [their] own personal sinfulness and the need for God."[5]

Evangelization is first and foremost a human encounter—the story of women and men sharing and receiving the gospel in a given moment and a particular space, in their most concrete and vulnerable reality. The first thing one shares in any evangelistic situation is oneself with one's human limitations. One never evangelizes as "an angel," or a "better than thou" heavenly creature. Rather, one approaches the evangelistic task as a human being who shares the same precarious existence as everyone else, and who is part of the same world of sinners and victims of sin. One may be a victim, or one may be part of a process that has victimized others, but "all have sinned and fall short of the glory of God" (Rom. 3:23).

Evangelization and the Divine Initiative

My second proposition is that *evangelization involves persons addressed by a holy and loving God with the liberating news of Jesus Christ in the power of the Holy Spirit.* Every evangelistic endeavor assumes a divine initiative and engagement. The great presupposition of the Christian faith is that in the gospel God has spoken a redemptive word to the world. Indeed, the gospel assumes that the God whose creative handiwork we witness all around us (Ps. 19:1) is not an "absentee landlord" but has in fact communicated a word of salvation to the world. God has spoken and addresses us.

It was not easy for the early Christian community to arrive at the conclusion that in the life, ministry, and work of Jesus, God had sent a unique, definitive saving message to the whole world. According to the Gospels, when Jesus was crucified some of his followers were discouraged and went away thinking that it was all over. They found it impossible to believe the report of the women who went to the burial ground early Sunday morning and not only discovered that the tomb where Jesus had been laid was empty but heard a divine messenger (an angel) announce that Jesus had indeed risen, and a while later witnessed his appearance before them. The news that such an undeniable happening as the crucifixion had been toppled by the Resurrection plunged the early community of Jesus into havoc. At first they did not know what to make of the amazing news that the one whose death had been witnessed by all residents of and visitors to Jerusalem was indeed alive. At last they saw and heard him for themselves and became bold witnesses of his death and resurrection. But it took a while longer before they could begin to understand in depth and articulate in breadth the meaning of what had actually transpired in Jesus' death and resurrection.

According to the Gospel traditions, the Resurrection made the early community of Jesus re-evaluate their first impression about his death and passion. They came to the conclusion that he had not been a mere victim of a historical accident. They became convinced that he had died willingly as part of his service to God, Israel, and the entire human race. They accepted the claim that he had died in accordance with God's will and purpose. Eventually they came to the realization not only that the one who had risen was the same Jesus who had been crucified, but also that his life and ministry had been the expression of the mystery *par excellence*—namely, the incarnation of the eternal Son of God. Thus the Fourth Gospel describes Jesus as the eternal Word of God who "became flesh and dwelt among us" (John 1:14). For its part, the Epistle to the Hebrews acknowledges that in the past God had spoken through the prophets "in many and various ways" to the forebears of Israel, but it affirms categorically that in the person of Jesus God had spoken a definitive word (Heb. 1:1-2). The Incarnation became "the point of arrival"[6] of the Christian faith, as the ecumenical consensus in the developing tradition of the universal church indicates.[7] This climactic affirmation of Christian faith is in fact the point of departure for the communication of the gospel.[8] There cannot be evangelization without incarnation.

The evangelistic task is always carried out under the assumption that the God who has spoken in Jesus Christ addresses each and every human being in his or her time and space. The gospel is not a generic message, although it has a universal and social dimension. It is a personal word from God for all and for each human being. The fact that this message has been embodied in Jesus as part and parcel of a particular social, cultural, and historical reality speaks for itself. The one who rose from the dead and is proclaimed as Savior and Lord is Jesus of Nazareth, the Galilean, who was crucified. Thus the gospel was first proclaimed in the language and culture, in the space and time of a first-century Galilean Jew.

This is not a mere coincidence but the very intention of the God who sends good news of salvation to the world. This God communicates only in the vernacular and addresses persons and communities in the particularity of their sociocultural and historical situations. The God of the Incarnation is not a supracultural, supratemporal, and supraspatial deity with a universal language and a "homogeneous mass" as interlocutor. Rather, the God of the Incarnation is the God who chose in sovereign freedom not only to be contextualized in the history and sociocultural reality of a first-century Galilean Jew but also to become available, through the transmission of the gospel in the power of the Spirit, to every person and community in their concrete reality. In the words of the Afro-Brazilian mass entitled *Misa dos Quilombos,* the God of the Christian faith is

> . . . the God of all names
> —Yahweh
> Obatala
> Olorum
> Oio[9]
> . . . who makes all [people]
> of tenderness and dust.
> . . . the true God
> who loved us first
> without divisions.
> . . . the Three
> who are one only God.
> The one who was,
> who is,
> who shall be.[10]

A contemporary British hymn writer has expressed the same conviction in the following hymn:

> God of many Names
> gathered into One,
> in your glory come and meet us,
> Moving, endlessly Becoming;
> God of Hovering Wings,

Womb and Birth of time,
joyfully we sing your praises,
Breath of life in every people—
Hush, hush, hallelujah, hallelujah!
Shout, shout, hallelujah, hallelujah!
Sing, sing, hallelujah, hallelujah!
Sing, God is love, God is love!
God of Jewish faith,
Exodus and Law,
in your glory come and meet us,
joy of Miriam and Moses;
God of Jesus Christ,
Rabbi of the poor,
joyfully we sing your praises,
crucified, alive for ever—
Hush, hush, hallelujah, hallelujah!
God of Wounded Hands,
Web and Loom of love,
in your glory come and meet us,
Carpenter of new creation;
God of many Names
gathered into One,
joyfully we sing your praises,
Moving, endlessly Becoming—
Hush, hush, hallelujah, hallelujah![11]

This God of many Names, known to Africans and Jews and made known to Christians through Jesus, speaks all languages and is aware of every kind of nuance and peculiar accent, especially among those whom the dominant cultures have denied the privilege of an extensive vocabulary, and whom society has condemned to a limited social space. Since God's Son took flesh in the person of a baby born in a manger, grew up in the household of a carpenter, and lived the social and cultural experience of the poor, the marginalized, and the oppressed, we can state that in the gospel God not only speaks to humanity from its lowest and humblest situation but also takes advantage of its own symbols and creations to communicate the good news of salvation in a contextually relevant manner. This is the extraordinary affirmation made in the theme song of the Nicaraguan Peasants' Mass:

You are the God of the poor,
the human and sensitive God
the God who sweats in the street
the God with a sun-scorched face.
That is why I speak to you
Just as my people talk,
For you are the God who labors
You are the worker, Christ.[12]

It is not an atheistic and materialistic philosophy that enables the author of this mass to appropriate such suggestive symbols but the New Testament itself, which states,

> Have this mind among yourselves, which is yours in Christ Jesus, who, though he was in the form of God, did not count equality with God a thing to be grasped, but emptied himself, taking the form of a servant, being born in the likeness of men [and women]. And being found in human form he humbled himself and became obedient unto death, even death on a cross. (Phil. 2:5-8)

Elsewhere the Apostle Paul writes that "our Lord Jesus Christ . . . became poor, so that by his poverty [we] might become rich" (2 Cor. 8:9).

These two texts, among others, give theological justification to the claim of the Nicaraguan mass. In Jesus Christ, God became part of history, identifying with its most humble expression and suffering its deepest pain. The one who suffered and died was a humble carpenter in whom the Son of God was revealed. The Son of God emptied himself of his glory, taking upon himself the human condition, submitting himself to a state of weakness and suffering death. He was born into a poor family and environment, lived in poverty, and in his ministry gave preferential option to the poor (cf. Luke 4:18-20) to save humanity from sin and death. As Paul reminds us, "God was in Christ reconciling the world to himself" (2 Cor. 5:19). In him and through him God assumes the identity of the poor, and becomes known as a "human and sensitive God," the "God with a sun-scorched face" who "sweats in the street." This is why Karl Barth said that "since God became [human]," humanity has become "the measure of all things."[13] We need to understand both humanity and the Son of God from the perspective of the poor, given the double fact that humankind is a social reality and that, in the story of Jesus, the Christ of God assumed the identity of a poor person. The poor are, consequently, a central reference to God's identity.[14] In them we see God's human face.

The God of the poor addresses women and men by the power of the Holy Spirit in their alienation from themselves, the divinely created world, and God's own fellowship. The Spirit is the loving "breath," the creative "energy," the liberating "agency" that makes Christ present and glorifies God, his Father. The Spirit enables women and men to hear God's voice both personally and collectively and to respond to God's call in creation, history, and the conscience. The Spirit breaks barriers and facilitates the communication of the Word of God, seeking and finding lost women and men who are scattered like sheep without a shepherd. The Spirit opens their ears that they may hear God's saving message, illuminates their minds so that they may understand the gospel, and moves their hearts to trust in God so that these once-lost will make a life commitment to the kingdom and bear personal witness to salvation.

To hear the gospel is in itself an act of faith, because faith comes by hearing the good news (Rom. 10:17). It is the Holy Spirit who leads women and men to hear and know the gospel. It is through the Spirit that the gift of faith is transmitted and received. The Spirit prepares the way, creates the encounter, and makes possible the response of faith. It is by means of such faith (trust) in Christ, by the acceptance of what God has done in and through the Son for humanity, and by the confession of Christ as Lord and Savior that those who are being evangelized are transformed. There is a passage from death to life, entrance into the kingdom of God, and incorporation into the new creation. Whoever is in Christ is a new creation (2 Cor. 5:17).

Evangelization is the process by which God, through the power of the Holy Spirit, makes possible the hearing and reception of the gospel concerning Jesus Christ. This process takes place in history. God does not offer salvation to angels. Those who are being transformed into new creations are themselves situated in the conflicts and struggles of history. This "Passover" experience and rebirth is not an escape into another world but rather an event that represents a promise and a call to the transformation of history. The promise is the hope of ultimate liberation from sin and death and of a new heaven and a new earth. That is why the Apostle Paul speaks of our being saved in hope (Rom. 8:24). That is to say, in Christ we receive the promise of a new life and the possibility of overcoming the hardships that besiege us as human beings. This promise is extended to all of creation, including nature and the whole of human society. In the words of Emilio Castro, "Because we trust in God and believe in God's plan for us today and in eternity, . . . because we look to the future with expectation and eagerness; we can, in faith, offer a cup of water, a word of love, the open hand of communion, all in God's name."[15]

For the Christian community, hope is translated into a call to obedience, and obedience is manifested in the labor of love, in Christian praxis, which means participation in the liberating transformation of the world.

In evangelization we bear witness to the gospel of Christ as a message of hope and a call to prophetic action. With the Argentine hymn-writer Federico Pagura we make the following declaration:

> Because [Jesus] came into our world and story,
> because he heard our silence and our sorrow,
> because he filled the whole world with his glory,
> and came to light the darkness of our morrow,
> because his birth was in a darkened corner,
> because he lived proclaiming life and love—,
> because he quickened hearts that had been dormant,
> and lifted those whose lives had been downtrodden.
> Because he drove the merchants from the temple,
> denouncing evil and hypocrisy,
> because he raised up little ones and women,
> and put down all the mighty from their seats,
> because he bore the cross for our wrong doings,
> and understood our failings and our weakness,
> because he suffered from our condemnation
> and then he died for every mortal creature.
> Because of victory one morning early,
> When he defeated death and fear and sorrow,
> so nothing can hold back his mighty story
> nor his eternal kingdom tomorrow.
> So we today have hope and expectation,
> so we today can struggle with conviction,
> so we today can trust we have a future,
> so we have hope in this our world of tears.[16]

Evangelization and Praxis

I have argued heretofore that evangelization involves, first, situated human beings, and second, persons found, addressed, and transformed by God. To these two assertions I shall now add a third: *Evangelization involves persons and communities working for the transformation of their respective life situations.*

Any person or community who cannot give evidence (through the efficacy of love) of a transformed life is not capable of evangelizing others. To participate in the transformation of one's life situation implies, first and foremost, having experienced God's grace, forgiveness, restitution, and liberation for service.

A personal experience of God's liberating grace, however, is not enough to give authenticity to evangelization. Communicators of the glad tidings of salvation ought to be persons committed to and engaged in the process of positive change in their respective life situations. Since the gospel is addressed to persons socially and historically situated, it follows that the gospel's transforming impact ought also to be evidenced in these contexts. Once in Christ, "business" cannot remain "as usual." The gospel is saving power—that is, the historical and transcendent energy of the kingdom of God, which is neither a theory nor a subjective ideal but rather God's efficacious transforming action in the world and beyond it (cf. 1 Cor. 4:20).

Such an impact can become evident only through the conscious action of those who have been reborn into a new life and hope. An evangelizing witness cannot be neutral or passive when it comes to his or her reality. Christians live by the spell of the Spirit. They need to demonstrate the power of the Spirit's presence through a new lifestyle of freedom, service, justice, and peace.

It is to such a lifestyle of discipleship that I refer when I speak of Christian praxis. Christian praxis is the creative and transforming action of God's people in history, accompanied by a critical-reflective and prophetic process that seeks to make Christian obedience ever more effective. Only to the extent to which Christians commit themselves to participate redemptively in their respective life situations are they able to bear efficacious witness to the gospel and be authentic instruments of the Holy Spirit in the evangelization of their neighbors. Authentic evangelistic witnesses establish their apostolic credentials through their praxis.

That is why I began this chapter by describing evangelization through the analogy of a beggar sharing with another beggar the news of where to find bread. But if, instead of the bread of life, which is the Son of God becoming part of our world and story, our neighbors find stones, evangelization will lose its credibility as the announcement of *good news.* A tragic gap will arise between what Mercy Amba Oduyoye has described as "Christianity preached" and "Christianity lived." According to Oduyoye, this is the gap that Christians are having to deal with in Africa. But as she herself admits, Africa is not the only place where "Christianity lived" has not measured up to "Christianity preached."[17] Such a gap has existed for far too long among too many Christians all over the world.

Those who have heard the call of Christ and resolved to share his message with the world need to answer this question: What do those whom we evangelize find in our witness—the living bread or stones? They will find the bread of life only if we follow the example of the Apostle Andrew: "He first found his brother Simon, and said to him, 'We have found the Messiah' . . . [and] brought him to Jesus" (John 1:41-42). Simon then discovered that Jesus was truly and indeed the bread of life—the real Messiah, the eternal Word of God who "became flesh and dwelt among us, full of grace and truth." And, with the other disciples, he "beheld his glory, glory as of the only Son from the Father" (John 1:14).

The gospel cannot be shared in a sociocultural vacuum. It is not a message without a social referent. Indeed, the gospel revolves around the divine condescension in the most precarious situation of human reality. This implies that if the gospel needs to be proclaimed contextually, it is no less essential that it be located in the most vulnerable point of each situation. To maintain its theological integrity and historical efficacy, evangelization needs to be undertaken from below—that is, from the depth of human suffering, where we find both sinners and the victims of sin. Such a situation constitutes a fundamental point of reference in evangelization. The communication of the gospel presupposes a common human base and a single "passover" of liberating grace from death into life. Thus it is a witness both personal and social that has as a primary condition the common sharing of human reality as experienced in suffering and hope, and that extends the call to participate in the transformation of a world of fears and tears into a new order of peace and justice, laughter and joy.

In the next two chapters we shall consider two biblical cases (from the Old Testament and the New Testament respectively) in which evangelization may be seen as a contextualized personal and social witness, carried out in two distinct yet similar situations. And we shall note the common denominators of these situations: the human condition and the announcement of the liberating grace of the gospel.

CHAPTER III

The Prophetic Character of Evangelization

A Perspective from the Jewish Diaspora

Contextual evangelization is a holistic witness to God's liberating grace in a given sociohistorical situation. Such a theological understanding calls for reflection on the biblical roots of evangelization. In this and the next chapter we shall explore two biblical models of contextual evangelization, one from the Hebrew Scriptures and the other from the New Testament. The *New Encyclopedia Britannica* defines a model as a "familiar structure or mechanism used as an analogy to interpret a natural phenomenon." It adds that "scientific models" are used to develop or modify theories or to render them more intelligible.[1] In theology, as Avery Dulles points out in his *Models of the Church,* models are used "in a reflective, discriminate, critical way to deepen one's theoretical understanding of a reality."[2] The two biblical models we shall reflect on are means to help us get a critical handle on the biblical roots of contextual evangelization. In this chapter we shall consider a prophetic model.

The Prophetic Evangelization of Deutero-Isaiah

The source of this model is that evangelizing prophet identified by scholars as Deutero-Isaiah. The prophetic work of Deutero-Isaiah is contained in chapters 40–55 of what might be described as the Isaianic collection. This section represents a prophet from the Babylonian exile who wrote around 540 B.C.E. but within the tradition of Isaiah of Jerusalem, to whom is ascribed the major part of chapters 1–39, written some two hundred years before chapters 40–55.[3]

The key text in Deutero-Isaiah's theology of evangelization is found in Isaiah 52:7:

> How beautiful upon the mountains
> are the feet of him who brings good tidings,
> who publishes peace, who brings good tidings of good,
> who publishes salvation,
> who says to Zion, "Your God reigns."

While the notion of heralding good news is already present at the outset of Deutero-Isaiah (cf. Isa. 40:9), it is 52:7 that is quoted by the Apostle Paul to describe the task of those sent to evangelize (cf. Rom. 10:15). The Gospels and Acts are inspired by the same image when they describe the evangelizing ministry of Jesus and the apostles (cf. Acts 10:36). Isaiah 52:7 is, therefore, a foundational text for the New Testament, for the work of the New Testament evangelist is patterned after Deutero-Isaiah's description of the divine herald, who brings glad tidings of peace, proclaims salvation, and declares that God reigns.

It is interesting to note how Deutero-Isaiah introduces evangelization at the outset of his literary work. He personifies the evangelization of the Babylonian captives on Mount Zion:

> Go up on a high mountain,
> messenger of Zion,
> Shout as loud as you can,
> messenger of Jerusalem!
> Shout fearlessly,
> say to the towns of Judah,
> "Here is your God."
> Here is Lord Yahweh coming with power,
> his arm maintains his authority,
> his reward is with him
> and his prize precedes him.
> He is like a shepherd feeding his flock,
> gathering lambs in his arms,
> holding them against his breast
> and leading to their rest the mother ewes.
> (Isa. 40:9-11, JB)

Zion was the southeast mountain of the old Jerusalem (which, according to 2 Samuel 5:7, had been the fortress of the Jebusites conquered by David) where Solomon built the temple. This mountain, which became synonymous with the Holy City, is designated by Deutero-Isaiah as a center of evangelization. From there the good news of peace is to be announced to the towns of Judah: God reigns! God is coming to rescue and shepherd the captives of Babylon. In the words of the New Testament, Zion is sent "to preach the gospel" to God's oppressed people.[4]

If we follow the argument of the prophet, we discover that one of the ways in which God comes to the people with an outstretched, redemptive arm is through the activity of Cyrus, the Persian king, who conquers Babylon and initiates the return of the captives (Isa. 41:2). Although Cyrus is not aware of it, God calls him and anoints him to liberate God's people from their Babylonian slavery and give them peace. Thus it is through a historical and political event that the peace and salvation which are to be proclaimed from Zion begin to be accomplished.

In Deutero-Isaiah evangelization is the collective and historical announcement that will be proclaimed from Zion for all of Judah. Thus the prophet says,

> The voices of your watchmen!
> Now they raise their voices,
> shouting for joy together,
> for with their own eyes they have seen
> Yahweh returning to Zion. (Isa. 52:8, JB)

We are dealing here with an *event* in which the messianic peace is manifested, the acquired redemption is revealed (Isa. 43:1ff.), and God's sovereign presence is declared throughout the land.

By *peace (shalom)* is meant social well-being, productivity, creativity, and harmonious relations with the neighbor and the environment. This is made possible by a just ordering of life, which guarantees that the weak and oppressed shall be lifted up and put alongside the strong and mighty. Similarly, *salvation* means liberation from captivity and restoration of that which has been destroyed; it means straightening the crooked ways, leveling the uneven ground, and making plain the rough places (Isa. 40:4). In short, it means holistic reconciliation —with God, the neighbor, and the land.

The one who guarantees and makes peace and salvation possible is God, the redeemer of the captives and the creator of the earth. Where God's reign is affirmed and his redemptive presence hoped for, salvation is experienced and peace is anticipated. By the same token, where God is denied, judgment and its consequences are suffered: adversity, brokenness, and darkness. God's judgment is the reverse side of God's liberating reign of peace. Therefore, in evangelization it is not necessary to proclaim God's wrath and judgment; they are assumed.

For Deutero-Isaiah the hour demanded a word of consolation, not of condemnation. To be sure, the captivity had raised a profound theological query: "Where is God, and what is he doing?"[5]; or, as the psalmist put it, "How shall we sing the Lord's song in a foreign land?" (Ps. 137:4). The answer of the prophets of exile was that the captivity represented God's judgment of the covenant people for their disobedience and idolatry (cf. Isa. 42:18-25; Jer. 25:3-11). To this radical question and answer, Deutero-Isaiah adds the glad tidings of peace and salvation—the confirmation that God does indeed reign and is soon to extend a mighty and merciful arm. Evangelization is thus a positive and not a negative task, a joyful rather than a tearful announcement, a communication of hope instead of damnation. The renewal of faith will make of Zion an evangelizing mountain. In the day of its liberation, Yahweh announces through the prophet, "My people . . . shall know that it is I who speak; here am I" (Isa. 52:6). For Deutero-Isaiah the renewal of the covenant is the restorative obedience of faith, which prepares the way to bring good tidings of peace, publish salvation, and say to Zion, "Your God reigns" (Isa. 52:7).

From Babylon to Persia

Prophetic Evangelization and the Story of Esther

Situated a century after Deutero-Isaiah in Persia is the prophetic story of Esther,[6] one of the most interesting characters of the Hebrew Scriptures. She is especially attractive to people in exile, foreigners, and ethnic minorities.[7] The fact that the Book of Esther presents a minority heroine in a male and politically dominated society adds to the prophetic significance of the story.[8]

The importance of Esther is reflected, above all, in the collective memory of Jewish people. She is remembered for her role in the providential liberation of the Jews in Persia from what could have become the first recorded holocaust. This is, in fact, the rationale for the annual Jewish feast of Purim. This feast remembers the irony (or tragic humor) of that event. The date for the proposed massacre of the Jews had been fixed by the Persian method of casting Pur, or lots (Esther 3:7; 9:24). However, thanks to God's providential intervention through Esther's faithful endeavors, the lot fell upon Haman, the very person who had devised the wicked plot to exterminate the Jews.

The Epic of Esther

The story, according to the biblical text, takes place in Susa, capital of the empire, which was witnessing a great feast that Ahasuerus was holding for the most important functionaries of the empire. Subsequently he gave a seven-day banquet for all the people present in Susa. "When the heart of the king was merry with wine," he commanded Queen Vashti to present herself "in order to show the peoples and the princes her beauty" (1:10-11). According to the custom of the time and culture, women covered themselves with a veil. If Queen Vashti were to show herself to the guests of the king, she would lower her dignity and be publicly humiliated. Accordingly, Vashti refused to obey the king's command. For this reason "the king was enraged, and his anger burned within him" (1:12).

According to the king's advisors and ministers, what Vashti had done was embarrassing not only for the king but for the entire empire. Besides, they feared that the queen's deed would reach the ears of women and cause them "to look with contempt upon their husbands" (1:17). Therefore, they advised the king to depose and get rid of Vashti and search for a better woman to serve as queen. Vashti was punished; her dethronement was promoted as an example for all the women of the empire. Several days later, the king ordered that a "beauty contest" be undertaken, a gathering together of the most beautiful young women of the empire so that he might choose a new queen. From among hundreds of beautiful women, the king chose Esther.

Esther was a beautiful young woman whose father and mother had died early in her life. She had been reared by her cousin and adoptive father, Mordecai, one of many Jews "who had been carried away from Jerusalem among the captives carried away with Jeconiah king of Judah, whom Nebuchadnezzar king of Babylon had carried away" (2:6). Conscious of what it could mean for the Jews to have one of their own near to the king, Mordecai encouraged Esther and trained her to enter the contest. He advised her, however, not to reveal to anyone her ethnicity or nationality. In divine providence, Esther, a Jew, was selected to be the queen of the Median-Persian Empire.

One day the future of the Jews was endangered. Haman, the king's prime minister, demanded that all the king's subjects and servants bow before him — "but Mordecai did not bow down or do obeisance [to Haman]" (3:2). In revenge, Haman sought "to destroy, to slay, and to annihilate all Jews, young and old, women and children" throughout the empire (3:13). He managed to get the king to sign a decree condemning to destruction all the Jews.

As soon as Mordecai heard of the decree, he "rent his clothes and put on sackcloth and ashes" (4:1). He went all over the city, "wailing with a loud and bitter cry" (4:1).

Esther learned of Mordecai's odd behavior and sent him clean clothes so that he could enter the palace and explain to her what was wrong. But Mordecai refused the clothes. Then Esther sent her chief personal guard to ask Mordecai what had happened. Mordecai relayed the news of the decree and asked that Esther intercede before the king on behalf of her people:

> Then Mordecai told them to return answer to Esther, "Think not that in the king's palace you will escape any more than all the other Jews. For if you keep silence at such a time as this, relief and deliverance will rise for the Jews from another quarter, but you and your father's house will perish. And who knows whether you have not come to the kingdom for such a time as this?" (4:13-14)

Esther hesitated at first, but upon reflection she decided to go directly to the king. She did so notwithstanding the law that forbade anyone from approaching the king unsummoned; the violator faced the penalty of death unless the king graciously held out "the golden scepter" and allowed the violator to live (4:11). Before appearing before the king, however, Esther ordered Mordecai to "gather all the Jews to be found in Susa" to fast for three days on her behalf. She and her maids would also participate in the fast, she told him. After the three days of fasting, she would go to see the king, even though it was against the law; if she should perish, so be it (4:16).

God responded favorably to the fast of Esther and her maids, Mordecai, and all the Jews of Susa. Not only did the king receive Esther and make it possible for the Jews to be spared, but he brought Haman to judgment and rewarded Mordecai's faithfulness by making him prime minister:

> Then Mordecai went out from the presence of the king in royal robes of blue and white, with a great golden crown and a mantle of fine linen and purple, while the city of Susa shouted and rejoiced. The Jews had light and gladness and joy and honor. And in every province and in every city, wherever the king's command and his edict came, there was gladness and joy among the Jews, a feast and a holiday. And many from the peoples of the country declared themselves Jews, for the fear of the Jews had fallen upon them. (8:15-17)

The epic of Esther is meaningful for Jews, and they have given it a high place in their collective history (as symbolized by the Feast of Purim and the canonical place given to the book at the Council of Jamnia).[9] But the story of Esther is also meaningful for oppressed people everywhere. For Esther—and, we should add, Mordecai—represent what J. B. Metz has called a "subversive memory." Her example and that of Mordecai live in the memory of oppressed and powerless people in every society where they are threatened by annihilation through the wicked machination of unscrupulous, idolatrous, and unjust power-brokers.What was particularly remarkable about Esther was her obedient character. Even though she rose to the throne by way of an event that could be described as alienating and opportunistic, she managed to put her resources at the service of the oppressed. The courageous Vashti disobeyed the king in legitimate protest but succeeded only in opening the way for Esther (a contribution, however, that is to be viewed as rather significant from the "providentialist" perspective of the narrative). But Esther distinguished herself by her submission and subversion. Esther is remembered, therefore, as a strong and courageous woman who disobeyed the law of the empire in order to obey God. In such a context, obedience must be understood not simply as blind acceptance of an order imposed from above but rather as the grace to hear sensitively the liberating word of God (implicit in the unfolding of the story), the wisdom to understand it, and the strength to fulfill it, to do what is right and just in God's sight.

The Prophetic Praxis of Esther

What was the secret of Esther's daring and courageous obedience? A close scrutiny of her prophetic action will reveal that her secret lay in her ability to remember the several aspects that are foundational in the life of every human being.

First, Esther did not forget her roots. She remembered that before she was the king's wife, she was the daughter of Mordecai's uncle, the girl Mordecai adopted as his own daughter when her father died (2:7). That is why, when she learned that he had put on sackcloth and ashes and had gone throughout the city wailing and crying (4:1-2), she "was deeply distressed" and sought to help him (4:4). However, it is interesting to note that at this point, although Esther acted out of family love, she behaved in a manner that was more befitting of a queen than of a relative; perhaps she was embarrassed by Mordecai's attire and behavior. She sent her servant with proper clothing so that Mordecai "might take off his sackcloth" (4:4). When Mordecai refused the clothes, Esther sent her chief servant, Hathach, to find out what was happening and why (4:5). Mordecai told him what had happened and extended an appeal to Esther "to go to the king to make supplication to him and entreat him for her people" (4:8). Initially Esther hesitated because of the law of the land. Besides, it had been thirty days since Esther had been called into the king's presence. She acted, therefore, in accordance with her royal role. She did what any politician would do—she thought of the consequences of the proposed action. She acted as a realist. Mordecai was asking her to commit political suicide!

Mordecai reminded Esther, however, that she was a Jew *before* she was queen: "Think not that in the king's palace you will escape any more than all the other Jews. For if you keep silence at such a time as this, relief and deliverance will rise for the Jews from another quarter, but you . . . will perish." Then he added the punch line: "Who knows whether you have not come to the kingdom for such a time as this?" (4:13-14). It was *then,* according to the narrative, that Esther *remembered* that the liberation of her people took precedence over both her individual well-being and her political office. In such a time as this, she needed to remember that it was not her individual attributes as a beautiful woman or even her political sense as the queen that mattered. What was important was that she was a Jew, that her people were condemned to death, and that she was in a position to do something about it. She *remembered* her roots and thus realized that the lives of others, and especially the salvation of her people, took precedence over her personal survival and well-being.

Esther's story reminds us how difficult it is for us to remember who we really are and where we come from when the waters get rough. It is such a great temptation to deny our roots, our families, and our collective self in order to "make it big." This is particularly true if we happen to be members of an ethnic minority, which means there is always the pressure to forget who we really are in order to win the acceptance of the dominant sectors of society and be free from bigotry and prejudice.

There is no shame in proceeding from a humble origin, in being the son or daughter of an immigrant, in being black or white, yellow or brown, a Yankee or a Southerner, an Easterner or a Westerner, an Arab or a Jew, an Ashkenazi or a Sephardi. But there is shame and tragedy in forgetting where we come from—for sooner or later it will catch up with us. Those we deny will manage to live without us, but we will not be able to live with ourselves. Remembering who we are and where we come from is, therefore, essential to living at peace with ourselves.

The second key to Esther's obedience was that she remembered the nature of her calling. Her vocation was not simply to be a queen and thus enjoy the "goodies" and privileges of royal life. Her winning the crown in the "beauty contest" was not meant to be an opportunity for her to succeed financially, socially, or politically; it was, rather, an opportunity given to her so that she might serve her people in a moment of crisis. Indeed, Esther's vocation was to represent her people in the royal court when the need and occasion arose. For "such a time as this" she had come to the kingdom. She had not attained the crown so that when the crunch came she and her father and mother's house might survive. She had been brought to the kingdom as a sign of hope and as an instrument for life among her people.

There are people who come from the "under and outerside" of

life and manage to make it in the centers of power only to forget the plight of those they have left behind. They see their success as a private affair. They develop a deformed vocation—a selfish, individualistic desire for survival and success.

Jesus taught that people who think only of their personal survival end up losing their lives: "Whoever would save his [or her] life will lose it. . . . For what does it profit [a person], to gain the whole world and forfeit . . . life?" (Mark 8:35-36).

The fact of the matter is that the life vocation of the people of God is to be one of service rather than of survival or achievement of personal success. We are called not to be trouble free and enjoy the good life but rather to represent the cause of the oppressed and be a sign of hope among them. God has indeed shown us what is good and acceptable: "to do justice, and to love kindness, and to walk humbly with . . . God" (Mic. 6:8).

We need, therefore, to keep our priorities straight. It is too easy in consumer-oriented societies to set our goals on wealth and power rather than on justice and righteousness. It is too tempting, especially in times such as ours, to forget about the plight of others and think only about ourselves.

Take contemporary North American society. If one is a Hispanic-American in this context, it is a great temptation to ignore the plight of illegal aliens from Mexico, Central America, and the Caribbean because if they were allowed to stay in this country they would compete for the jobs that would otherwise go to legal residents and U.S.-born Hispanics. Protecting one's own interests seems far more attractive than helping our neighbors from the other side of the border with the grim prospects they face—deportation, abject poverty, and sometimes death. If one is a successful black American, it is far more enticing to be concerned with one's next step on the stairs of upward mobility than to struggle on behalf of the growing number of urban blacks who are becoming part of a permanent underclass in North American cities. If one is a white feminist, it is so much more appealing to work for the empowerment of white professional women than to advocate Hispanic and black female leadership in North American religious and social institutions. If one is a successful member of the mainstream in the late 1980s, it seems far more logical to sustain the economic bonanza that the federal government has made possible for the well-to-do than to be an advocate for the thousands who are still jobless, the economically depressed farm family, the poor, and the elderly. In sum, if one enjoys power and wealth, it seems far more attractive and realistic to worry about maintaining it than sharing it with the poor, the powerless, and the oppressed.

We can become so enamored with our rights and privileges and so pragmatic about the limits of our resources that we consider offensive any suggestion of giving our lives away to others without expecting anything in return.

In the fall of 1984, Mortimer and Esther Arias learned that Esther did not have long to live. They decided to leave immediately the School of Theology at Claremont (in Claremont, California), where Mortimer had been teaching, and return to their homeland in Bolivia to await Esther's death. Late in December 1984 Esther finally rested from her labors. A poem entitled "Gastar la Vida" ("To Spend Life") by Father Luis Espinal, the Bolivian martyr of human rights, was read at the funeral. It is a poem inspired by the teachings and example of Jesus; the words express quite vividly the point I have been trying to make.

> Jesus Christ has said, "Whoever does not want to spend life will lose it." . . . But we are afraid to spend our life, to give it away without reserve. To spend life is to work for others, even without pay, to make a favor without expecting return. To spend life is to throw yourself ahead, even to fail, without false prudence. It is to burn your bridges for the sake of the neighbor. We are torches that have no meaning except burning out for others.

Such was the case with Esther Arias, who for years gave everything she had for the dispossessed children of Bolivia. And such was also the example of Queen Esther, who remembered her call to service and put her future on the line for the cause of her condemned people. "I will go to the king, though it is against the law; and if I perish, I perish" (4:16). That was her final answer to Mordecai. Both of these women kept their priorities straight. They were faithful to their vocation. They were willing to spend their lives in the service of others.

The third key to Esther's obedience was that she remembered to whom she really belonged. The fact of the matter is that ultimately she did not belong to herself, to her husband-king, to her adopted father, or even to her own people. She belonged to God. It was out of this deep conviction that she called for a fast and opted to go before the king. She demonstrated her loyalty to God not in words or in religious actions. Instead she showed her commitment to God in an almost suicidal political deed.

Interestingly enough, the Book of Esther has no direct reference to God. Nowhere does it mention God explicitly. Esther's call for a fast and Mordecai's claim that "deliverance will rise for the Jews from another quarter," should Esther refuse to help, are the only indirect references to God to be found in the original story.[10] This is congruent with a basic conviction of the Hebrew Scriptures: commitment and loyalty to God are best demonstrated not through lip service and "religious" gestures but by following the path of justice. The Lord himself said, "Did not your father . . . do justice and righteousness? Then it was well with him. He judged the cause of the poor and needy; then it was well. Is not this to know me?" (Jer. 22:15-16).

In many contemporary situations we run the risk of confusing a "pious" vocabulary and a "religious" lifestyle with faith and spiritual commitment. The real crisis of faith in societies with a religious tradition is not secular humanism but rather the lack of a radical obedience among those who profess commitment to the living God. "Whoever does not do right [and justice] is not of God," says the Apostle John (1 John 3:10).

Tomás Borge, minister of the interior of Nicaragua and the lone surviving member of the original Sandinistas, was leaving his office one day shortly after the overthrow of Somoza's regime (in July 1979). On his way out he noticed a former member of Somoza's guard who had been captured and was being brought to trial. Borge recognized him immediately as the man who had tortured him. Borge looked the guard straight in the eye and asked him, "Do you recognize me?" The guard answered, "No." Borge insisted, "Look at me! I was one of those you tortured! And now you will see what the Revolution will do with people like you. Shake my hands! *I forgive you!*"

Borge is an avowed Marxist who makes no pretense of being a believer in God. Yet he was the Sandinista who immediately, upon the triumph of the Revolution, began to speak of "generosity in victory." Here is someone who, while not professing to be religious, demonstrated the most profound expression of what faith in the living God is really all about—"I forgive you!" Without professing to believe, he showed what true faith is all about. He showed mercy and did what was right and just in God's sight. Like Esther, he demonstrated that which the Apostle Paul called the "obedience of faith" (Rom. 1:5).

True faith means obedience, and obedience means doing what is right and just in God's sight. By remembering her roots and thus accepting her Jewish identity in a time when it was very dangerous to do so, by being faithful to her vocation of service and thereby risking her own well-being, and by expressing her loyalty to God in an act of unlawful disobedience for the cause of justice, Esther demonstrated an obedient—indeed, a subversive—faith, a relationship of trust in God's liberating power and commitment to God's justice that went beyond words and religious deeds. Such a faith transcends traditional categories and makes concrete the providential and liberating presence of the living God whom ancient Israel worshiped, the prophets proclaimed, and Jesus embodied.

The Legacy of Prophetic Evangelization

In her radical obedience Esther also fulfilled the authentic mission of an evangelist as described by Deutero-Isaiah (52:7-9). In her prophetic praxis Esther became a messenger of good news. She struggled, along with Mordecai, for the peace (the spiritual and social well-being) of her people. She bore public witness to salvation. She declared that the God of Israel reigned, even in a strange land!

In the prophetic tradition of Deutero-Isaiah, authentic evangelization consists of a joyful announcement around God's liberating work on behalf of the people. This announcement is not mere words; it is distinguished by the force of the joyful news it heralds. It is a message of hope and jubilee because it affirms the sovereignty of a merciful God who creates new things—particularly the liberation of the captives and the establishment of *shalom* (well-being), a new order of life grounded in divine justice.

By the time of the Third Isaiah, or Trito-Isaiah (chapters 55–66), who prophesied a generation later, the glad tidings are not addressed to all of Zion. Rather, the addressees are now "the afflicted (or poor), the brokenhearted, the captives, the prisoners, the mourners—all the faceless, forgotten ones who have lost hope, if indeed they ever had any [61:1-3]. It is to *them* that God has directed his prophetic word."[11] Small wonder that, according to the Gospel of Luke, Jesus chose this passage to describe his own evangelistic ministry (4:18-19).

The prophetic perspective is foundational for a theology of contextual evangelization. For, on the one hand, the roots of evangelization in the New Testament are found in the prophetic literature that originates in the Diaspora. And, on the other hand, evangelization is not a mechanical practice unrelated to specific situations; it is an announcement clearly linked to God's liberating action in a specific social space and historical moment.

In a world threatened by death, where life is devalued by poverty, economic exploitation, sociopolitical oppression, racism, sexism, the arms race, and plain human selfishness, evangelization cannot be limited to religious gestures and verbal formulas. The situation requires that evangelization fulfill its fundamental intention—namely, to transmit the good news of *shalom,* to declare publicly God's salvation and to affirm God's righteous and liberating reign. Thus evangelization today, like that of yesterday, needs to be linked to the obedience of faith. For only by living the faith at its roots—that is, by doing the will of God—can one bring to people in crisis good news of peace, proclaim God's deliverance in their midst with credibility, and demonstrate that God does indeed reign on earth as in heaven.

In the tradition of the New Testament, both faith and the announcement of the gospel are linked to Jesus. He is seen as the promised Messiah, the faithful witness, the perennial agent of peace, the liberator. An evangelist can do nothing more or less than announce the gospel (the good news of peace and salvation that has been incarnated in the life and work of Jesus). This announcement can be implicit (as it is in the case of Esther and of Deutero-Isaiah) or explicit (as it frequently is in the New Testament). This, too, demands a renovating obedience of faith in the concrete situation of daily life. It is not possible to announce good news without going through a personal conversion. For evangelization presupposes a call to commitment and the demonstration of faith.

The obedience of faith is not so much a biblical imperative as a historical exigency all over the Western world, especially in the Americas. To be sure, we lack neither believers (at least nominally) nor evangelists (witness, for example, the high number of evangelistic radio and television programs in the majority of capitals and cities throughout the Caribbean, Mexico and Central America, and North and South America). It seems, however, that we really have few doers of the will of God. How else are we to explain the scandalous fact that in a planetary space occupied by so many Judeo-Christians there are so many physical, social, and spiritual ills — hunger, malnutrition, ignorance, inadequate education, shortage of housing, unemployment, torture, unjust imprisonment, people who disappear not to be heard from again, wars, invasions and military threats, political dictatorships, racism, sexism, mistreatment of children, and psychological and spiritual alienation? What can we say about an evangelistic practice that does not take into account either the short-range or the long-range consequences of socio-economic and political systems established for a few, whereby millions of human beings are wasted, condemned to live or die without any value? The tragedy of Christianity in the Americas and the Western world, the tragedy of Christian churches is that they seem to have more heralds of war, nationalism, imperialism, oppression, and injustice than communicators of peace and salvation.[12]

That is why I would insist that perhaps the greatest challenge before the contemporary church is to repossess the prophetic notion of evangelization as both a joyful announcement to Christians and people of other faiths as well as a contextualized witness in secular society. For it seems that there are more *practical* atheists (that is, people who confess God with their lips but deny God with their deeds) inside communities of faith than there are ontic atheists (who deny the existence of God's being) outside of them. We have churches that are filled with formal believers who deny in practice what they affirm inside the community of faith. The church, as a community and an institution, needs to be evangelized in the same way that Deutero-Isaiah described and Esther undertook. In other words, the church needs to hear time and again the good news and be called to the renewal of the obedience of faith.

The evangelistic legacy of Esther lies in the manner in which her deeds actualized the evangelistic vision of Deutero-Isaiah among the Jews who had remained in Persia (supposedly of their own free will and for socio-economic reasons). As a story of courageous witness in the eastern dispersion, the Book of Esther demonstrates Deutero-Isaiah's prophetic model.

Thus evangelization is seen as a contextual witness that announces the good news of peace, publishes salvation, and declares that the God of the covenant, of redemption and providence, reigns. From this perspective, evangelization implies living in obedience to the kingdom of God and serving thereby as an agent of transformation in given life situations. The contextuality of this witness further implies the need to reclaim and cultivate our respective roots. If we deny our personal and sociocultural identity, if we are ashamed of who we are and where we come from, if we do not live for service, it will be difficult (if not impossible) to communicate the gospel. Evangelization is undertaken through our human and Christian vocation of service to the neighbor.

Our objective in this chapter has not been to engage in a literary analysis or "scientific" exegesis of either Deutero-Isaiah or the Book of Esther. (For that we can always consult the many exegetical and critical commentaries which are available.) Rather, we have sought to reflect theologically on Deutero-Isaiah's model of prophetic evangelization and to demonstrate how the story of Esther fulfilled this model several centuries later among Jews in the Persian diaspora. We have also noted how the legacy of Deutero-Isaiah is further contextualized by Third Isaiah, who provided the text that Jesus used in describing his own prophetic evangelizing ministry. The concepts thus introduced inform and illuminate the evangelizing mission of the church in our time and life situations. For we live in a period of history in which the church finds itself in sociohistorical situations similar to the one described in the Book of Esther and the Isaianic tradition.

In the light of this prophetic perspective, evangelization should be understood as the sharing of the message of *shalom* (justice and well-being) which God has made known through the story of Israel, and which for Christians has been revealed in Jesus the Messiah. This message is above all a witness to the liberating God who reigns in justice and grace, and it carries an implicit invitation to faith and obedience. It is expressed in the disposition to serve, to defend and promote the cause of justice, and to identify with those who suffer, knowing that God reigns and promises to forgive and to lift the fallen and lead them to the enjoyment of a new life of spiritual and social well-being.

CHAPTER IV

The Evangelistic Legacy of Jesus

A Perspective from the Galilean Periphery

One need not engage in a very profound study of evangelization in the New Testament to be convinced of the importance of Jesus' ministry in the apostolate of the early church. It is clear from both the canonical Scriptures and other sources of early Christianity[1] that the early church did not limit itself to a passing, illustrative reference to Jesus. Rather, it found in his message and ministry the inspiration and source for its evangelizing mission. Accordingly, in the Gospels, Acts, and the Epistles, we are given a picture of evangelization as grounded in Jesus' own ministry. Indeed, it was the starting point and model for the later development of the church's missionary vocation.

In the Gospel of Mark, which according to many scholars represents the oldest of the four Gospels,[2] we find a model of evangelization rooted in the ministry of Jesus. This model is framed in a Galilean perspective. It is, therefore, no accident that a reference to Galilee appears in the Prologue (1:1-13) and in the summary statement of Jesus' ministry (1:14-15).

Following the clue of various scholars and theologians,[3] I have concluded that Galilee is a "key" not only to understanding Mark but also to recovering and interpreting Jesus' evangelistic legacy. I see in Mark a model of contextual evangelization from the periphery.

By "periphery" is meant not just the region of Galilee located on the fringes of the Palestinian Jewish world. In the context of Mark's Gospel, the term also refers to "the disciples," or the Twelve, and "the other followers" of Jesus. In his study of Mark Juan Mateos notes that the first group came from institutional Israel.[4] They are called at first "the disciples" (2:15, 18, 23; 3:7, 9), and later are constituted into messianic Israel under the symbol of "the Twelve" (3:13-19). The "other followers" are those "who do not proceed from institutional Israel, be they ethnic Jews or not; they are not called disciples and have not been integrated into messianic Israel."[5] According to Mateos, the Gospel of Mark constructs a picture of "disciples" and "followers" that corresponds to "the double denomination found in the early Christian tradition: *Eclesia ex circumcisione, Eclesia ex gentius.*"[6]

These two groups, notwithstanding their different calls (the Israelites are typified in 1:16-20; the others in the call of Levi [2:14ff.]), shared similar peripheral experiences. The first group represented the Jewish minority who accepted Jesus. It existed on the periphery of institutional Israel. The second group represented those who were not an integral part of the covenant people. It was made up of "tax collectors and sinners" (2:1ff.), "the crowd" (3:32), or simply those "who were near to Jesus."[7]

For both groups Jesus appeared as an "evangelist of the periphery." He evangelized on the periphery of institutional Israel, gathering a minority of what we might call "messianic Jews." He also evangelized "outside" the covenant community and "open[ed] the good news to all the peoples who neither belong[ed] nor under[stood] the [Israelite] tradition." "The good news," says Mateos, is focused "on the person and work of Jesus."[8]

Bearing in mind this double understanding of periphery, and without pretending to engage in a "scientific" exegesis or literary analysis of the text (though attentive to the works of exegetes and scholars of Christian origins), we shall reflect theologically on Mark's Galilean model and its implications for contextual evangelization. We shall turn our attention first to Jesus the Galilean. Next we shall analyze Galilee as an evangelistic landmark, then follow the movement from Galilee to the nations anticipated in the missionary commission of "the Twelve" and "the other followers" of Jesus. We shall conclude with several universal implications of particular relevance for evangelization in our time and life situations.

Jesus the Galilean

Galilee was a cultural crossroads.[9] It was a commercially oriented region that had long been inhabited by Gentiles as well as Jews. During the time of Jesus, Jews lived side by side with Phoenicians, Syrians, Arabs, Greeks, and Orientals. This racial mixture had given it the name Galilee (literally "the circle"), which came to mean "circle of heathens." Thus Isaiah of Jerusalem speaks of "Galilee of the nations" (Isa. 9:1-12; cf. Matt. 4:15-16).

In such a society there was a natural, ongoing biological and cultural mixture. Jews from the area had a peculiar accent and lacked cultural sophistication. In addition, they had a slightly unorthodox theology and maintained a vigorous independence from the Jewish hierarchy in Jerusalem. Because of their impurity, Galilean Jews were looked down on by the southern Jews of Jerusalem and Judea (particularly Pharisees and priests). The Jews of the south saw themselves as the heirs of cultural and religious purity. For them "Galilee" was synonymous with "fool." This explains Nathaniel's response (John 1:46) and the reason why the claim of a Messiah from Galilee seemed ridiculous to the Jerusalem leadership. "Search and you will see that no prophet is to rise from Galilee," said the Pharisees to Nicodemus (John 7:52ff.; cf. Matt. 21:11).

Yet, despite its being a melting pot in some ways, Galilee produced some of the most militant and exclusivist Jews of the time. While some Jews readily mixed with Gentiles, others intensified their exclusivism, seeing any type of collaboration with Rome as a sellout. According to Virgilio Elizondo, "The name *Galilean* came to be associated with 'hard-line hawk'—*Zealot* or *Galilean* came to mean the same."[10] Accordingly, Romans despised Galilean Jews and forbade them to proselytize Gentiles.

Jesus came from this rejected and despised land, this "circle of heathens," to be baptized by John in the river Jordan in "the wilderness" (1:4-5). The reference to the wilderness in John's ministry (1:4) reminds us of Israel, which, according to the biblical tradition, was first called "God's son" in the wilderness (Exod. 4:22f.; Jer. 2:2). It is interesting to note the contrast between Mark 1:5 and Mark 1:9:

> And there went out to him all the country of Judea, and all the people of Jerusalem; and they were baptized by him in the river Jordan, confessing their sins. (1:5)
>
> In those days Jesus came from Nazareth of Galilee and was baptized by John in the Jordan. (1:9)

William Lane, following E. Lohmeyer, notes,

> In Ch. 1:5 *all* of the people come forth to be baptized by John; in Ch. 1:9 *one* single representative is introduced, the only Galilean mentioned by Mark who heeded John's call to the wilderness. By this correspondence and contrast Mark suggests that all of those from Judea and Jerusalem who came out to John prove to be yet rebellious and insensitive to the purpose of God. Contrary to expectation, only the one from Galilee proves to be the unique Son who genuinely responds to the prophetic call to the wilderness.[11]

According to the Markan text, Jesus assumed the identity and vocation of the whole of Israel. He came to do what Israel was not able to do—namely, to be God's faithful covenant partner, the Servant of Yahweh (cf. Isa. 52:13–53:12), suffering redemptively for the nations in order to bring into being a new humanity. This is why the recording of Jesus' baptism is preceded by a reference to the baptism of the Spirit: "I have baptized you with water; but he will baptize you with the Holy Spirit" (1:8). According to these words, Jesus had to suffer death before he could bring into being a new humanity. Before he could baptize with the Spirit, he had to rise from the grave. Thus his baptism was an anticipation of his suffering experience as a true, obedient Israelite. The Father expressed his approval of Jesus' faithfulness and obedience by sending the Spirit upon him (1:10-11).

The fact that this narrative appears at the very beginning of Mark (in the Prologue) indicates that Mark believed Jesus to be the revelation of the eternal Son, the bearer of salvation, and thus the restorer of creation. He is the Messiah. As such he has penetrated "the wilderness," symbol of evil and death, to affirm God's intention to bring about a new earth. Mark's reference to Jesus being in the wilderness for "forty days," where he was "tempted by Satan," lived with "the wild beasts," and was ministered to by the angels (Mark 1:13), is not without theological significance. Commenting on this passage, Hendrikus Berkhof states, "As the Son of the Creator of this threatening world he [Jesus] lived in it as the lord and master, and he used his freedom to make the love of the Father triumph even in the dark shafts of reality, as a sign of the coming kingdom of peace."[12]

For Mark, the fact that Jesus came from Galilee and not from

Jerusalem seems to be charged with profound theological significance. Mark sees in Jesus the eternal Son of God who became a "nobody" in order to make women and men "somebody" and bring into being a new creation. Paul expresses a similar idea when he states that God chose the world's nobodies to save the world (1 Cor. 1:18-31). By becoming an obscure, "foolish" Galilean, Jesus was able to open the way for a new exodus for Israel—indeed, for the whole world. And it is this historical and theological reality that makes Galilee such a symbolic reference in the Gospels and a landmark in the evangelistic praxis of Jesus.[13]

Galilee as an Evangelistic Landmark

In the Markan text Jesus is presented not only as the one who came *from* Galilee but as the one who came *into* Galilee. He returned to his province, after John had been arrested, to preach "the gospel of God" (Mark 1:14). Following the Markan tradition, all the Gospels assert that Jesus spent the majority of his ministry in Galilee. Even Luke—who develops in both his Gospel narrative and the Acts of the Apostles a theology of "no return," with Jerusalem as its goal (Luke 24:52), and with the aim to go from there "to the end of the earth" (Acts 1:8; 28:14-31)—uses Galilee as a landmark for the Ascension (Acts 1:11) and refers to it as the place where he was baptized and began his ministry (Acts 10:37). In other words, Luke incorporates the Galilean references of Mark in his own theological construct. Likewise, in John's Gospel, Galilee is given a place of prominence at the beginning (John 1:43) and the conclusion (John 21:1).[14] Thus the Fourth Gospel uses Galilee not only as a point of departure for its narrative of Jesus' mission but also as the point of arrival of the risen Christ. It is understandable, says Virgilio Elizondo, that in the Gospel narratives "many of the incidents that are best known to ordinary Christians took place in Galilee, or near it, or on the road between Galilee and Jerusalem."[15]

Galilee was the stage of Jesus' public proclamation of the gospel, a fact that is affirmed not only in the Gospel narratives but also in the liturgical tradition of the church. Very early in the church's history its liturgy was structured around two Christological moments. The first was focused on Jesus' Galilean ministry. It was dedicated to the proclamation of the gospel. The second moment was centered on Christ's death and resurrection. In the words of J.-J. von Allmen, this moment "explains, justifies and elicits the true content of the first."[16] This explains why Christian worship came to be understood as a celebration of the ministerial life and work of Jesus as the focal point of salvation history. It was only natural, therefore, that the first part of the liturgy be a celebration of the proclamation of the gospel as embodied in the public ministry of Jesus, and that the second part be a confirmation of the good news through the celebration of the Eucharist, the memorial of Jesus' suffering death and his continuing presence in the church as the risen Lord.

According to Mark, Jesus came to Galilee proclaiming the kingdom of God. He summarizes Jesus' missionary message in 1:15: "The time is fulfilled, and the kingdom of God is at hand; repent, and believe in the gospel." Scholars generally agree that the theme of "the kingdom" is the most certain datum we have of the content of Jesus' evangelistic ministry.[17] Both in the prophetic literature and in the Psalms, the kingdom theme represents God's active and sovereign rule over all creation (see Ps. 145:10-13). It was proclaimed and celebrated in the temple (see Ps. 24:7-10). It was also taught in the home and later in the synagogue. In fact, the whole life of Israel was to be a continuous affirmation of God's creative and sustaining sovereignty over the world and of the accountability of every living creature to its Lord. God was not an absentee landlord for Israel. God was Yahweh, the Covenant God, the Shepherd King.

There is also in the Hebrew Scriptures (especially in the prophets) the idea of God's kingdom as a future hope: the promise of a radically *new* world order. This new order involves the overcoming of all antagonisms, whether between humankind and nature, whether between people, nations, sexes, generations, or races (see Isa. 11:6ff.). It implies an era of love expressed in an environment of freedom, justice, and peace (well-being) (see Amos 5:24; Jer. 31:33; Isa. 11:12ff.; 19:18ff.; 42:4; 51:4; 60:1ff.). In short, it anticipates the transformation of the entire created order—a new heaven and a new earth (see Isa. 65:17).

While Jesus presupposed (like most Jews) the sovereign rule of God, it was the hope of the kingdom as expressed by the prophets that became the focus of his missionary message. The good news he came proclaiming on God's behalf was the announcement of the messianic age, a new world order. For Jesus, as for the prophets, this new order was the goal of God's mission. God was in the process of inaugurating the kingdom.

Jesus (and the early church) went *beyond* the prophets, however. He announced the breakthrough of the new world. In him that new world had come within the reach of everyone. This is vividly demonstrated in the miracle narratives: they were signs of the new creation; they proclaimed that creation will be made whole—brand new. The proclamation of the kingdom was a witness to the emergence of the new world.

The most outstanding sign of the coming into being of the new world was Jesus' death and resurrection. This event unveiled the mystery of the age to come—an age of life and well-being, not of death and decay. It made possible the anticipation of the kingdom in history (Mark 4:30-32; John 11:25), and yet kept the messianic future open to a final consummation (Mark 13:32).

In summarizing the missionary message of Jesus around the concept of the kingdom, Mark tells his readers that the totality of Jesus' ministerial life and work was a continuous kerygmatic event (a public message). To be sure, it was also a personal message, "the gospel of Jesus Christ, the Son of God" (Mark 1:1). The *locus* of this message was the open space of Galilee. This is why Mark concentrates every major aspect of Jesus' messianic ministry in Galilee. Thus, for example, Jesus called his disciples and other followers (1:16-20; 2:14ff.; 3:13-19) and sent them forth to preach and heal (6:7-13) in Galilee. He began to be rejected in Galilee (3:21; 6:1-6), and from there he launched his pilgrimage to Jerusalem, where he was crucified. In other words, Galilee is the place where Jesus established his messianic credentials, built the base of the messianic community, and began to experience his messianic sufferings for the world.

From Galilee to Jerusalem

From Mark's perspective, Galilee represents the base of Jesus' ministry. Jesus' goal, however, was to confront the powers centered in Jerusalem with the radical message of the kingdom of God. If Galilee was the place of the rejected and the marginal, Jerusalem represented established power, judgment, and death.[18] Not only was it a geographic center; it was the cultural, social, religious, political, and ideological hub of the entire Jewish world. Jews considered Jerusalem to be the center of Israel—indeed, of all the inhabited world. In the words of Ezekiel, God had placed it at the center of the nations (Ezek. 5:5). It was "the center of the earth" (Ezek. 38:12).[19]

The heart of Jerusalem was the temple. The Mishnah required that certain types of tithes be invested only in Jerusalem. Thus three times a year, and especially during Passover, thousands of Jews were drawn to the Holy City from the entire Diaspora. These multitudes of pilgrims came specifically to pray at the temple. It was their business that gave commercial importance to the city. That business not only supported the priestly nobility, the regular clergy, and the temple employees, but also brought great profits to the artisans and the business community.[20] Another reason for the central role of Jerusalem was the fact that it was the seat of the Sanhedrin. This senate of seventy-one members was the highest authority in world Jewry. After Judea became a Roman province in the year 6 C.E., the Sanhedrin became its chief political influence. As the highest Jewish court of law, it not only joined administratively every Judean village but also had links with the entire Diaspora.[21]

The Sanhedrin was made up of three groups: the elders, the scribes, and the chief priests. The elders were, according to Joachim Jeremias, "the heads of the most influential lay families."[22] They were wealthy landowners and represented the secular nobility. Unlike the elders, the scribes did not have a hereditary claim to power. Their power base lay in their knowledge. They were experts of the law—the guardians of the written tradition and its foremost interpreters. They had achieved a prestigious place in the Sanhedrin not only because of their knowledge of the law (Scripture), but especially because, as Jeremias has observed, they were "possessors of divine esoteric knowledge . . . the deepest secrets of divine being," a knowledge that could only be transmitted secretly to a select few (the brightest and choicest rabbinical students).[23] It was the scribes (the majority of whom belonged to the Pharisaic party) who made Jerusalem the most important theological center in world Jewry. Young Jews from all over the world came to the Holy City to study law and theology at the feet of the rabbinical masters of the day.[24]

But by far the most influential sector in the Sanhedrin was the priestly aristocracy. Not only was the Sanhedrin presided over by the high priest, but it was also heavily influenced by its priestly members and the prestige of the temple. "Israel at the time of Jesus," adds Jeremias, "was a pure theocracy, and the priesthood was the primary representative of the nobility."[25] This is all the more significant when we consider the fact that during this period the high-priest families were, by and large, illegitimate. In the words of Jeremias, they had climbed to their posts through sheer "power politics, exercised sometimes ruthlessly . . . sometimes by intrigue."[26]

During the time of Jesus, the high priest was the most powerful Jewish figure in Jerusalem. He and his family controlled not only the temple, the cultus, and the priestly court, but also a considerable number of the seats in the Sanhedrin. Without question he had in his hands the political leadership of the nation. This explains why the Roman authorities negotiated all matters pertaining to Jews with the high priest.

Given this reality, we see why Jesus of Nazareth and his Galilean movement would be such a threat to the Jerusalem establishment. His messianic claims were grounded not in wealth, social status, or power politics but rather in the call of God and the anointment of the Spirit. Furthermore, they were verified by the power of the kingdom at work in his ministry.

By the same token, it is clear why one goal of Jesus' evangelizing mission was to confront the socioreligious leadership of Jerusalem with the message of God's kingdom. Such confrontation unmasked their moral corruption, religious hypocrisy, and oppressive leadership. In so confronting these rebellious and oppressive "powers and principalities," Jesus sought to liberate for the new creation everyone who had fallen under the yoke of sin and death (cf. Matt. 11:28-30). This appears to explain Luke's statement that Jesus "made up his mind and set out on his way to Jerusalem" (Luke 9:51, TEV). Nothing could detain him from fulfilling the redemptive mission entrusted to him by his God and Father (cf. Mark 9:30-32).

The inevitable consequence of Jesus' evangelizing mission, according to Mark, was suffering and death. Jesus anticipated the results of his pilgrimage to Jerusalem; he taught his disciples about it (9:31). But his faithfulness to his mission was such that he was willing to offer his life, if need be, as a redemptive sacrifice (14:36). This vocation of liberating, prophetic service is the predominant focus of the Gospel of Mark, indicated by the verse many scholars consider the "key text" of Mark: "For the Son of man also came not to be served but to serve, and to give his life as a ransom for many" (10:45). Accordingly, Jesus expects his followers to follow in his footsteps. Confronting the authoritarianism and ambition of James and John, Jesus warns his disciples, "Whoever would be great among you must be your servant" (10:43).

The fundamental problem of the disciples ("the Twelve") was understanding the meaning of the redemptive service that accompanied Jesus' evangelizing mission. According to Mark, this was in fact the fundamental problem of all of Israel, and not least of the Israelites who followed Jesus. On the other hand, "the other followers," the majority of whom came from "a 'peripheral' Judaism, on account of their lack of or little commitment to Jewish traditions, . . . accepted without difficulty the message of Jesus."[27] This is the group that, according to Mark, effectively fulfilled the mission (cf. 9:38-41), although it did not represent messianic Israel (which had a temporal priority since it was called first to follow Jesus). That is why Jesus rebuked John when he (symbolizing the intolerance of the Israelite group, which saw itself as privileged) forbade someone not of "the Twelve" to cast out demons in Jesus' name: "Do not forbid him; for no one who does a mighty work in my name will be able soon after to speak evil of me. . . . For . . . whoever gives you a cup of water to drink because you bear the name of Christ, will by no means lose his reward" (9:39, 41).

To this Jesus adds, "Whoever causes one of these little ones who believe in me to [stumble], it would be better for him if a great millstone were hung round his neck and he were thrown into the sea" (9:42). The "little ones who believe" are those who serve in the name of Jesus, those who do what Jesus expects his followers to do. The scandal associated with them could be provoked by the ambition of James and John (9:34) and the desire to dominate (9:38).[28]

While one of "the Twelve" betrays Jesus, another denies him, and all abandon him, "the other followers" accompany him to the end. Simon of Cyrene, who came from the periphery ("the country") and was therefore a prototype of the non-Israelite follower, helped Jesus carry the cross (15:21).[29] The women who "followed him, and ministered to him" in Galilee "and also many other women who came up with him to Jerusalem" (15:41) accompanied him to the cross. Two of them, Mary Magdalene and Mary the mother of Joses, "saw where he was laid" (15:47). Finally, Joseph of Arimathea, "a respected member of the [Sanhedrin], who was also . . . looking for the kingdom of God," daringly "went to Pilate, and asked for the body of Jesus" and "laid him in a tomb" (15:43, 46).

The same situation is repeated in the narratives of the passion and death of Jesus. When the passover meal was concluded, Jesus predicted that "the Twelve" would abandon him: "You will all fall away; for it is written, 'I will strike the shepherd, and the sheep will be scattered'" (14:27). Later, Peter denied him three times (14:72), and Judas betrayed him to "the chief priests, with the elders and scribes, and the whole council," who turned him over to Pontius Pilate (15:1), which indicates that Jesus died as *persona publica* under the official representative of the Roman Empire.

From Galilee to the Nations

According to Mark, Jerusalem was not the end of Jesus' evangelizing mission. Prior to his arrest, he had promised to "go before" the Twelve "to Galilee" after his resurrection (14:28). That promise was fulfilled when an angel announced to the women who had come to the tomb early Sunday morning that Jesus had risen, and commanded them to "go, tell his disciples and Peter that he is going before you to Galilee; there you will see him, as he told you" (16:7).[30]

The expression "going before" in Mark corresponds to the "follow" associated with the call to discipleship. One can observe a parallel between 1:17ff., where the call is given for the first time, and 16:7, where the three women are commanded to go and tell "his disciples and Peter" that Jesus is going ahead of them to Galilee, where he will meet them. The point to make here is that the disciples had to leave Jerusalem and follow Jesus to Galilee in order to "see" him.[31] Jerusalem was neither the place to meet Jesus nor the end of his evangelizing mission. The disciples had to return to the place where they first met Jesus in order to be restored (baptized with the Holy Spirit) and continue his mission (13:10; 14:9). Only by following him faithfully to Galilee, a missionary bridge to the nations, could they re-establish their relation with Jesus and carry on his evangelizing work.

It is not without significance that women were the first to receive the news of Jesus' resurrection and the mandate to relay the message to the disciples and Peter. It is said of them, however, that "they went out and fled from the tomb; for trembling and astonishment had come upon them; and they said nothing to any one, for they were afraid" (16:8). Since the oldest and most reliable manuscripts of the Gospel of Mark end with this verse,[32] it has been conjectured that "the women did not transmit the message to the disciples," which means that "they had not gone out of Jerusalem, that is, that they had not broken with the nationalist ideology and . . . undertaken the mission."[33]

Elisabeth Schüssler Fiorenza has rightly questioned that interpretation. She argues that it fails to take into account the fact that the women fled not from the *angel* but from the empty *tomb.* Their fear was well founded, since to be found in the empty tomb of a condemned person was to run the risk of being arrested. According to Schüssler Fiorenza, the fact that the women fled and did not tell anyone what they had seen and heard "does not imply that they did not obey the command of the angel."[34] She notes that in Mark 1:44 Jesus orders the leper who had been healed to be sure to "say nothing to any one," but sends him to show himself to the priest. The fact that Jesus orders him to keep silent

> does not exclude the information that must be given to the priest. Similarly, the silence of the women *vis-a-vis* the general public does not exclude fulfilling the command to "go and tell his disciples and Peter," and communicating the resurrected Lord's message of his going ahead to Galilee where they shall see him. Mark 16:7 and 8b, therefore, should not be related as command and disobedience of the command, but as command and obedience which brings the message to special designated persons but does not inform anyone else.[35]

This argument, seen in the light of the entire content of Mark, leads us to conclude not only that the message of the Resurrection was communicated to the disciples but that they followed Jesus to Galilee, where they met him and were restored to his fellowship. It was in Galilee that fulfillment of the promise to make them participants, as it were, in his project of world evangelization (1:17) was made possible. In their last encounter, the disciples as well as the other followers of Jesus received the decisive key to understand "the secret of the kingdom of God" (4:11). They began to understand why the cross was necessary when they met the risen Christ. Above all, they realized that Jesus was God's kingdom in person. With this new understanding they were now ready to evangelize the nations. Their meeting with the Lord in the same place where the first disciples had been called to follow him was a "final demonstration" of what Jesus had repeatedly taught them — namely, that he had come "to give himself for the many."[36] Likewise, it was a reminder of the servant character of the evangelization they were to undertake in his name throughout the world. Not only were they reconciled with one another and with the Lord, and restored to his community, but they were liberated and empowered to make known the gospel in all the nations.

The Universality of Galilee

The fact that Mark locates Jesus' evangelizing mission in Galilee is not an accident. The location of Jesus' ministry on the Galilean periphery is congruent with the witness of the New Testament as a whole, which sees Jesus as a poor person who identified with the oppressed and died as one of them to liberate humanity from the power of sin and death and make possible a new order of life—of love, justice, freedom, and peace. If, as the various books of the New Testament teach, evangelization is addressed in the first place to the poor, the dispossessed, and the oppressed,[37] and if they are the ones who are most able to understand the meaning of the gospel (cf. Matt. 11:25), then it follows that Galilee, as a symbol of the periphery, should be understood as a universal in relation to the theology of evangelization. Thus the particularity of the periphery should inform all and each evangelizing context. From this foundational premise, we can say that the Markan model offers three implications for contextual evangelization.

The Sociohistorical Foundation of Evangelization: The Periphery as a Base

Mark's Galilean model implies, first, that contextual evangelization should have a sociohistorical foundation based on the periphery. The communication of the gospel presupposes a base. It does not originate from a tabula rasa; it is not carried out in a vacuum. The base, however, is not simply the point of departure for an action or the place where it is carried out. The base is especially a *fundamental association rooted in the lowest level, or most marginal spaces, of society.* To say that evangelization needs a base rooted in the periphery is to advocate the popular or grass-roots sectors as evangelization's starting point and fundamental point of reference—sectors that in any society constitute, by and large, those rendered marginal in life and powerless in decision-making.[38]

If evangelization starts on the periphery of society, if it works from the bottom up, the good news of God's kingdom is vividly demonstrated and credibly announced as a message of liberating love, justice, and peace. When the gospel makes "somebody" out of the "nobodies" of society, when it restores the self-worth of the marginalized, when it enables the oppressed to have a reason for hope, when it empowers the poor to struggle and suffer for justice and peace, then it is truly good news of a new order of life—the saving power of God (Rom. 1:16). When evangelization begins at the centers of power, working from the top down, its content usually ends up being an easy and cheap accommodation of the vested interests of the mighty and wealthy. In such instances, evangelization suffers reduction, because the content of the gospel is truncated, turned into a private whitewash, manipulated to soothe the conscience of those who, by virtue of their position and power, control—economically, socially, politically, or culturally—the destiny of those on the fringes of society. An evangelistic endeavor geared in the first place to the "elite" of society usually ends up being absorbed by their power systems.

Evangelization is prophetic, and thus liberating, when it has a communal base, a basic, witnessing faith-community. Such a basic community is built from the periphery. The gospel seeks to set men and women free *from* all godless, dehumanizing, alienating, and oppressive forces *for* the service of God's kingdom of liberating love, justice, and peace, to enable them to live freely, obediently, and in solidarity for God and humankind. It follows that evangelization should be able to challenge and transform all absolute and centralizing power systems. This can be achieved by forming faith communities among the marginalized and rejected, the sick and uneducated, little children and alienated women, publicans and sinners, who will be transformed by the saving power of the gospel into a prophetic witnessing movement.[39]

The Public Character of Evangelization: Proclaiming the Kingdom amid the Multitudes

The second thing implied by the contextual model of evangelization that we discover in Mark—and its sociohistorical grounding in Galilee —is that evangelization is by its very nature public. Not only does it have a public message (the presence and promise of God's kingdom in Jesus), but it takes place amid the multitudes. The gospel is a public message of personal concern for each and every human being. The gospel is personal because it is public. It is good news for everyone, not just for a chosen few. Accordingly, it needs to be proclaimed in the "circles of pagans" that comprise our human mosaic. Wherever there are people who do not have a knowledge of the God whose Son was revealed in Jesus, wherever people are trapped in structures of sin and death and are the powerless victims of injustice, suffering, oppression, and poverty, there is to be found the arena of evangelization, and there the gospel is to be proclaimed, Jesus Christ exalted, and the power of the kingdom demonstrated.

The public sphere is the arena of evangelization because it is the arena of the multitudes. It is there where human need is most overtly and nakedly revealed. It is there where women and men are most conscious of their human predicament and vulnerability, and where their solidarity in the face of sin and death is most clearly revealed.

According to Mark, Jesus had compassion on the multitudes (Gr. *ochlos*) "because they were like sheep without a shepherd" (6:34). That is, they were leaderless, without a goal, uncertain of the future. He evangelized them by announcing the dawning of the messianic age and demonstrating its liberating power by feeding them, healing the sick among them, restoring their hope, and inviting them to repent and believe in the gospel.

Proclaiming the good news of the kingdom among the multitudes is without question one of the most pressing evangelistic challenges of our time. Multitudes of human beings around the world find themselves "like sheep without a shepherd," harassed and helpless and threatened by the material and spiritual reality of sin and death. Here it is important to distinguish between numerical multitudes and theological multitudes. Of course, quantitatively speaking, it is not difficult to determine who the multitudes are. What qualifies people as multitudes in the theological sense, however, is their social and spiritual condition—their bearing the brunt of injustice, powerlessness, oppression, and poverty on this planet. Thus oppressed minorities in North America, Europe, Japan, and Australasia, although they are not multitudes in the numerical sense, nevertheless function as a concrete referent of human alienation and vulnerability. In their material condition we see the spiritual reality of sin and death.

The Galilean multitudes can be found everywhere. There is not a neighborhood, town, city, state, nation, or continent that does not have a Galilee. One must always look for the powerless, the marginalized, and the voiceless to discover the concrete reality of Galilee. In the United States, for example, Galilee is particularly evident in the barrios and ghettos of the great urban areas and in the *ranchos* and plantations of rural communities. Without coming to terms with these multitudes, we cannot discover the Galilees that lie on the fringes of powerful and affluent communities in North America. Evangelization in Galilee makes it possible for the gospel to be heard in Jerusalem, in the center of power.

To evangelize the multitudes is to announce the glad news of God's action in Christ to radically change the frail, unjust, and death-prone patterns of human existence by bringing into being a new world. Such an announcement cannot but be public. To keep it private, to announce it only to a select few, is to deny the very content of the gospel. Furthermore, it is to shield its privileged addressees.

When the multitudes are evangelized, everybody hears about it: the press, government authorities, the business community, the religious leadership, the army, the comfortable and secure individuals who usually remain aloof from the cry of the multitudes. Very often such groups and institutions become irritated and threatened, joining forces as a sort of "counter-multitude" to try to quench the hope and aspirations that rise among the harassed multitudes when they hear the gospel and appropriate it by faith in Christ.

We see this borne out in Jesus' ministry. Mark records that when Jesus entered the Holy City accompanied by his followers, his first act was to drive the merchants from the temple (11:15). "Is it not written," he said, quoting Isaiah 56:7, "'My house shall be called a house of prayer for all the nations'? But you have made it a den of robbers" (11:17). When the chief priests and the scribes heard what Jesus had done and said, they immediately "sought a way to destroy him." They feared him because the multitude "was astonished at his teaching" (11:18). The next day Jesus and all of his followers returned to the city. When Jesus told the parable of "the wicked tenants" (12:1-11), the chief priests, scribes, and elders tried to arrest him, perceiving that the parable was against them. But they were prevented from doing so by their fear of the multitude (12:12). A few days later, the chief priests, scribes, and elders managed to organize a "contra multitude" on the basis of a religious coalition of all who could not accept a new age of freedom, fraternity, and peace, an age in which the uncultured and marginalized could live at the same socioreligious level as the privileged few (14:43). It was the "contras" of Jerusalem, the counter-crowd —not the multitudes from Galilee and the periphery—who angrily asked Pilate to release Barnabas and crucify Jesus (Mark 15:8ff.; cf. Matt. 27:15ff.; Luke 23:1-5, 13-21; John 19:6-7, 12, 14-16).

Something similar has occurred in our time in regions like Latin America and South Africa. After centuries of political repression, economic exploitation, racial discrimination, and social marginalization, the multitudes have begun to hear the liberating message of the gospel and appropriate its promises. As a result, the oppressed and dispossessed have begun to anticipate the transforming hope of God's kingdom. The poor have truly begun to receive (at last!) the good news. In addition, a significant minority from the privileged sectors of society —including professionals, intellectuals, students, and religious, business, and political leaders—have progressively ceased to be scandalized by Jesus' identity with the poor and oppressed. Never before have so many Latin American and South African multitudes demonstrated so much openness to the gospel and been so inspired by its promises. And never have the powers and principalities that rule these regions been more irritated and threatened. It is no wonder that they have unleashed a brutal and repressive offensive that has seen literally thousands follow in the path of martyrdom,[40] even as Jesus suffered outside the gates of Jerusalem (Heb. 13:12).

When the multitudes are evangelized, the whole creation hears about it! Indeed, men, women, and children have the opportunity to respond both personally and collectively to the gospel and commit their lives to the Galilean Messiah who cast his lot with the wretched of the earth and made possible a new future for all. And when this occurs, the "powers and principalities" are threatened because business can no longer be done as usual: a new world is in the making, and the old is served notice that it *will* pass away.

This underscores the importance of giving evangelization a strong communitarian base on the periphery of life. For only by establishing a strong base of men, women, and children from the marginalized multitudes, the *ochlos,* can evangelization acquire the authenticity and spiritual vitality necessary to be an efficacious instrument of the kingdom of God. Evangelization can be prophetic and therefore liberating only if it has a committed witnessing base in the trenches of history. The evangelizing practice of our Lord Jesus Christ, corroborated by the work of the Holy Spirit in the life and mission of the church, demonstrates that such evangelistic ministry is possible when one starts from the periphery.

The Global Scope of Evangelization: Communicating the Gospel from the Periphery of the Nations

The third thing implied by the contextual model we find in the Markan analysis of Jesus' Galilean-rooted ministry is that evangelization has a global scope. The fact that in the Markan narrative Galilee became the launching pad for world evangelization should not be taken lightly. As has been noted, evangelization is not a ghetto affair; it takes place in the open space of the multitudes. As an apostolic mandate, it can be fulfilled only through a worldwide pilgrimage. Evangelization is the outgrowth of the movement of Jesus' messianic community through the nations, the response to the Great Commission in Matthew's Gospel: "Go therefore and make disciples of all nations" (28:19).

Evangelization is the communication of the good news to the

multitudes near and far. No individual Christian, local congregation, or denomination can be content simply with ministering to the multitudes that lie geographically and/or culturally near. They should always seek to extend their witness beyond their frontiers. To be evangelistically concerned with those within one's geocultural context while remaining aloof from those who lie beyond one's frontiers is selfish and hypocritical. If the gospel is important for those who are geoculturally close, it should be equally valuable for those who are afar. In short, contextual evangelization should not be limited to local situations. It should be globally contextual, addressing women and men in their sociohistorical reality everywhere on this planet.

This affirmation should not be interpreted as a relativization of the Galilean principle—the evangelistic perspective from the periphery. If this were the case, we would be erasing in a single stroke everything we have been advocating in the previous sections of this chapter. In effect, we would be arguing for a return to an acritical and prophetically mutilated contextualization.

In insisting that contextual evangelization has a global scope, we are building upon our previous arguments. The global scope of contextual evangelization should correspond to the Galilean principle. This means, concretely, that evangelization should be geared, first and foremost, to the nations' peripheries, where the multitudes are found and where the Christian faith has always had the best opportunity to build a strong base. Whenever the Christian faith has been geared to the centers of power (as it has been, for example, in those situations of mission history in which the first to be evangelized was the monarch, the head of state, or the ruling elite), the result has usually been what has been called the great "massification"[41] of the faith. The gospel has been cheapened and devalued. Evangelization has become the propagandistic arm of the ruling classes, focusing on mandatory mass conversions and thereby losing its critical, prophetic edge.[42]

When the gospel is communicated from the periphery of the nations, the outcome is, by and large, much different. The critical, liberating thrust of the gospel comes forth in one way or another, given the similarities between the situation of today's marginalized and the historical situation portrayed in the biblical texts. Indeed, for the poor and the oppressed it is not possible to "demythologize" the gospel, as was proposed several decades ago.[43] For people on the periphery, it is not difficult to relate the Christ of the gospel with Jesus of Nazareth. They have no problem in understanding the life and saving message of Jesus or his death and resurrection because they have no other historical instruments to mediate the gospel message besides their experience and reality.

At the popular level the theoretical postulates of any religion are relativized. For people who live on the fringes of society, the fundamental theological question is, Does religion have a liberating word to say to us? From the perspective of Jesus and the gospel, the answer is affirmative, even if the answer given through the behavior of Christians and the church in history has often been negative.

This question was vividly articulated during a visit I made several years ago to the Republic of Sri Lanka. I participated, with several colleagues from around the world, in an "immersion exposure" to urban Colombo from the perspective of the shantytowns where half of the population live. We saw Buddhists, Hindus, Muslims, and Christians living side by side, suffering and experiencing together the effect of a dehumanized social, economic, and political reality. This situation is powerfully described in a local song:

> Cardboard and tin cans all straightened out
> Patched up with these and blocked round about
> Everyman's junk we've built up our house
> That's one of many in old shanty town.
>
> A million mosquitoes, we wait for the rain
> To wash away all the dirt-filled-up drains
> The water we get comes down from the skies
> But the drought's going on and our home's full of flies.
>
> A slum is where the world forgets who you are
> They close their eyes, no time to care
> They pass you by, faces full of frowns
> Turned up noses at our shanty town.

This same song extends a moving invitation:

> Come, take my hand
> Some time can you give
> To open your heart and see how we live
> Visit my home, I'll take you around
> The Forgotten People of old shanty town.

We visited the "forgotten people of old shanty town" and saw ourselves deeply interrogated from the very heart of the Christian faith. How is it that the ruling elite can be satisfied with the dehumanization that occurs in these slums? How have religious communities in general and Christians in particular allowed themselves to become so dehumanized that they can go to sleep peacefully despite the millions around them who live and suffer in the shantytowns of the world? We discovered the shantytown—which is found almost everywhere in the world, including the Americas—as a new universal. (It is simply called different names in different places. In the United States, it is called the urban barrio or ghetto; in Puerto Rico, it is called *arrabal;* in Central America, *tugurio;* in southern Brazil, *favela;* in Peru, *pueblo joven;* in Argentina, *villa miseria.*) Most importantly, however, we professors, who came from around the world to learn about and reflect theologically on the problem and challenge of religious pluralism, left feeling that we had been evangelized by the risen Christ shining forth from the suffering faces of the residents of the shantytowns of Sri Lanka. We heard a message of liberating love, justice, and peace, accompanied by a call to a praxis of transformation among the poor and dispossessed of the earth.

Our urban barrios and ghettos are without a doubt a fundamental point of reference in evangelization. They are also a disturbing sign of the dehumanizing effect of sin, and a liberating possibility for those who take the gospel sincerely. My experience in Sri Lanka reconfirmed my conviction, derived first of all from the evangelistic praxis of Jesus, that an authentic contextual evangelization should start from the periphery with an immersion in the pain and agony of the people who live on the fringes and the bottom of society. In such an immersion experience, one encounters the risen Lord, enlarging and deepening one's limited vision of human reality, challenging one's presuppositions, renewing one's mind, and liberating and empowering one's life for service as a channel of grace in the "Galilees of the nations."

Some make the mistake of starting in Jerusalem rather than Galilee and end up frustrated or co-opted by the ruling "powers and principalities."[44] They gear the message to a select few rather than the harassed multitudes and end up with a historically harmless church, a private gospel, and a plastic Jesus. When this happens, evangelization loses its dynamic and ends up fossilized, crippled as a vital, worldwide, transforming force.

But if we take Galilee as a serious evangelistic context, our praxis will never be alienating, dull, static, or without challenge. For we will be forced to ask, *Where* is our base, *who* is our target audience, and *what* is the scope of our evangelistic praxis? These are the types of questions that help us recover the prophetic, liberating, holistic, and global apostolic legacy in the tradition of Jesus, our Messiah and Lord, Savior and Teacher.

CHAPTER V

The God of the Evangel

The Trinitarian Community as an Evangelizing Presence

Evangelization is the storytelling of God's saving message as it has become an integral part of our lives as people of faith. This understanding proceeds not only from the Markan narrative of Jesus' evangelizing ministry, which tells us that he "came into Galilee, preaching the gospel of God" (1:14). It is also rooted in the evangelistic ministry and theology of the Apostle Paul, that great missionary evangelist of the early church. At the beginning of the Epistle to the Romans, Paul declares that although he was "a servant of Jesus Christ, called to be an apostle," he was nevertheless "set apart for the gospel of God" (Gr. *euangelion theou*; Rom. 1:1). As an apostle, he was dedicated exclusively to the communication of God's saving message, especially among the Gentiles. He interpreted his evangelizing mission as a perennial witness to the God of Abraham, Isaac, and Jacob who had sent good news of eternal salvation through Jesus the Messiah in the power of the Spirit. Paul grounded his calling and mission, therefore, in God.

How different was Paul's understanding from ours! For God is often the one we least think of when reflecting on evangelization. We worry about knowing the right scriptural texts. We make sure that our hearers know the meaning of sin and salvation, grace and works, heaven and hell, Christ, the Holy Spirit, and the church. We get concerned about having the proper evangelistic environment in our churches. But God . . . well . . . we take the Dear One for granted—even though the evangel originates with and is intended to lead the world to God, despite the fact that the church is God's assembly (Gr. *ekklesia*) and exists for God's praise, and notwithstanding the fact that the meaning of Jesus Christ and the Holy Spirit becomes clear only in the context of the mission of God.

We need to repossess the biblical understanding of evangelization as a witness to God. Indeed, to communicate the gospel faithfully, we need to bear in mind that it proceeds from God, has Jesus the Messiah as its content, and is transmitted by the dynamic power of the Holy Spirit. In other words, we need to remember that God is the spiritual reality that surrounds and undergirds the evangelistic event.

The Bible bears witness to a God who is not a static, fixed being removed from us, who points to a divine reality which has a history that has become part of our history and yet transcends it. This is an affirmation to which the Apostle Paul bore eloquent witness in his sermon at the Athenean Areopagus, according to the narrative in Acts 17:22-31.[1] In this sermon Paul underscored four dimensions of God's history: (1) God before all (v. 24), (2) God for all (vv. 25-27), (3) God in all (v. 28), and (4) God after all (v. 31). For Paul, God is not an unknown, abstract being. God has a historical identity, a past as well as a present and a future. God is above and beyond us but also among us. Therefore, all evangelistic efforts are not only preceded but accompanied and completed by God. By the same token, all historical events have an evangelistic cutting edge. They witness to God's presence in and sovereignty over history.

The Scriptures also indicate that God is not solitary but exists in community. The biblical Christian God has a communal identity: he is one-in-relation. Thus the New Testament speaks of God as the Father[2] of our Lord Jesus, who is himself the begotten Son of God sent to save the world through the power of the Holy Spirit. The Father is glorified in the reconciliation of the world by the power of the Spirit through the death and resurrection of the Son. In other words, we can know this God only as a Trinitarian community.

In this chapter I propose to underscore the relevance of God's communal identity for evangelization. I shall explore the Trinitarian foundation of the evangel in order to set forth its dynamic operation in evangelization, and thus demonstrate how it motivates, empowers, and corrects the church's evangelistic ministry.

Trinitarian Foundation of the Gospel

The gospel presupposes a twofold movement: from God to the world and from the world back to God.[3] The first of these movements discloses God as the holy and loving Father of Jesus, and as the loving and obedient Son of the Father. The second reveals God as uniting Spirit. This double movement refers us to God's inner life, where we discover God as holy love sending and seeking, or as a community of mission and unity.

From God to the World: Holy Love and Loving Obedience

The gospel is the story of the sending of the only begotten Son of the Father to redeem the world. In this action we see reflected the foundation of God's existence: holy love. God is both "light" and "love" (1 John 1:5; 4:8, 16). In other words, God exists in love—that is, in communion—and this love is holy, transparent, without variation, self-determined for communion. "God's love," says P. T. Forsyth, "is love in holy action, in forgiveness, in redemption."[4] It is "God's movement toward his creatures for the purpose of communion."[5] God's holiness fixes and assures God's love. Only "the holy can love for ever and for ever subdue the loveless; only the holy can thoroughly forgive so as to make his holiness dear."[6]

The God who exists in holy love is made known to us in the New Testament as the holy and loving Father of Jesus. This is the God of Israel whom Jesus called "Abba" and to whom we are to pray this prayer:

> Our Father who art in heaven,
> Hallowed be thy name,
> Thy kingdom come,
> Thy will be done,
> On earth as it is in heaven.
> Give us this day our daily bread;
> And forgive us our debts,
> As we also have forgiven our debtors;
> And lead us not into temptation,
> But deliver us from evil. (Matt. 6:9-13)

God is Jesus' holy Father whose kingdom Jesus came to proclaim and whose will he came to fulfill. He taught us, therefore, to pray in the same spirit, hallowing the name of the Father, seeking the promised kingdom, and doing God's will. Our prayers are to reflect our relationship to God in life. We are to pray even as we live: in reverence, hope, and obedience. Even more, the God of glory (heaven) and power (the kingdom) whom Jesus taught us to honor and obey is the God of love on whom we are to depend for our physical needs, whose redemptive grace is to be the foundation of our human existence, and on whose liberating power we are to depend for deliverance from the Evil One.

Jesus was so dependent on God. His whole way of life was one of dependent and confident prayer. The fact that he addressed God as Father is indicative not only of his dependence but of his confidence in the nearness of the Father. Jesus' God was not just the Holy One but the loving Father who was near to him. Jon Sobrino has rightly noted that "what characterizes Jesus is the way his whole life is concentrated in the confidence that the Father is near to him. Because God is not hidden at a remote distance, this familiarity and exclusivity is both possible and legitimate. Moreover, it heightens and brings out the whole drama of the cross, where Jesus is abandoned by the Father in whom he has placed all his trust."[7]

According to Scripture, it is precisely the Father's delivering Jesus unto death that shows par excellence the Father's holy love. For, indeed, the Father "did not spare his own Son but gave him up for us all" (Rom. 8:32). God is love because he gave up his most precious love for the unloved. God is holy because not even the only begotten Son of the Father was spared to make possible the redemption of a sinful and death-prone world. "In this the love of God was made manifest among us, that God sent his only Son into the world, so that we might live through him" (1 John 4:9). Thus the drama of the cross is the holy action of the Father's love delivering the Son for the purpose of communion with the world.

There is, however, another dimension to the first movement of the gospel story. For the Son is not passive in the drama of the cross. The holy love of the Father finds its correspondence in the loving obedience of the Son. Jesus was "obedient unto death" (Phil. 2:8). His love for the Father and the world was manifested in his obedient sacrifice. As we have noted, obedience in the biblical sense is not blind action but rather the disposition to hear and follow. Jesus was the faithful covenant partner who heeded God's holy word and followed through on God's will to communion. He was at one with the Father. Like Isaac, he gave himself fully to the will of his Father even at the price of death.[8] He humbled himself and followed through on the Father's holy determination to be honored and glorified in the faithful obedience of the human race. He took the place of the entire human race and willingly gave himself out of love to the Father for the world. Not "what I will, but what thou wilt" was his ultimate prayer to the Father (Mark 14:36). This is why Paul could state that Jesus loved him (and everyone)—because Jesus "gave himself" in atoning death (Gal. 2:20).

The cross shows a correspondence of wills between Father and Son: both act out of love and for love. Thus the cross discloses God's identity as the holy and loving Father and as the loving and obedient Son. There we see the Father passionately delivering the Son out of holy love for the world and the Son suffering death for the world in loving obedience to the Father.

The cross of Christ is, in the words of Jürgen Moltmann, "the material principle of the doctrine of the Trinity." Only at the cross can we understand the Trinitarian reality of God. Conversely, "the formal principle of knowledge of the cross is the doctrine of the Trinity."[9] We can comprehend the mystery of the cross only in Trinitarian terms. The cross can make sense only in light of the Father's holy love delivering the Son for the world and the Son's loving obedience in offering himself to the Father "through the eternal Spirit" (Heb. 9:14) to make possible the reconciliation of the world with God and the glorification of God by a redeemed world.

From the World to God: The Uniting Spirit

The gospel is not only the story of the sending of the Son by the Father to redeem the world, but also of the Holy Spirit bringing the world to God through the Son for the glory of the Father. The Spirit, who in the tradition of the Old Testament represents God-in-action, is the One who made possible the sending of the Son. Indeed, Jesus' identification with the world on behalf of the Father in his birth, baptism, and ministry; his suffering death as the Father's atoning offering for sin and the Father's true representative of the world who took upon himself the sins of the world; and his victorious resurrection, which confirmed the reconciliation of the world and set in motion a new creation—all of these aspects of the mission of Christ were accomplished by the power of the Spirit.

The Holy Spirit is the uniting member of the Trinity. The Spirit is not only the connecting link between the Father, who delivers the Son unto death, and the Son, who in his trust and obedience is abandoned by the Father; the Spirit is also the one who unites the mission of the crucified and risen Son with his future with the Father in glory. Moreover, the Spirit unites the community of faith with the Son and has made possible the unity of the world with God. Indeed, the Spirit keeps alive the redemptive hope of the entire creation (cf. Rom. 8:18ff.).

Just as the unity between the mission of Jesus and his future with the Father in glory is affirmed in his continuing presence as the Lord of history and the church, so the unity of the community of faith with the Son is demonstrated by its participation in his continuing mission through the power of the Spirit, even as promised in the New Testament (cf. John 14:26; 16:7; 20:22; Acts 1:4-8). This unity is also expressed by the Spirit's intercession for the believing community through the advocacy of the Son (Rom. 8:26-27; 1 John 2:1). Jesus has become one with the Spirit. The Spirit is now so linked with the risen Christ, who has become a life-giving spirit, that in the Epistles the Spirit is referred to as the Spirit of Christ. This "pneumatic Christ" (that is, the risen Christ acting through the Spirit) now has the mission to bring the kingdom to its final consummation and reunite the world with the Father, so that God may be at last "everything to everyone" (1 Cor. 15:20-28, 42-50; 2 Cor. 3:17-18).[10]

Love Sending and Seeking: God as Mission and Unity

The twofold movement presupposed in the gospel refers us to the internal life of the Trinity. Indeed, what in classical theology is known as the "imminent Trinity" finds its correspondence in the "economic Trinity." That is to say that our knowledge of the inner life of the Trinity is derived from the saving deeds of the Triune God.[11] We are able to discern the origin and motive of the mission of God in history—namely, holy love—from the reciprocal historical relations of the Son with the Father and his union with the Spirit.

The mission of the Father in the internal life of the Trinity is loving the Son. The mission of the Son is loving the Father. The mission of the Spirit is maintaining the bond of love between Father and Son. The imminent Trinity can be described, therefore, as a holy community of love, a Tri-unity.

The Trinitarian history of Father, Son, and Spirit reveals a self-giving and fulfilling God, eternally existing as holy love, sending and seeking. As Moltmann explains, "The sending of the Son for the salvation of the world, and the seeking of the Spirit for the union of the world with the Son and the Father can be summed up . . . as *the love of God* that goes out from itself"[12] for the purpose of communion. Accordingly, God should be thought of as mission and unity.

The gospel proceeds from this communal, missionary, and uniting God. The gospel is the story of the Father sending Jesus Christ the Son to lay down his life for a godless, broken, and death-prone world in order to redeem it, regenerate it, and restore it to communion with God. Hidden in this wonderful story is the reconciling activity of the Holy Spirit uniting the world with Father and Son in the all-embracing love of their eternal communion. God is glorified by the telling of and obedient response to the gospel story.

Trinitarian Dynamics in Evangelization

Whereas in our reflection on the gospel story we start with the sending of the Son by the Father, in thinking about the communication of that story we have to move from the opposite direction. Instead of starting with the sending of the Son, we have to begin with the arrival of the Spirit, which implies the dawning of the "eschaton," the coming into being of the new creation. Therefore, the first point to be made in reference to evangelization as such has to do with the reconciling action of the Holy Spirit through the cross of the Son. This event discloses the Spirit as the power (or creative energy) of evangelization.

The Reconciling Action of the Spirit as the Power of Evangelization

Evangelization is the province of the Spirit. Outside of the Spirit's dynamic operation there cannot be any effective communication of the gospel.

The New Testament speaks of the Holy Spirit as the *external force* of the evangelistic process. As we have noted, Jesus came into Galilee "in the power of the Spirit" (Luke 4:14). The Spirit anointed him "to preach good news to the poor . . . to proclaim release to the captives and recovery of sight to the blind, to set at liberty those who are oppressed, to proclaim the acceptable year of the Lord" (Luke 4:18-19). In Luke and Acts, we see Jesus urging his disciples not to leave Jerusalem until they were clothed with the Spirit's power (Luke 24:49; Acts 1:4). He said to them, "You shall receive power when the Holy Spirit has come upon you; and you shall be my witnesses . . . to the end of the earth" (Acts 1:8). The Book of Acts is the story of how this promise was fulfilled in the earliest church.

The Spirit is also the *internal force* of the evangelistic process (John 6:63, 65; 15:26; 14:26; 16:13, 8; Rom. 8:9, 14; Eph. 1:13). Without the Spirit, evangelization becomes an exercise in futility. For one thing, the human mind is in itself incapable of understanding the mystery of God's love revealed in Christ. For another, women and men are in themselves unable to turn away from their sins and commit their lives to Christ in response to his saving deed. The reconciling work of the Spirit in evangelization is evidenced in at least four areas.

First, the Holy Spirit brings awareness of the history and meaning of Christ. The Spirit is the fundamental witness to the historicity of Jesus and the teacher par excellence of the truth of Christ's saving work. Only by the Spirit's power can women and men experience salvation through Jesus Christ.

Second, the Spirit of God convicts men and women of their fundamental alienation from God and their need of reconciliation through the Son. The Spirit convinces them of their moral and spiritual failure, the holiness of God, and their ultimate accountability to the Lord Jesus Christ. The Spirit creates faith where there is no faith and starts the people of faith on a new life-journey, enabling them to turn from the power of selfishness and greed to the freedom of service and community, liberating them from the captivity of an old order of death and injustice for the freedom of a new order of life and justice.

Third, the Holy Spirit anticipates the future freedom of the kingdom of glory wherein creation shall be made whole and brought to its consummation, a liberating existence shall be universally established, and the promised messianic peace shall be at last fulfilled.[13] The Spirit is "the guarantee of our inheritance" (Eph. 1:13-14). By the Spirit's power we are regenerated (Titus 2:5) and born anew into a living hope (1 Pet. 1:3) for the praise of the Father and the Son (Eph. 1:6, 14, 17).

Fourth, the Holy Spirit makes the new life a sign of hope *for* the world.[14] In the new life in the Spirit, the whole creation finds a sign of its liberation from death and decay. Thus the entire creation finds reason to hope for its future salvation through the Spirit's witness to the promised glorification of the children of God (cf. Rom. 8:16-23).

The reconciling action of the Spirit does not take place in a vacuum—isolated, as it were, from the tangible and concrete. Nor is it limited to the inner life of believers. The sphere of action of the Spirit in evangelization is history, the concrete history of women and men. The experience of the Spirit finds its correspondence in the life according to the Spirit. In biblical Christian faith, subjectivity is verified objectively.

Thus, for example, the Spirit's witness to the history and meaning of Jesus Christ needs to be seen in connection with the objectivity of Scripture. Scripture is the primary source of the Spirit's witness. No one can claim to own the Spirit; rather, each one's perception of the Spirit of truth is judged by that foundational witness which the church has recorded in Scripture, preserved in its tradition, and transmitted in its mission.

The Spirit's transformation of the personal lives and social existence of women and men finds its correspondence in their outward behavior in society and the transformation of their reality. They that testify to have been born of the Spirit must demonstrate the fruits of the Spirit in their personal lives and their social environment.

Similarly, the anticipation of the future freedom of the new life in Christ is made evident in the ongoing life of the community of faith. The liberating love, justice, and peace that characterize the life of the kingdom of God are also to characterize the personal and collective lifestyle of believers. Indeed, they are to be the criteria by which the church evaluates its mission in general and its ministries in particular.

The Spirit's signal of hope for the world in the ecclesial community is confirmed in the liberating service of the people of God on behalf of the world. To speak of hope for a new world without engaging in concrete attempts to make this world a better place to live in is to deny that very hope; indeed, it is to escape into a vague and otherworldly abstraction that paralyzes the transforming force of the eschatological mission of the gospel and ends up sacralizing the status quo. Hope for the transformation of the world without liberating action in the world is blasphemy.

The Cross of Christ as the Mediating Sign of Evangelization

If the Spirit's reconciling action is the power of evangelization, the cross of the Son is its mediating sign. In this context, a sign is a material object that points beyond itself to a spiritual and eschatological reality. Paul describes the gospel in terms of the cross. For him, preaching the cross is the same as communicating the good news (1 Cor. 1:18). What is it that enables such an ugly, contradictory, and scandalous object to be a mediating sign of the good news that is communicated in evangelization? How can a symbol of suffering and death be a sign of life and hope? Just why is the cross so important in evangelization?

Both the Gospels and the Epistles see the cross as central to the good news because it is the place where God's work for the reconciliation of the world took place. The cross discloses God the Father of Jesus sparing a godless world by the deliverance of his only begotten Son. It reveals the Son offering himself in a godforsaken death through the Spirit in order to justify a godless world and reconcile it with the Father (Rom. 8:24, 32; Heb. 9:14; 2 Cor. 5:19). This marks a deep abyss between Father and Son and yet an inward unity: the Father forsakes the Son, and the Son feels himself forsaken; the Father delivers the Son unto death, and the Son willingly offers himself as a sacrifice for sin. At the cross we see the Father suffering because of the death of his beloved Son, the Son suffering because he is forsaken by the Father, and the Spirit proceeding from the deliverance to death by the Father through the forsaken agony of the Son in order to fill with love the despised, rejected, and lonely, and liberate the world from the power of sin and death. Thus the Spirit sets the world free through the crucified Son.

The cross explains the significance of the reconciliation proclaimed in the gospel and is itself the basis of the evangelistic mandate. The content of this mandate is the message of reconciliation. The God who through the Son suffered death for the reconciliation of the world has given the church the ministry of reconciliation (2 Cor. 5:18-19) to be carried out through the power of the Spirit.

Earlier I quoted Moltmann in his designation of the cross as the "material principle of the doctrine of the Trinity." (In that same context, Moltmann quotes two well-known statements by Immanuel Kant: "Concepts without perception are empty" and "Perceptions without concepts are blind."[15]) We can say that the cross is the material principle not only of the doctrine of the Trinity but also of the message of reconciliation. The cross discloses the basis of the evangelistic mandate—namely, the deliverance of Christ unto death for the reconciliation of the world.

The cross is, therefore, the criterion by which we may evaluate our evangelistic performance. Our evangelistic practice flows from our union with Christ. Christ "died for all, that those who live might live no longer for themselves but for him who for their sake died and was raised" (2 Cor. 5:15). This "living for him" is not to be conceived in personalistic terms, as a mere "I-thou" relationship. Rather, it is to be understood as a living for him *in the world*, in the service of the "others" for whom Christ died (Heb. 13:14-15). Participation in the ministry of reconciliation is the evidence of the sanctified life.

If our union with Christ is measured by our participation in the ministry of reconciliation, our evangelistic performance must also be evaluated by the cross. How else can we test the faithfulness of our ministry except by the place where it was concretely revealed? We need to pay close attention to the exhortation of the writer of Hebrews: "Jesus . . . suffered outside the gate in order to sanctify the people through his own blood. Therefore let us go forth to him outside the camp, and bear the abuse he endured" (Heb. 13:12-13). This is a concrete exhortation. We are not to carry our evangelistic ministry inside but rather outside the comfortable walls of our secure churches. We are to go to the crossroads of life, among the outcast, the unsanctified, proclaiming Christ with sweat, blood, and tears.[16] Lesslie Newbigin captures this image when he describes the church's evangelistic mission as "sharing the life of the Son."[17]

The problem with many of the activities that today pass for evangelization is that they fail to meet the test of the cross. The gospel they proclaim has been made such a marketable message—offering a plastic Jesus and an inoffensive call to a terrific, happy life that guarantees an unending good time—that it has become unrecognizable. The churches and groups that advocate such evangelization appear to be carbon copies of the consumer society. It is difficult to differentiate them from sophisticated social clubs, cultural associations, and businesses that specialize in providing a variety of religiously oriented services. Indeed, one of the most serious problems facing the community of faith today (at least in the Americas) is that evangelization has become so popular with people in the mainstream that it has turned out to be a powerful ideological weapon in the hands of those who are more interested in maintaining their social, economic, and cultural privileges than in responding affirmatively to those who are on the bottom of society—namely, the poor, the powerless, and the oppressed. When people claim to be born of the Spirit and then icily continue to turn their backs on the outcast and disenfranchised, then it is time for us to ask whether they have been born of the Spirit of the crucified Christ or born of the spirit of the Antichrist. When churches report phenomenal numerical growth as a result of their evangelistic endeavors and then continue to sacralize the status quo, failing to demonstrate a qualitatively distinct style of life and obstructing the transformation of the social, economic, cultural, and political institutions of society, then we have every right to question the evangelistic performance of such churches and ask whether they are being faithful to the message of the cross.

The Kingdom of God as the Goal of Evangelization

The goal of evangelization is not simply to promote the growth of the church or merely to help individuals come to salvation. Rather, the all-encompassing goal of evangelization is to make known God's kingdom as embodied in Jesus Christ and made present by the Holy Spirit. In so doing, evangelization prepares the way for the revelation of the kingdom of glory. We can isolate three specific contributions that the church makes in its evangelistic witness toward that end.

First, through evangelization the church leads women and men to confess Jesus as Messiah and Son of God. To confess Christ is to believe in the kingdom, since Christ embodied it in his life, proclaimed it in his ministry, and made possible its anticipation in history through his death and resurrection. In the resurrection of the crucified Jesus, God his Father revealed the liberating rule of the kingdom and thus inaugurated a new order of life. The kingdom involves both the present anticipation of that new order and its final consummation in glory. The Lordship of Christ stands for that rule and that order. In confessing Jesus as Christ and God's Son, we acknowledge Jesus to be in himself the kingdom—the liberating sovereign of history.

Second, through evangelization the church builds itself up—but only as a sign and an instrument of the kingdom. The church is the community of those who have confessed Jesus as the Christ and the Son of God. It is the fellowship brought into being by the Spirit of the new creation. The church is recognized by at least three characteristics: (1) obedience to (or faith in) the Word of Christ, (2) the sharing of his love both with those inside the household of God and with those outside it, and (3) bearing witness to the hope of the kingdom in and for the world. Faith, love, and hope find their correspondence in (1) the church's calling to the perpetual refusal to acknowledge as Lord and Savior anyone else but Christ, (2) the church's representation of and intercession for those who are still outside the kingdom, and (3) the church's selfless commitment to the future and well-being of the world.

Third, evangelization serves the kingdom by enabling the church to celebrate its fulfillment in the Spirit. In Christ, women and men are transformed into a worshiping community that lives "for the praise of his glory" (Eph. 1:12). They are constituted "a spiritual house, . . . a holy priesthood" (1 Pet. 2:5), a living temple that renders a perpetual song of praise to "the wonderful deeds" (1 Pet. 2:9) of the God of the kingdom.

Contextual Evangelization in Light of Its Trinitarian Framework

What, then, is the meaning of contextual evangelization in light of its Trinitarian foundation and dynamic? What does it imply for our evangelistic witness in our respective situations? I offer the following response.

Witness in the Presence of the Triune God

First, *contextual evangelization implies witnessing everywhere and at all times in the presence of the total activity of the triune God.* The Christian church bears witness not to a static God but rather to a dynamic divine community that makes itself known in history as Father, Son, and Spirit, sending and seeking in love, redeeming and uniting the unloved. God is, therefore, present in every situation of life.

This implies that we cannot separate God's redemptive activities in the evangelistic process from what Father, Son, and Spirit are doing in the secular affairs of life. The same God who created the world redeemed it. The same God who provides for the well-being of the earth judges those who exploit and destroy its resources. God is one, but one in community, a Tri-unity. Communicating the good news of salvation with integrity in our respective life situations means relating that message to God's involvement in all the spheres of human life and to the totality of God's concern for the well-being of our planet and the universe.

Further, since evangelization is a witness that is borne in the presence of the God who precedes us and is beyond us, whose love has been revealed in the mystery and passion of the cross, and who seeks tenderly and persistently those who have sinned as well as those who have been sinned against, those who do justice and those who practice injustice, the communication of the good news needs to be carried out in *faith* and *prayer.* The ecclesial community does not exercise control over the evangelistic process. No individual believer, church, local congregation, or parachurch group can program success in evangelization or predict its failure. We can only reach out in faith, trusting God to bless our witness and honor the word of the gospel. We can only pray that God will prepare the hearts of women and men, use our witness for their conversion, and help us to have courage and patience when things don't work out according to our expectations. But faith and prayer are no small things! Indeed, they are extraordinary resources that God puts at the disposal of the evangelizing community. Only a technologically conceited church would be unwilling to accept its limitations, confess that as far as the communication of the gospel is concerned it is totally dependent upon God for effectiveness, and resist the temptation to program and manipulate God's mysterious work.

Human History and the History of God

The second point to make is that *contextual evangelization involves an immersion of the evangelizing community into both the depth of human history and the history of the Triune God.* Since the gospel is centered on the cross, evangelization must incorporate humankind's history of death, abandonment, and godlessness as part of the history —or life—of God in the Trinity. Human suffering and death were taken up into God's suffering at Golgotha. They have become part of the economy of salvation and the inner life of the Trinity.[18] Therefore, human suffering and death must be a fundamental referent of the kerygma. In other words, they should be part of the story of the cross whenever the gospel is proclaimed. That is why evangelization should start with those who lie at the bottom, those who are the representatives par excellence of the tragic human history of selfishness, injustice, greed, alienation, and despair. In every society they are specific groups in specific locations. In North America, for example, they are nonwhite ethnic minorities, exploited farm workers, and the permanent underclass of the urban ghettos. They are also prostitutes, convicts, drug addicts, and alcoholics; they are lonely elderly, frustrated youth, denigrated women, rejected handicapped, and despised homosexuals. They are *los de abajo*—the poor, the powerless, and the oppressed in affluent North America.

Those who are so designated are also the privileged addressees of the gospel—those whom Jesus called blessed and to whom he gave the promise of the kingdom (Luke 6:20). The poor, the powerless, and the oppressed are privileged not because they are better than the rest of us but rather because in their destitution they are a living witness to the magnitude of God's suffering love. They are blessed because they have no one else but God and are, therefore, more willing to put their faith in him alone. Evangelization must take place "outside the camp," because it is there that we can meet these people, the wretched and the outcast, and come face to face with the crucified Messiah who is present in their midst (cf. Matt. 11:25-27; 25:31ff.).[19]

Reconciliation of the World

The third point to make is that *contextual evangelization should be understood by the community of faith as an opportunity to make a significant contribution toward the reconciliation of the world with itself and with God.* The church is able to make such a contribution through the faithful proclamation, anticipation, and celebration of the liberating rule of God and the new creation that came into being through the resurrection of Christ.

Evangelization cannot be divorced from the ecumenical task of the church. As firstfruits of a new humanity, the community of faith is called to be "perfectly one" to enable the world to be reconciled with God and with itself (John 17:23). The church ought not to forego any opportunity to work for world peace and Christian unity. The argument that in working toward these goals the church may divert its energies from its primary task of evangelization constitutes a basic misunderstanding of the heart of the gospel and a lack of appreciation for the seventh beatitude: "Blessed are the peacemakers, for they shall be called [children] of God" (Matt. 5:9). Working for world peace and Christian unity is a mark of the church. If it is true that the best credential the church has in its evangelistic witness is the way in which it lives the gospel, then if the church fails to work for its own unity and the unity of the world, it denies its essence and thus renders itself incapable of bearing witness to the gospel. An evangelistic church should also be an ecumenical community, and an ecumenical church should always be an evangelizing community—if they are not, they will deny the ground and meaning of evangelization and ecumenicity.

The Ministry of the Whole People of God

The fourth point to make is that *contextual evangelization should not be seen as an activity that is done on a part-time basis by a group of specialists. Rather, it should be understood as a ministry that belongs to the whole people of God.* God's people exist as communities of worship and witness. They are gathered out of the breadth and depth of human life for the praise of God's glory, and are sent into the world as bearers of the good news. In the gathered community they celebrate the gospel; in their respective life situations they share it with their neighbors from the depth of their common struggles, a broad range of human endeavors and values, and the groaning hope of the entire creation.

While it is true that some among the people of God are given a special gift of evangelization, it should be remembered that the church as a whole has been entrusted with the ministry of evangelization. This means that the whole people of God are to be responsible for the communication of the gospel at all times and in all places, using all the means at their disposal. This requires continuous motivation, recruitment, instruction, organization, and support at the grass-roots of the life and mission of the church. Such a task is possible only if the church understands evangelization as its base and sees itself as a basic evangelizing community, and only if the church rediscovers the evangelistic cutting edge of all its ministries and makes a conscious effort to make that part and parcel of its everyday life.

We began this chapter by addressing the importance of God in the communication of the evangel. We have noted that God is not only the foundation of evangelization but also the spiritual presence that permeates it. God is not a solitary monarch existing apart from us. Rather, God is the eternal community of Father, Son, and Holy Spirit whose holy love, loving obedience, and reconciling action are the source, content, and power of the gospel. The Trinitarian foundation of the gospel is made evident at the cross, where we see the Father delivering the Son unto death and the Son offering himself to the Father through the Spirit as an atonement for a godless, godforsaken, and unloved world. The coming kingdom of the Triune God is the goal of the gospel message and the hope that feeds its communication in the world.

It is in light of the reconciliation effected at the cross, confirmed in Christ's resurrection, and experienced in the church that the Holy Spirit re-unites the world with God for the glory of the Father. New life is now communicated to the world by the preaching of the gospel in the power of the Spirit through the life and mission of the church.

This Trinitarian understanding of the God of the gospel offers a vision of God as a universal and yet particular community—transcendent and imminent—of mission and unity. This is the spiritual context of evangelization, the formal principle of the salvation announced in the gospel, and the basis of the church's witness as the basic evangelizing community.

CHAPTER VI

The Message of the Cross

Life and Hope through Suffering and Death

In the previous chapter we noted that the Apostle Paul equates the gospel with "the word of the cross." For Paul, preaching the cross was identical with the communication of the gospel (1 Cor. 1:18). Such an identification is characteristic of apostolic evangelization in general.[1] It denotes the importance of the cross for the apostolic church and its centrality in the New Testament interpretation of the economy of salvation. For the historical Jesus the gospel was the good news of God's coming kingdom; for the early church the gospel was the good news concerning Jesus the crucified Messiah who was himself the embodiment of the kingdom. To this the Resurrection bore witness. Jesus' death was not a tragic accident but the revelation of God. Indeed, it revealed the mystery of his life and ministry —namely, the provision of a redemptive service for the many. Thus the cross became fixed to the identity of Jesus. Is it any wonder that the cross became the central symbol of the Christian faith and the sign of its message?

From the perspective of the New Testament and of the early church's apostolate, the gospel was understood as God's liberating news through the cross of the risen Jesus. Its proclamation was the redemptive memory of the risen Messiah who was crucified for the sins of the world and declared the Son of God in power by the Holy Spirit —indeed, the gospel proclaimed the Galilean Jew in whom the eternal Word of God became flesh. The cross is central, therefore, not only for understanding the mystery of the person and work of Christ but also for the significance of the gospel as a message of liberation.

Evangelization is the communication of the gospel as the apostolic message of the cross. In this chapter we shall explore further the meaning of this message for our respective sociohistorical contexts.

Life through Suffering and Death

The message of the cross is, first, a witness to Jesus' atoning death. That Jesus died on a cross is a fact of history, but that he died as an atonement for sin is a foundational claim of the gospel and a central fact of its communication (cf., for example, Rom. 4:25; 8:32; Gal. 1:4; 2:20; 3:13; Heb. 9:12-14; 10:10, 12).

The English word "atone" is derived from the phrase "at one," which means to be in harmonious personal relationship with someone. Originally, "atonement" meant "at onement" or "reconciliation." In modern usage, "atonement" has taken on the restricted meaning of "the process by which the hindrances to reconciliation are removed" rather than indicating the end achieved by the removal. Therefore, "to atone for a wrong is to take some action which cancels out the ill effect it has had."[2]

The notion of atonement in the sense of reconciliation permeates the Hebrew Scriptures. The term *kippur* is used in reference to the removal of "the effect of sin."[3] It is linked with the ritual system of ancient Israel and is the heart of temple worship. It can be said that a fundamental purpose of the latter was to provide the means of "atonement" for the people in their relationship to God—that is, to remove the sin that separated the covenant community from God and made it impossible for them to be in communion ("at one"). Thus an elaborate system was provided for daily, weekly, monthly, yearly, and occasional "offerings." These offerings involved, by and large, the sacrifice of animals, although on the Day of Atonement (Yom Kippur) a goat was "sent away" with the sins of the people, and another was sacrificed.

There are other types of offerings specified in the Torah, such as offering money for the house of God (Exod. 30:16), burning incense (Num. 16:47), and saying prayers (Exod. 32:30). Of the five main types of offerings stipulated in the early chapters of Leviticus, only one (the cereal offering mentioned in Lev. 2:1ff.) does not involve the sacrifice of a victim; all other offerings involve the shedding of blood. This is based on the principle that "life is in the blood." Thus the dictum of Leviticus

17:11: "For the life of a creature is in the blood, and I have given it to you to make atonement for yourselves on the altar; it is the blood that makes atonement for one's life" (NIV). The symbolism is clear: God provides atonement for life through blood. Life is in the blood (Deut. 12:23). Only through the shedding of blood can there be life; only where there is life can there be a right relation with the living God. To be estranged from God is to be cut off from the source of life. Blood is a symbol of life, and life is a symbol of full communion with God. The point of such "blood sacrifices" in temple worship was to be "at one" with God.

When Israel found itself in exile without access to the temple, it discovered that it was possible to re-establish communion with God through penitent prayer and obedience. The unwritten Law *(halakhah)*[4] became Israel's way of life, the dynamic factor of change that interpreted the written Law in new historical circumstances[5] and kept alive the memory of God's dealing with Israel through the telling and retelling *(haggadhah)*[6] of the great salvific moments of the past, especially the Passover.

In fact, the sacrificial system of temple worship, grounded as it was on the Torah, was a development of Israel's foundational event—namely, the Exodus, which had as its central act the Passover meal. Yahweh commanded that the remembrance of the first Passover inaugurate Israel's annual calendar. It was the moment when God redeemed Israel from the long Egyptian bondage. This redemptive event led to the renewal of the covenant on Mount Sinai and the institution of the Law (cf. Exod. 12:2ff.). Of all the things that Israel was commanded to observe, one stood out: each household was to choose a lamb "without blemish, a male a year old" and kill it on "the fourteenth day of this month" (12:5-6). They were then to sprinkle the blood on the doorposts and lintel of the house. The family was not to go out of the house that night, and they were to eat the flesh of the lamb, roasted and served "with unleavened bread and bitter herbs," in haste, remembering their affliction and liberation from Egypt. On the night of the first Passover, Yahweh "passed through" Egypt in judgment and "passed over" every blood-marked house, protecting it from destruction. In celebrating the Passover feast, Israel was to remember the first Passover, when Yahweh was disclosed as the redeemer and covenant-keeping God of Israel and the judge of the oppressors. The Passover became foundational to Israel's self-understanding as a covenantal community. Its annual observance became a reliving of the Exodus and a call to the renewal of the covenant.

That is why Deutero-Isaiah links the return of the exiles from Babylon with the Exodus by calling Judah to the renewal of the covenant. He sees the return of the exiles from Babylon as a second Exodus. The glad tidings of peace proclaimed by the prophet (52:7) find their correspondence in the liberating double command to "depart" and "go," "touch no unclean thing" and "purify yourselves" (52:11). Then follows a startling affirmation: "For you shall not go out in haste, and you shall not go in flight, for the Lord will go before you, and the God of Israel will be your rear guard" (52:12). Unlike the first Exodus, with its Passover meal to be eaten "in haste," as a symbol of the soon-to-be-undertaken flight from the hands of Pharaoh, the second Exodus was not to be a flight by night. For a Passover lamb had been offered through the sufferings of the servant of Yahweh (52:14ff.) during the years of Babylonian captivity.

The image of the suffering servant as a Passover lamb is patterned after the notion of the righteous remnant proclaimed years before by Isaiah of Jerusalem (Isa. 6:13; 10:20ff.). Through its suffering the nation of Israel was to be redeemed, and the mission of Israel as "a blessing" to the nations (cf. Gen. 12:3; Isa. 9:2; 11:10) was to be renewed.

Personifying the righteous remnant (the Babylonian captives of Judah) as Yahweh's suffering servant (cf. Isa. 42–43, especially 42:18-25; 43:1ff.), Deutero-Isaiah states, "His appearance was so marred, beyond human semblance, and his form beyond that of the sons of men" (52:14). It was difficult, therefore, to believe this astonishing revelation: "Who has believed what we have heard? . . . For he grew up before him like a young plant, and like a root out of dry ground; he had no form or comeliness that we should look at him, and no beauty that we should desire him" (53:1-2). His contradictory appearance notwithstanding, he was the victim Yahweh offered to make atonement for an unfaithful and idolatrous nation that had willfully and consciously broken the covenant:

> Surely he has borne our griefs
>   and carried our sorrows;
> yet we esteemed him stricken,
>   smitten by God, and afflicted.

> But he was wounded for our transgressions,
> he was bruised for our iniquities,
> upon him was the chastisement that made us whole,
> and with his stripes we are healed. (53:4-5)

For Deutero-Isaiah the just judgment of Yahweh was counterbalanced with a gracious, liberating alternative. The nation as a whole had indeed "gone astray" like shepherdless sheep. Everyone had turned to his or her own way. Yahweh had no other choice than to judge such a rebellious and stubborn people. That had been the essential message of Isaiah of Jerusalem (Isa. 1:2ff.). Now Deutero-Isaiah states that in Yahweh's infinite mercy—indeed, in the midst of the shattering experience of judgment—Yahweh had provided a way of deliverance. The Lord had laid on the righteous remnant "the iniquity" of the whole nation (53:6).

The suffering of the righteous in Babylon was thus a new Passover. The tragedy of captivity had a hidden redemptive significance that was now beginning to surface. In their silent oppression and affliction, the righteous remnant were led "like a lamb . . . to the slaughter" (53:7). They were taken away by "oppression and judgment" and no one considered that their "generation" had been "cut off out of the land of the living, stricken for the transgression" of the people of the broken covenant (53:8). Indeed, although they had done "no violence, and there was no deceit in [their] mouth," for they were the faithful few in Israel, yet they ended up in the "grave with the wicked" (53:9). But "it was the will of the Lord to bruise" them, putting them through "grief" (53:10a). Through their suffering and death they became the Lord's offering for the sins of the nation (53:10b). And having thus atoned for the sins of the nation, they were to rise with the new nation. The righteous remnant would indeed return and see their "offspring." They would "prolong" the days of the nation. The "will of the Lord" would "prosper" in their faithful deeds (53:10c). They would be "satisfied" with "the fruit" of their "travail" (53:11a). Through their "knowledge"—that is, their faithful obedience to God in suffering and death—they would make the "many" (the nation and the nations) "to be accounted righteous," bearing their iniquities (53:11b), and thus fulfilling the promise of Isaiah of Jerusalem that "the earth shall be full of the knowledge of the Lord as the waters cover the sea" (11:9b).

In this poem Deutero-Isaiah announces the resurrection of Israel and the renewal of its universal redemptive mission through the historical atonement effected by the righteous remnant during the Babylonian captivity. The righteous remnant became the Passover victim of the new Exodus. New life was given to Israel through the remnant's suffering and death. Their faithfulness and obedience enabled them to be an atoning sacrifice for the nation. In their satisfactory mission, they also reaffirmed Yahweh's promise to the nations. The knowledge of Yahweh would thus be imparted to the nations through a faithful and obedient Israel made righteous by the suffering and death of the righteous remnant (53:12).

Deutero-Isaiah's theology of exodus and atonement became a fundamental referent for early Christians as they began to interpret the meaning of the suffering and death of Jesus. We noted in Chapter IV that the Gospel of Mark begins with a reference to the Exodus motif. Moreover, its central text (10:45) reflects the servant motif, which was probably the earliest image used in the apostolic church for the passion of Christ.[7] According to Joachim Jeremias, "No other passage from the Old Testament was as important to the Church as Is. 53."[8] John Stott has noted that "eight verses out of the chapter's twelve (verses 1, 4, 5, 6, 7, 8, 9 and 11)" are quoted by the New Testament as "having been specifically fulfilled in Jesus."[9] And Martin Hengel has further observed that "there are ten literal quotations from the fifteen verses of Isa. 52:13–53:12, and thirty-two allusions to it" in the New Testament.[10]

Some critical scholars of the New Testament have argued that the application of Isaiah 53 to Jesus reflects a later Christological development of the early church and not an interpretation of the earliest church or the historical Jesus. Other scholars, however, have traced the linkage of Isaiah 53 with the suffering and death of Christ to the historical Jesus himself.[11] In fact, it may be argued, with Stott, that Jesus' "public career, from his baptism through his ministry, suffering and death to his resurrection and ascension" is seen in the Gospels "as a fulfillment of the pattern" of Isaiah 53.[12] The eucharistic words "This is my blood of the covenant, which is poured out for many" (Mark 14:24)—which according to Jeremias and Zimmerli are "preserved in all versions of the Words of the Institution which the New Testament hands down to us, although with some variations as to position and phrasing"[13]—bear evidence to the claim of Jesus' own understanding of his passion as an atoning death "for many" in the tradition of Isaiah 53. This foundational referent to the suffering servant of Deutero-Isaiah needs to be placed in the context of the New Testament affirmation of Jesus' messiahship as the eschatological prophet.

Deutero-Isaiah's theology of exodus and atonement did not achieve its glorious expectations. The third section of the Isaianic collection (chapters 56–66) reflects a "contrast between high anticipation on the one hand and inadequate fulfillment on the other."[14] A generation later, Deutero-Isaiah's glorious vision had yet to be realized. Thus Trito-Isaiah began his prophecy by declaring that salvation and deliverance would "soon" be revealed. In the meantime, the people were to "keep the sabbath" (56:2) and accept foreign converts and eunuchs into the covenant community (56:3-7).

The fact remains that Judah was still plagued by corrupt leaders who walked in the same path as the corrupt in the time of Isaiah of Jerusalem (56:9-12). The sense of the law was again forgotten (58:1ff.; 66:1ff.); Judah was once again separated from God on account of its iniquities (59:1ff.). Judgment was once again proclaimed against those "who forsake the Lord" (65:11) along with the call to repentance (58:13ff.).

In light of this situation, Trito-Isaiah tried to concretize the vision of Deutero-Isaiah by making it "a *program* for the re-creation of life in Jerusalem"[15] (cf. 60:1ff.). This program was predicated on Yahweh's visit "to Zion as Redeemer" (59:20) to renew the covenant (59:21), thereby guaranteeing the permanent presence of God's spirit and words. It was inspired by the prophet's anointment by "the Spirit of the Lord God"

> to bring good tidings to the afflicted
> . . .to bind up the brokenhearted,
> to proclaim liberty to the captives,
> and the opening of the prison to those who are bound;
> to proclaim the year of the Lord's favor,
> and the day of vengeance of our God,
> to comfort all who mourn;
> to grant to those who mourn in Zion—
> to give them a garland instead of ashes,

> the oil of gladness instead of mourning,
> the mantle of praise instead of a faint spirit;
> that they may be called oaks of righteousness,
> the planting of the Lord, that he may be glorified.
> (61:1-3)

Building upon Isaiah and Deutero-Isaiah, Trito-Isaiah proclaims a message of judgment and hope. He points to a year of jubilee and a day of judgment, and looks forward to the renewal of the whole earth (cf. 65:17ff.) "in harmony with a reborn Israel (66:6-9)" and "the universal recognition of the glory of God (66:18-24)."[16]

The prophetic message of Trito-Isaiah, especially the pericope in 61:1-3, which originally referred to a post-exilic historical situation but with eschatological overtones, became a definite eschatological reference in the Second Temple period, as James A. Sanders has demonstrated.[17] According to Sanders, the Essene community at Qumran[18] "applied it to Melchizedeq, a heavenly judgment and redemptive figure, perhaps the chief figure in the Qumran view of the heavenly council" (cf. Ps. 110:1ff.). Sanders states that in 11QMelch,

> it is Melchizedeq who proclaims or announces the End Time . . . and it is also Melchizedeq who executes the judgment of God of the Eschaton. Melchizedeq is also identified as the evangelist . . . who is anointed by the spirit. . . . What he proclaims, in effect, is the "acceptable year of Melchizedeq" . . . . Four times is Melchizedeq called the *'elohim* . . . or heavenly being who on that day will reign and execute judgments against the forces of Belial but redemption for the "captives" . . . or Essenes.[19]

It is the Essene reinterpretation of Isaiah 61:1-3 that in Sanders' view lies behind Jesus' inaugural sermon at Nazareth in Luke's Gospel (4:18ff.). The sermon is based on Isaiah 58:6 and Isaiah 61:1-2 and is characterized by Jesus' claim to be the fulfillment of that prophecy; he is subsequently rejected by his own people (4:28-29). Given the foundational place that the sermon occupies in Luke's Gospel, which addresses the question of "why Jesus was crucified,"[20] it is all the more striking to note both the similarities and the dissimilarities between Jesus' interpretation and Qumran's interpretation of the Isaianic text. Sanders argues that there were two hermeneutical axioms at work in

Qumran—eschatological and constitutive. The former "had as its content the End Time,"[21] while the latter was the requirement "that scripture be so interpreted as to show that in the Eschaton God's wrath would be directed against an out-group while his mercy would be directed toward the in-group."[22] Jesus used the "End Time" axiom when he applied it to the present: he was the fulfillment of the messianic figure of Isaiah 61. But he rejected the second axiom and substituted for it a "prophetic realism" which challenges "from within the group's own self-understanding."[23] Sanders further points out that

> Jesus' citation of the gracious acts of Elijah and Elisha toward the Sidonian widow and the Syrian Leper [Lk. 4:25-27] shows that he does not subscribe to the Essene second axiom. Far from it, by this enriching juxtaposition of the acts of Elijah and Elisha and Isa. 6l, Jesus clearly shows that the words meaning poor, captive, blind and oppressed do not apply exclusively to any in-group but, on the contrary, apply to those to whom God wishes them to apply. God sent Elijah and Elisha to outsiders, the Sidonian Widow and the Syrian Leper.[24]

One valuable aspect of Sanders' comparative Midrashic study of Isaiah 61 and Luke 4 is the light it casts on Jesus' life and work as an eschatological prophet. He is rejected by his own not because he is a prophet but rather because he stands in the tradition of the *true* prophets, casting "a light of scrutiny upon his own people from the very source of authority on which they rely for their identity, existence and self-understanding."[25] Thus "Jesus turned the very popular Isa. 6l passage into a judgment and a challenge to the definitions of Israel of his day."[26] He was "the eschatological prophet, anointed by the spirit . . . who so challenged his compatriots' assumptions about divine election that he met the prophet-martyr's end."[27]

The New Testament claims that Jesus died as a prophet-martyr *and* the suffering servant of the Lord, as a Passover lamb *and* a "sin-bearing" offering. Moreover, the New Testament affirms that he overcame the power of sin and death and established a new pattern of existence for those who believe in him. This pattern is called "the way of the cross."

The apostolic preaching of the cross affirms his life of faithful obedience to the Word under the anointment of the Spirit of God. He fulfilled the law in his life and applied it to the social context of his ministry. His way of life was an authentic *halakhah,* the way of righteousness and justice. Thus John's Gospel calls him the true and living way to the Father (14:6).

It was on the basis of Jesus' righteous life, his faithful witness to the Word of God, his absolute commitment to God's holy love, and his outstretched hand of mercy to "sinners, publicans, and outcasts" that the apostolic church proclaimed a message of life through his suffering and death. The New Testament uses all possible imageries from the Hebrew Scriptures and extra-canonical literature to make this point. Thus Paul refers to the crucified Jesus as "our Passover lamb" (1 Cor. 5:7-8, NIV) and God's obedient servant (Phil. 2:8). Mark and Matthew describe him as "the Son of man" who came "to serve, and to give his life as a ransom for many" (Mark 10:45; Matt. 20:28). The Book of Revelation calls him "the faithful and true witness" (1:5; 3:14; 19:11) and identifies him as the Lamb no less than twenty-eight times.[28] John's Gospel speaks of him as "the Lamb of God, who takes away the sin of the world" (1:29), perhaps combining in this description both the Passover lamb and the sacrificial victim of the Day of Atonement as well as the goat that was led into the wilderness with the sins of the people.[29] In 1 John Jesus is called "the righteous" who is "the expiation for our sins, and . . . for the sins of the whole world" (2:1-2). Luke's Gospel adds that he suffered and died in fulfillment of the law, the prophets, and the Psalms, "that repentance and forgiveness of sins should be preached in his name to all nations" (24:44-47). Hebrews sees him as both the high priest (after the order of Melchizedek!—cf. Ps. 110:4) who "offered up himself" in the heavenly sanctuary (7:27), securing an "eternal redemption" (9:12), and "the pioneer and perfecter of our faith, who . . . endured the cross, despising the shame" (12:2), and thereby set the example for us to "go forth . . . outside the camp, and bear the abuse he endured" (13:13) for the life of the world. In 1 Peter Jesus is described as God's sinless, suffering servant who "bore our sins in his body on the tree" (2:24), dying the death of a cursed criminal (cf. Deut. 21:22-23; Gal. 3:13) "that we might die to sin and live to righteousness." Thus he *descended* into hell and announced "the good news."

All these images, inspired by the very words of the historical Jesus and representing a developing tradition in the early church, bear witness to the message of the cross as an affirmation of life through suffering and death. Through Jesus' suffering and death, Israel has been set free and received new life to fulfill its historic mission as a light to the nations. Likewise, all of humankind has been promised new life. The basis for a reconciled existence under God has been established by God's crucified Messiah. His life has been offered as an atonement for the whole world.

It is in this light that we need to bear in mind the words of the Johannine Christ: "I came that they may have life, and have it abundantly" (John 10:10). Because God was not willing "that any should perish" (2 Pet. 3:9), Jesus came as God's gift of eternal life. Jesus came not just to make personal God's gift of life and not simply to let humankind know that God wills life for all, but especially to make it possible for all to experience life in all of its fullness. Life should be understood not only as personal and spiritual—that is, as living in communion with God—but also as global and social, as living a reconciled existence with our neighbors and the whole of creation. Accordingly, in John 10:10 Jesus was referring to life in all of its dimensions—life with God and in the world, life here and there, life for us and our posterity, life now and beyond.

The message of the cross is the announcement of God's gift of life through the suffering and death of the *Easter* Christ. His resurrection from the dead has given validity to the memory of his passion. The cross is a sign of life because it is the memory of the one who made new life available through his suffering and death. In him we have a "passover" into eternal life, we become a new creation, we enter a new order of existence, we are set free to live for God in the service of the world and become thereby signs and instruments for the renewal of the earth.[30]

Shame in Suffering and Death

Notwithstanding the glorious reality of the cross as a message of life, the fact remains that its proclamation has been associated from its inception with shame and scorn. It is not just the fact that the cross represents a barbaric and inhumane method of execution which repulses the human conscience but that it stands for weakness and impotence and appears in fact as an insult to the very God who is affirmed by biblical faith as the Living God. The message of the cross carries a stigma of shame and scorn. This shame has a threefold dimension that we will explore.

The Shame of a Crucified Messiah

The first dimension stems from the very religious and ethnic community of which Jesus and his early followers were bona-fide members. Jews were astonished — indeed, offended — by the affirmation that not only was Jesus the promised Messiah but that as such he was crucified. This was not acceptable to Jews for at least two reasons: first, the Messiah was to come in power and glory, not in weakness and suffering; and second, it was not possible for God's Messiah to die on a cross because of the curse of the law on anyone who hung on a tree (Deut. 21:23).

According to the New Testament, Jesus was handed over to Pilate as a messianic pretender. The Jerusalem leadership reasoned that the fact that he was crucified showed that he was bluffing. They were baffled, therefore, when they and their followers began to hear early Jewish-Christian preachers argue precisely the opposite: "The God of our fathers raised Jesus whom you killed by hanging him on a tree" (Acts 5:30; cf. 10:39-40). This was perhaps the reason for Saul's volatile reaction in the aftermath of Stephen's death, to which Saul consented (Acts 8:1). He found Stephen's proclamation of a crucified Messiah utterly blasphemous. This also explains why after his conversion Saul—that is, Paul—argued so strongly that it was precisely by Christ's death on the cross that redemption from the curse of the law was extended to everyone (Gal. 3:13). Only a former Pharisee could appreciate the radical implication of a crucified Messiah. He realized that by God's grace Jesus had taken upon himself the universal damnation of sin, thereby setting humanity free from eternal separation from God. This meant, further, that Christ made the temple offering unnecessary; he had become the definitive sacrifice for the permanent purification and ultimate reconciliation of Jews and Gentiles with God. Just as Paul had found such a claim offensive as a rabbinic Jew, so as a Christian missionary he understood why Jews rejected the message of the cross: it was "a stumbling block" (1 Cor. 1:23). Such a message was a scandal, an incredible claim, offensive to Jewish thought and belief!

Even though Jesus was himself a Jew, his disciples were all Jews, and the earliest church in Jerusalem was made up entirely of Jewish believers and remained Jewish for twelve years, the church's central message was rejected by the majority of Jews. Israel and the church parted ways, split over the scandal of Jesus as the crucified Messiah. The tremendous pain caused by the shame of the cross among Jews was deeply felt by a mature Paul in the Epistle to the Romans, where he said, "I have great sorrow and unceasing anguish in my heart" over Israel's rejection of the gospel (9:2). So great was his anguish that he wished he "were accursed and cut off from Christ" for the sake of his people (9:3): "They are Israelites, and to them belong the sonship, the glory, the covenants, the giving of the law, the worship, and the promises; to them belong the patriarchs, and of their race, according to the flesh, is the Christ. God who is over all be blessed for ever" (9:4-5). But they "pursued the righteousness which is based on law" and "did not succeed in fulfilling that law" (9:31). By rejecting God's gracious provision at the cross and pursuing instead their own way of achieving righteousness by seeking to keep the law, they failed to gain a right standing before God. They "stumbled over the stumbling stone" (9:32) —that is, over the crucified Messiah (cf. 9:33). Thus Paul prayed for Israel. Indeed, he bore witness to the Israelites' "zeal for God," but lamented the fact that it was not an "enlightened" faith: "For, being ignorant of the righteousness that comes from God, and seeking to establish their own, they did not submit to God's righteousness. For Christ is the end of the law, that everyone who has faith may be justified" (10:3-4).

The shame of the crucified Messiah, felt so keenly by Paul, has continued across the years. The Christian message of the cross carries with it the scorn of rejection by the very community to whom it was first addressed. With the message of the cross comes therefore a cry of anguish and a prayer for Israel, the legitimate heir to the gift of life through the suffering and death of Jesus the Messiah.

A similar sorrow can be expressed over the shame that the message of the crucified Messiah carries among Moslems. Notwithstanding the honorable recognition that Islam gives to the Torah and the gospel in the Koran, it rejects the need of atonement. Jesus is venerated as a prophet, but the saving significance of his death is denied. Even though Allah is merciful and forgives those who repent and do good, the Koran categorically declares that each human being is responsible for his or her own deeds. Each one shall reap the fruits of his or her actions, for "no one can bear the burden of another" (35:19).

While the Koran leaves the door open for the possibility of the Resurrection, many Moslems have interpreted the Koran as denying both the need of the cross and the fact of Jesus' death. The Koran states that the Jews claimed to have killed

> the Messiah, Jesus son of Mary, the Messenger of Allah; whereas they slew him not, nor did they compass his death upon the cross, but he was made to appear to them like one crucified to death. . . . Indeed, Allah exalted him to Himself. . . . There is none among the People of the Book but will continue to believe till his death that Jesus died on the cross, and on the Day of Judgment Jesus shall bear witness against them. (4:158-160)

In this passage the Koran denies that the death of Jesus was ultimately caused by the Jews. They spread the "grievous calumny" of his death, and they thought that they had killed him, but they actually had not, for "Allah exalted him to Himself." Is this not congruent with the saying of the Johannine Christ? "I lay down my life, that I may take it again. No one takes it from me, but I lay it down of my own accord. I have power to lay it down, and I have power to take it again; this charge I have received from my Father" (John 10:17-18). Whatever else others may claim, the fact of the matter is that no one actually determined the death of Jesus; he alone, by the power invested in him by the Father, decided to give up his life and "take it again." Like John's Gospel, the Koran makes an indirect reference to Christ's resurrection. Similarly, the Apostle Paul states that while Jesus "humbled himself . . . unto death . . . God has highly exalted him" (Phil. 2:8-9). The death of Jesus is, according to Paul and the Johannine Christ, not the last word about him, for he has been exalted "above any name." Therefore, says the Koran, whatever Jews may claim regarding the death of Jesus is not true. What is true is that Allah has "exalted him to Himself."[31]

It is striking, nevertheless, that this text has been traditionally interpreted by Moslems as denying the very reality of Jesus' death. They assume that just as the Koran does not attach an atoning significance to Jesus' death, so it also denies his death as such, when the fact of the matter is that all the Koran disputes is that Jesus' death was caused by human hands. Indeed, if anything the aforementioned text points to the fact of the Resurrection, which makes Islam's rejection of the saving significance of the cross all the more tragic. By defending the exalted role of Jesus, it denies his redemptive death. I agree, therefore, with John Stott that this is one of Islam's "saddest features."[32]

Yet, as Samuel M. Zwemer (1867-1952) noted after years of ministering among Moslems, when the gospel is read with Moslems, the apostolic emphasis on the cross resurfaces, and "although the offense of the Cross remains, its magnetic power is irresistible."[33] It is irresistible because it brings forth a missing dimension in the religion of Allah, the merciful and forgiving God. How can God be merciful and forgiving without acting in holy judgment against sin? God's love is holy or else it is not true love, outgoing and all-embracing. It is the holy God who makes a total claim upon human life in all of its modes and expressions, and who is determined to have communion with humankind, who is capable of being all-merciful and forgiving. Therefore, God's love is "love in holy action, in forgiveness, in redemption."[34] In the face of sin, of broken communion, God's holiness "makes sin damnable as sin and love active as grace."[35] It is in and through the cross that sin is judged and sinners can be forgiven. At the cross, God provides and accepts the sacrifice of Christ as God's judgment upon sin and the basis for its forgiveness. Only a holy God who judges sin can be loving and forgiving. Adds P. T. Forsyth, "It is the holiness in God's love that is the eternal, stable, unchangeable element in it—the holiness secured for history and its destiny on the Cross."[36] This is the irresistible attraction that the message of the cross has for Moslems, despite the rejection of the cross by Islam.

The shame of a crucified Messiah is also felt among Hindus. To be sure, Hinduism has no problem with the fact of Christ's suffering and death, but it rejects its saving significance. Thus Mahatma Gandhi, who greatly admired the person of Jesus, could not accept his death as a sacrifice for sin. "I could accept Jesus as a martyr," he said, as "an embodiment of sacrifice, and a divine teacher, but not as the most perfect man ever born. His death on the cross was a great example to the world, but that there was anything like a mysterious or miraculous virtue in it, my heart could not accept."[37]

There are many religious people all over the world who, like Gandhi, are attracted to the person of Jesus but reject his work upon the cross. They find the latter a religious offense. This is the shame that the apostolic message of the cross bears wherever it is proclaimed.

The Shame of a Foolish Logic

If the message of the cross is a scandal to Judaism, Islam, and other religious communities, it is foolishness to humanists and secularists. This was the conclusion that the Apostle Paul reached when writing to the church in Corinth: "Christ crucified," he said, is "folly to Gentiles" (1 Cor. 1:23)—that is, to the nonreligious, the "Hellenists" for whom human wisdom, or secular knowledge, is the ultimate criterion for truth. For such people the message of the cross is a foolish *logos* (word, statement, or logic); it makes no sense. How is it possible, they reason, to redeem the world through the death—let alone death on a cross—of an obscure Galilean craftsman?

Paul's Gentile audiences in Antioch, Ephesus, Corinth, and Rome, influenced as they were by Hellenistic culture and thought, had a difficult time accepting the message of the cross—although, as Martin Hengel has noted, they were familiar with the notion "of vicarious dying for others out of love . . . a voluntary death as an atoning sacrifice," and could understand it in their own way. They knew what it was all about "through myth, patriotic sagas and dramas." However, customs like this one appeared "archaic or barbaric" to them.[38] Indeed, Hengel notes, the message of a crucified Christ

> must have seemed aesthetically and ethically repulsive to them and to be in conflict with the philosophically purified nature of the gods. The new doctrine of salvation had not only barbarian, but also irrational and excessive features. It appeared to contemporaries as a dark or even mad superstition. For this was not the death of a hero from ancient times, suffered in the glow of religion, but that of a Jewish craftsman of the most recent past, executed as a criminal, with whom the whole present and future salvation of all men was linked. Because of this, the earliest Christian mission always spoke also of the teaching, the action, and the passion of the Messiah from Galilee. The narrative about his messianic person was part of the preaching of the cross.[39]

It is a fact that secularists and humanists have found it easier to accept the message of Jesus' life of service to the world than of his death for the life of the world. The centrality of the cross to the Christian faith has made Christianity appear to some to be an intellectually weak and ridiculous faith. Friedrich Nietzsche's rejection of Christianity as the religion of the weak is a modern example of the scorn that Christianity has suffered on account of its central message. For Nietzsche, the Christian conception of God was a decadent one: it proposed a "God of the sick," "God as spider" and "spirit" with an impotent Messiah, whom Nietzsche scornfully dismissed as a dead God hanging on a cross.[40]

Skeptics and rationalists have waged such a strong attack on the Christian message of the cross that theology, especially since the Enlightenment, has found itself on the defensive, trying to make the cross appear intellectually viable to those who consider it foolish and unreasonable. But from the earliest moments of the Christian mission, the message of the cross has had no truly effective intellectual response to the charges that reason has brought against it. God "chose" precisely "what is foolish in the world to shame the wise, God chose what is weak in the world to shame the strong," answered the Apostle Paul (1 Cor. 1:27). The foolish logic of the cross is precisely its message. It is not meant to be intellectually analyzed and rationally understood but intended to save the world by the power of God. For the kingdom of God, revealed in the cross and confirmed in the Resurrection, is demonstrated not by the logic of human wisdom but by the transforming power of God's Spirit (1 Cor. 4:20). It is not possible, therefore, to offer a convincing *apologia* for the message of the cross. The loftiest, most coherent and precise discourse falls short of a convincing explanation of the logic of the cross. Only God's Spirit can enable women and men to hear and understand the message of the cross. Thus Paul did not come to Corinth proclaiming the mystery of God in "lofty words or wisdom"; rather, "in weakness and in much fear and trembling" he proclaimed "Jesus Christ and him crucified" (1 Cor. 2:1-3). His message, he adds, was not "in plausible words of wisdom, but in demonstration of the Spirit and of power," so that the faith of Corinthians and other Christian believers "might not rest in the wisdom of men but in the power of God" (1 Cor. 2:4-5).

Whatever else the church in history might have learned about the mystery of the cross and its proclamation after the Apostle Paul, it has not been able to find a more adequate theological response to those who dismiss its message as intellectual folly. Although the God of the cross is also the creator of the human mind and is in fact the ultimate reality of the world, and although all true knowledge is ultimately grounded in God's wisdom, God refuses to subject the mystery of the cross—indeed his strategy for the salvation of humanity—to the judgment of human wisdom. Thus the shame of the cross before the world is the very glory of God in the world, for it is through its message that God has chosen to save the world from its foolish and self-destructive ways.

The Shame of Historical Betrayal

The message of the cross has also suffered the shame of its various distortions in the course of Christian history. Just as the Father's delivery of Jesus unto death for the salvation of the world was accompanied by the betrayal of the disciples, so the communication of the message of the cross to the world in the church's mission has been accompanied by the betrayal of that message. Interestingly enough, the very word (Gr. *paradidomi*) that the New Testament uses for the deliverance of Jesus unto death as a redemptive offering is used to describe his betrayal (e.g., Mark 14:10, 11, 18, 21, 41, 42, 44; Matt. 10:4; 17:22; 20:18; 24:10; 27:3, 4; 26:2, 16, 21, 23, 24, 25, 45, 48).[41] The liberating service announced in the message of the cross was replaced with a message of power and domination as Christianity passed "from a scarcely tolerated and often persecuted minority movement into an established social institution with the power to determine (sometimes by persecution) life within its own ranks as well as in society."[42]

The event symbolizing this change is, of course, the Edict of Milan, issued in 313 C.E., which proclaimed full toleration for all religions and the restitution of wrongs done to Christians. This event was preceded by Constantine's defeating his rival, Maxentius, at Milvian Bridge in 312. According to Lactantius, Constantine had a dream shortly before the battle wherein he received "instruction to paint the Christian monogram . . . on his troops' shield."[43] In Eusebius's version, however, Constantine is said to have received a vision during the campaign against Maxentius in which "the Christian sign appeared in the sky with the legend, 'In this sign, conquer.'"[44] The versions of this story differ on some points, but both underscore the fact that the symbol of the cross became a sign of power and conquest instead of a sign of liberating service and abundant life.

Thereafter, the message of the cross became not only the symbol of the empire but the rallying point of military conquest. Thus, when the Byzantine empire lost the Holy Land to the forces of Islam, it was the sign of the cross that was invoked to launch a military campaign for the land's reconquest. From 1095 to 1291, eight major expeditions were launched by the military forces of the Latin Christian West; these were followed by other lesser ventures to recover what had been lost. The Crusades (literally "campaigns of the cross") not only identified Moslems and Jews as the enemy, and thus set out to conquer them and wipe them out, but also became a point of hostility between Western and Eastern Christians. In the name of the cross, Moslems and Jews were massacred in Jerusalem (the Holy City, the City of Peace!) and other parts of the Middle East. This was also the basis upon which the Holy Office of the Inquisition was established in Spain in 1492; by this tool Jews were threatened with expulsion from the country if they did not convert. Moslem territories were finally reconquered in Spain as part of the Crusades. Moslems and Jews who tried to remain in Spain after 1492 were either driven out or forced to renounce their respective faiths and convert to Christianity. The Crusade mind-set became so ingrown in medieval Western Christianity that even those Franciscan and Dominican missionaries who advocated voluntary conversion through the preaching of the cross suggested that it be accompanied by a campaign of "military force."[45]

The conquest and colonization of the Americas (16th-19th centuries) amounted to an extension of the Crusades. Spanish and Portuguese Christians came to the Americas with the cross in one hand and the sword in the other. They were followed by the French, the British, and the Dutch, who acted in a similar manner. The challenge that Bartolomé de Las Casas posed to Spanish Christendom—that it was crucifying Christ anew by enslaving and oppressing the aboriginal population—is applicable to *all* the European powers. Not only were they responsible for the human holocaust of millions of aborigines, but, as I have pointed out elsewhere, they were also responsible for "the enslavement of Africans and their descendants, the exploitation of natural resources, the political and cultural domination of the emerging societies and the continually increasing impoverishment" of the peoples of Latin America, the Caribbean, and the minority racial populations of North America.[46]

Something similar has taken place in Africa, Asia, and the Pacific. In the name of the cross, Western Christian civilization has expanded across the globe. And was this not the same rationale behind the Holocaust—the attempted extermination of all Jews by the Third Reich?[47] Whatever positive word can be offered on behalf of Christian Europe, history offers the undeniable judgment that it (together with its various extensions around the world—North America, Australasia, and white Southern Africa) has betrayed the crucified Messiah, crucifying him anew in the crosses of suffering and death imposed upon millions of innocent people around the world. This is a greater shame than the scandal of Jews, Moslems, and other religious communities who reject the saving message of the cross, and the scorn of those who consider the cross an intellectual folly. For this is the shame brought about by Christians themselves!

Wherever the cross is preached today, it carries the stigma of scorn and shame. It is proclaimed in sorrow, with recognition of its rejection by religious and nonreligious people alike, and in penitent confession, with remembrance of its betrayal by the Christian church in history. The message of the cross on the lips of the Christian church the world over can be a credible instrument of the saving power of the gospel only if it is proclaimed in humility and penitent confession.

Hope beyond Suffering and Death

There is a further word to be said about the message of the cross. Notwithstanding its shame on account of Christ's suffering and death at Golgotha and the shame of its various distortions in the course of human history, the cross still conveys a message of hope. For, as we have noted, the crucified Messiah is the Easter Christ who has broken the chains of suffering and death through his resurrection. He was indeed crucified outside the walls of Jerusalem. Tragically, this city, known as a sanctuary of peace, had become the deathbed of prophets and apostles. As Jesus himself noted, it was the city that killed the prophets and stoned those who were sent to it (Matt. 23:37). But through his resurrection, Jerusalem was put in an entirely new perspective; it became a city of the future, to be rebuilt not by human hands but by the work of the living God who raised Jesus from the dead (Heb. 10:20; 13:14).

To be sure, the cross of Jesus forces us to take suffering and death seriously, as we noted in the previous chapter. The cross of the risen Christ, however, reminds us that suffering and death are no longer ultimate. God-in-Christ has dealt decisively with them by taking them upon himself and thereby breaking their ultimate grip on human history. Therefore, the cross is a sign not only of life everlasting but of hope beyond the continuing presence of suffering and death in human history. The message of the cross announces the overcoming of suffering and death through the life made available in Christ's suffering and death. Life is not only a present possibility but a future promise.

There is hope for a way beyond the shame of suffering and death because God's gift of life is not dependent on us—not dependent on the credibility of our discourse, on our spiritual superiority, or even on the consistency of our historical deeds—but rather on what God-in-Christ has accomplished and will bring to pass. This is, in fact, Paul's concluding argument in his discussion of the problem of Israel and the church.

Although Israel found the cross a stumbling block and therefore rejected Christ, God did not reject Israel (Rom. 11:11). For Israel was beloved of God "for the sake of their forefathers" (11:28). After all, "the gifts and the call of God are irrevocable" (11:29). Without determining Israel's stumbling or hardening their hearts in unbelief, God nevertheless used this sad reality positively for the salvation of outsiders (the Gentile world). Israel's rejection of Christ made possible "the reconciliation of the world" (11:15). This turn of events provoked Israel to jealousy (11:11). Yet Gentiles were not to look at Israel's stumbling as something to boast about, since Gentiles were included in the economy of salvation through the *root* of Israel. The fact that in the universalization of salvation the natural branches were cast off because of unbelief did not mean that the "wild olive shoot" (the Gentiles) had now replaced Israel. On the contrary, "if their trespass means riches for the world, and if their failure means riches for the Gentiles, how much more will their full inclusion mean!" (11:12). Therefore, in this passage Paul looks forward to the salvation of "all Israel," when God will take away their sins and renew the covenant with them (11:26-27). When will this take place? In God's good time! How will it come about? Through God's infinite mercy and wisdom! "O the depth of the riches and wisdom and knowledge of God! How unsearchable are his judgments and how inscrutable his ways!" (11:33).

Meanwhile, there were Israelites who did believe in Christ, just like Paul and so many before and after him. They were a sign of the salvation promise for "all Israel." There were also Gentile Christians who proudly forgot the special place that God in his mercy and wisdom had granted to Israel as his elect for the salvation of the world. These Gentiles boasted that they did what God had refused to do—rejected the people of the promise! Their "anti-Semitic" behavior brought shame and disgrace to the Christian message of the cross, disfiguring its representation and blurring its sign.

But this shame is not the whole of the Christian story. For although there have been far too many who have shamed the memory of both the church's root and its message of the cross, other Christians have honored and defended with their lives their dignity and promise.

There is, for example, the story of Father Maximilian Kolbe, a Polish Franciscan who ended up in Auschwitz. One day, after a number of prisoners had been selected for execution, one Jewish man among them shouted out that he was a married man with children. At this point Kolbe stepped forward and offered to take the place of this man. According to Trevor Benson, Father Kolbe's offer "was accepted by the authorities, and he was placed in an underground cell, where he was left to die of starvation."[48]

There were many other Christians like Father Kolbe in the Netherlands, Sweden, and other European countries who risked their lives to shelter persecuted Jews. There were Christian Jews who were thrown into the gas chambers and died in concentration camps not because they were Christians but rather because they were Jews, and yet they died as both faithful children of Israel and followers of Christ. They served and gave their lives in hope, knowing not only that God was with them in their suffering and death but that he would uphold them as he had Jesus—he would not let them rot in Sheol. Indeed, they died confessing that their "Redeemer lives, and at last he will stand upon the earth," and after their skin "has been thus destroyed, then from [their] flesh [they] shall see God" (Job 19:25-26). They suffered and died with an unshakable faith in the crucified Messiah, who is also "the resurrection and the life" (John 11:25).

Their testimonies stand among those of a long chain of believers in the living God who suffered and died serving others and their God. For their faith led them to hope beyond suffering and death. The list is long and wide. Their blood has been the seed of the true church, correcting its many distortions and transcending the many instances in which many of its members, leaders, communities, and institutions have betrayed the message of the cross.

Over against the enslavement and oppression of the American aboriginal community there was the witness of Christian prophets. The Dominican Antonio de Montesino was the first to protest the mistreatment of the aborigines in Hispaniola and the "encomienda" system created by Spain to "civilize" and "Christianize" them while exploiting their labor, expropriating their lands, and treating them like subhuman beings. It was Montesino who evangelized Bartolomé de las Casas. The latter became, in turn, the champion of human rights in early colonial America and an advocate of prophetic evangelization and voluntary conversions. Along with the witness of Montesino and Las Casas, there was the witness of Louis Bertran, the first of the Spanish missionaries to the New World to be canonized; he rebuked the Spaniards for living off the blood of the aborigines.[49] In eighteenth-century Paraguay, Jesuit missionaries helped create an environment of hope for the aboriginal community by enabling them to organize in villages where most "of the fields and all of the animals and tools were held in common." Not only did they learn "how to manage their own lives, but also they practiced such specialized art as the buildings of organs for their churches."[50] These courageous and dedicated missionaries did everything they could not only to enable the Paraguayan aborigines to survive the menace of slave hunters but also to establish a liberating, just, and peaceful environment for them.

With the coming of black slaves, "ecclesiastical authorities found very little wrong with the institution" of slavery. But God raised from within prophets of compassion and hope such as Pedro Claver, a Catalonian Jesuit who gave his life to change the plight of the slaves of Cartagena, brought from Africa, who suffered "broken families, broken bodies and broken lives."[51] Adding to the vows of poverty, chastity, and obedience, he vowed to be "forever a slave to blacks," and developed a courageous and compassionate ministry of evangelization. He took care of lepers abandoned by their masters and organized the freed blacks of the city to provide relief for them and other blacks in need. He humbly greeted the poorest of slaves and crossed the street to avoid greeting a slaveowner. In listening to confessions, he followed "the evangelical order, beginning with the slaves, then the poor, and finally the children." According to Justo González, he was sure that "the rich and slave-owners . . . could find another confessor who had time for them"; his time was completely dedicated to the destitute and downtrodden. Claver died "unable to move and made to lie in his filth"; in this situation "he thanked God for the opportunity to experience something of what his flock had experienced in the slave ships."[52] He bore the cross to the very end of his life. He suffered and died as a witness of hope, knowing that neither his suffering and death nor that of the slaves to whom he became a slave was the end. His future and their future were in God's hands. Ultimately, life, freedom, justice, and well-being were in the hands of God.

That is what the message of the cross is all about: life through suffering and death and hope beyond it. There is shame, to be sure, but shame, like suffering and death, is not and cannot be ultimate. Where there is life in all of its fullness, there is hope, and where there is hope, there is the certainty of love, because there is God—the Alpha and Omega, the Great One from whom no one and nothing can separate us (cf. Rom. 8:31ff.). The proclamation of the cross is, therefore, the communication of liberating news—a message of life, of hope and love through faith in the one who suffered death and shame for all that all might live, look to the future with hope, and be assured of God's love, which surpasses all odds. We live accordingly, hoping and loving. In evangelization we invite the peoples of the world to experience true life, hope, and love through faith in the risen Christ who was crucified for Israel and the world.

CHAPTER VII

The Call to Conversion

New Life in the Spirit

The communication of God's liberating news is centered on the cross of Jesus Christ and leads to a call to conversion. The gospel issues an invitation to experience new life in the Holy Spirit through repentance and faith in Christ. Jesus' own evangelizing ministry was characterized by such a call (Mark 1:15), and the apostles who followed in the tradition of Jesus issued a similar appeal as part of their message (cf. Acts 2:38; 3:19ff).

In this chapter we shall explore the meaning of the gospel's call to conversion. We shall note its biblical roots, its soteriological comprehension and specificity, its pneumatological source, and its spiritual dynamic as an outgrowth of the work of the Holy Spirit in evangelization and the praxis of the faith.

Conversion as a Spiritual Awakening

A New Beginning and a Transformative Process

The root of conversion, like the root of evangelization, is found in the prophetic literature. Therein the Hebrew verb *shub,* meaning "to turn," appears over a thousand times.[1] It is linked with the prophetic call to Israel to turn from its sins, to return to Yahweh, and to renew its vows. This word also appears in connection with God's acts toward Israel and the nations. In this context, the following comment from Christopher Barth is helpful:

> The prophet's call to "return" derives its special force and urgency from the fact that it confronts its addressees (who include

> the new people of God from among the pagans) not only with a demand from God, but with the reality of God. Man's return and renewal in the community of God's people is first of all a given event and reality through God's coming, the renewal of His covenant and the coming of His Kingdom. It is only then that conversion becomes an invitation, a call and a demand.[2]

In the New Testament, it is the word *epistrepho* that stands out. It is often used in the Septuagint to translate the verb *shub*.[3] It means "to turn, bring back, or return." It is often used in relation to the turning of unbelievers (for the first time) away from their sins (Acts 14:15) to God (Acts 3:19; 26:20).[4] But sometimes the word is linked to erring believers (James 5:19-20) who are brought back into a right relation with God.[5]

Another term that is often used in the New Testament is *metanoeo,* which means "to change one's mind," often with regret, and "to adopt another view."[6] It is used both in the context of the call to forgiveness of sin and liberation from future judgment (Acts 2:38; 3:19; 8:22; 17:30; 26:20) and in reference to the problem of apostasy within the church (Rev. 2:5, 16, 21-22; 3:3, 19).

Metanoeo is closely connected with *epistrepho,* as we see in Acts 3:19, where Peter calls the multitude to "Repent . . . and turn again." *Metanoeo* also appears in connection with *pisteuo,* which means "to believe," or "to adhere, to trust or rely on." Thus Jesus summoned his hearers to "Repent, and believe in the gospel" (Mark 1:15).

The uses of these different words in Scripture underscore several aspects of the biblical concept of conversion. First, conversion means a turning from sin (and self) to God (and God's work). Second, this act involves a change of mind, which implies the abandonment of an old worldview and the adoption of a new one. Third, conversion entails a new allegiance, a new trust, and a new life commitment. Fourth, conversion is but the beginning of a new journey and carries implicitly the seed of new turns. Fifth, conversion is surrounded by the redemptive love of God as revealed in Jesus Christ and witnessed to by the Holy Spirit.

We should think of conversion as a distinct moment, a new beginning, as well as a continuous transformative process. This seems clear from Paul's statement in 2 Corinthians 3:16-18: "But when a man turns to the Lord the veil is removed. Now the Lord is the Spirit, and where the Spirit of the Lord is, there is freedom. And we all, with unveiled face, beholding the glory of the Lord, are being changed into his likeness from one degree of glory to another; for this comes from the Lord who is the Spirit." In this passage Paul is referring to Israel's incapacity to understand the Torah because of spiritual blindness. Only "through Christ" can this blindness be lifted and Israel come to see the truth of the covenant (v. 14). This is true not only for Israel but for all people. We are all unable to see God because we are blinded by the veil of our sins. But when we turn—are converted—to Christ, that veil is removed. This turning to the Lord puts us in the sphere of the Spirit of Christ, who not only enables us to see "the glory of the Lord" but constantly transforms us "from one degree of glory to another."

Conversion is then both a distinct moment and the first in a series of transforming experiences. It is both a unique turn and a continuous transforming movement, made possible by the enabling power of the Spirit of freedom. The Spirit turns us toward the Lord, whose unfathomable glory is always being disclosed before our eyes.

Elsewhere in the New Testament (e.g., Mark 1:15), conversion is connected with the kingdom of God. This is the new order of life that God offers in Jesus Christ through the enabling power of the Spirit. It is a future reality that is nevertheless anticipated in the present. It is a reality that we experience both personally and collectively, in the community of faith. It is a reflection of what God has done, is doing, and will do, but it is basically discernible in the obedience of faith. Christian conversion revolves around this future-present, personal-communal, reflection-action reality. In the words of José Míguez Bonino, it is "the process through which God incorporates [women and men], in [their] personal existence, into an active and conscious participation in Jesus Christ."[7]

This process, which has a distinct although not a consciously uniform beginning, implies a constant turning from the self to God. Obsession with the self alienates women and men from their human vocation, from their calling in creation to be at the service of one another. The self is the idol that separates them not only from their vocation but from their creator. In turning to God, they are reconciled to the true source of life and are renewed in their vocation. Conversion is, therefore, a passage from a dehumanized and dehumanizing existence to a humanized and humanizing life. Or, to put it in other terms, it is the passage from death and decay to life and freedom. In conversion, women and men are liberated from the enslavement of the past and given the freedom of the future; they are turned from the god of this age, who passes away, to the God who is always the future of every past (Pannenberg).

Accordingly, such a passage cannot be limited to a single moment, for this would mean reverting to the static existence from which the gospel liberates. Rather, the dynamic life that is appropriated in conversion implies a series of new challenges, new turnings, and new experiences. On the one hand, it is a life that is appropriated in history, in the midst of history's precarious and evil reality. As historical beings, believers are always assailed by evil and are always tempted to go back to the past and fall into sin—thus the biblical reminder to be on the lookout, to resist temptation, to constantly turn away from evil and commit oneself to God. On the other hand, the new life is part of the "new creation" (2 Cor. 5:17) that God in Christ is bringing into being. Believers have been set on the course of God's coming kingdom. They have been made the pilgrim people of God, called to set their hopes on "the city which is to come" and to participate in the afflictions of Christ in the world (Heb. 13:13-14). Therefore, they are not to escape from history but rather to participate in its transformation through their witness and service. In so doing, they will encounter ever-new challenges and should expect ever-new turnings. This, says Paul, "comes from the Lord" who has "put his seal upon us and given us his Spirit . . . as a guarantee" (2 Cor. 3:18b; 1:22).

Conversion as a Socio-Ecclesial Reality

Social Context and Historical Engagement

We should further think of conversion as a socio-ecclesial reality. It is a social reality because it is a historical reality. Conversion is not something that occurs in a vacuum; it takes place in particular social contexts. These contexts bear witness to and are witnessed to by conversion. They are able to see and verify the change (and the changes) that God by his Spirit makes in the lives of those who trust in his Son. And these converts cannot help but name the One by whose power they have experienced wholeness and freedom (Acts 4:12, 20).

Conversion constitutes both a break with society and a new commitment to it. It places believers in a dialectical relationship with their environment. Society becomes penultimate in their scale of values but is given top priority in their Christian vocation. Free from its absorbing power, believers can give themselves completely to its service. But as with Peter in the case of Cornelius, so with all believers: perception of this new relationship often requires "new turnings"; its complexity makes new adjustments necessary. In fact, Christians are *always* in need of more clarifications from God in their relationship to society, and often need, as Peter did, to be transformed in their outlook in order to fulfill their calling.

Conversion is an ecclesial reality as well as a social reality. It is the result of the witnessing engagement of a visible, concrete community, and leads to incorporation into that community. This implies a new set of relationships, participation in a new fellowship, witnessing with others to a new social reality, and sharing in the hope of a new future. This is what Luke tells us occurred at Pentecost: "And all who believed were together and had all things in common; . . . And day by day, attending the temple together and breaking bread in their homes, they partook of food with glad and generous hearts, praising God and having favor with all the people. And the Lord added to their number day by day those who were being saved" (Acts 2:44, 46-47).

This community, however, is affected by the tensions of history. It is constantly threatened by what the New Testament calls the principalities and powers. This accounts for the situation described in Acts 5:1ff., where the fellowship of Pentecost was broken by the cheating of Ananias and Sapphira. Situations like this are repeated throughout the New Testament and the history of the church, and can be witnessed everywhere today. Not only individual believers but the church as a whole in a given geographical area can be trapped in sin. Therefore, the reminder to resist evil is given both to the individual believer and to the whole church everywhere. By the same token, the call to conversion is not limited to the unbeliever and the individual believer who has fallen into sin but is extended to the church in all of its range and complexity. Conversion will continue to be needed until the consummation of the kingdom.[8]

As an ecclesial reality, conversion is the means by which the church is brought into being and is constantly being brought back into right living. It is also the way to growth and maturity. Wasn't this what happened at the Council of Jerusalem (Acts 15)? And hasn't this been the case with the Protestant Reformation and with so many other *kairoi* in the history of the church? Indeed, conversion is God's way of renewing and changing the face of the church, so as to lead it along new paths and enable it to cross new frontiers.

Conversion has a definite "what for?" Its goal is not to provide a series of "emotional trips" or the assimilation of a body of doctrines, or to recruit women and men for the church. Rather, its goal is to put men and women at the service of the mission of God's kingdom. As Míguez Bonino has observed, "The call to conversion is an invitation to discipleship . . . whether it takes the direct form of Jesus' call to follow him or the apostolic form of participation through faith in the Messianic community. . . . It revolves around the kingdom. Consequently, it involves a community which is engaged in an active discipleship in the world."[9]

In the Matthean account of the Great Commission (28:19-20), the call to discipleship is *mediated* by baptism (which is the outward sign of incorporation into the body of Christ) and teaching. The *goal* of discipleship, however, is the observance of everything the Lord has commanded believers to do. All of these things can be summed up in the Great Commandment: "Love the Lord your God" and "your neighbor as yourself" (Mark 12:30-31). Christian conversion aims at putting women and men at the service of God and neighbor. It is that process by which they commit themselves to loving God and neighbor in "deed and in truth." Consequently, conversion can be verified only in concrete situations, in the efficacy of love. Here the words of John are extremely pertinent:

> This is the message which you have heard from the beginning, that we should love one another. . . . We know that we have passed out of death into life, because we love the brethren. . . . By this we know love, that he laid down his life for us; and we ought to lay down our lives for the brethren. But if any one has the world's goods and sees his brother in need, yet closes his heart against him, how does God's love abide in him? Little children, let us not love in word or speech but in deed and in truth. (1 John 3:11, 14, 16-18)

From the witness of the New Testament we can say that conversion is a complex experience. Not everyone experiences it in the same way; nevertheless, there is ample evidence to substantiate the idea that it is a qualified, open-ended process,[10] grounded in a vital initial encounter with and acceptance of Christ as Lord and Savior. As a new beginning, a spiritual awakening made possible by the Holy Spirit's inner work mediating the Word of the gospel and facilitating receptivity to it, conversion becomes a key that enables believers to unlock the many turning points that will take place in their new lives. Thus new conversions (sociocultural, political, spiritual) can be seen as having their root in Christ. As a new beginning, conversion becomes a fundamental reference in the interpretation and evaluation of other subsequent conversions that believers may have in the course of their Christian lives.[11]

It can be inferred from what has been said that the sociohistorical context plays an important role in conversion. The forms that conversion takes vary in accordance with the situation(s) of the person(s) that is (are) converted. Thus, for example, Jesus said to the adulterous woman, "Go, and do not sin again" (John 8:11), but to the rich young ruler he said, "Sell all that you have and distribute to the poor . . . and come, follow me" (Luke 18:22). It was not that Jesus had a double evangelistic standard but that different contexts demanded different forms of the call to conversion and the response to it. The woman had nothing and she knew it. The rich young ruler was also helpless, but his socio-economic situation inhibited him from recognizing his true need. Míguez Bonino has rightly commented that

> evangelism must . . . be related to the forms in which human groups place themselves in the world, their world-view, their forms of social representation, their class- and group-consciousness. And, on the other hand, it must be related to the way in which people act, their course of conduct. This means also that "conversion" may arise within the recognition of a verbally articulated message or through the engagement in a new form of conduct—consciousness may move through intellectual awareness to the form of life and action implicit in it or an accepted praxis into the self-understanding operation in it.[12]

This understanding of conversion implies, further, both a creative and a critical role for the convert in his or her social milieu. As the gospel is filtered through a person's sociohistorical situation, so conversion should arise in forms that correspond with his or her reality. Such a person will always enrich and critically evaluate his or her culture, class consciousness, group consciousness, and social representations. If it is true that the gospel frees one for creative service in society, it is no less true that it makes one critically aware of the reality of sin and evil. This leads Christians to fully share and participate in the joys and hopes, the values and life struggles of their society, and at the same time to maintain a critical distance from their society, a distance that enables them to detect any form of idolatry or any attempt to absolutize a given practice, person, group, institution, or vision.

A third implication of what has been said is the imperative of engagement that clearly differentiates Christian conversion from other types of human conversions. Christian conversion can be verified only in the concrete manifestation of a distinctive quality of life. This does not mean that there is a uniform pattern of behavior that distinguishes all believers in all sociohistorical circumstances. But it does mean that there is an "ethical minimum" which, although expressed differently in different contexts, nevertheless maintains a distinctive quality, easily recognizable everywhere. In the course of our discussion we have located this ethical minimum in the command to love God and neighbor through faith in Christ and in the turning that is continually translated into outward signs of loving service. Thus, for instance, whenever the rediscovery of one's cultural values or the acceptance of a political challenge enables one to deepen and make more efficacious one's service to God and neighbor, a new conversion can be said to have taken place. Likewise, conversion can be said to occur whenever believers fall away from this missional imperative (or "ethical minimum") and then "return" to their vocation.

Finally, what has been said implies not only that conversion confronts the church with an activity that takes place outside its walls, in the world, and for which its witness is vital, but that conversion confronts the church with the challenge of change in its inner life. A centrifugal theology of mission has enabled the church to come to terms with the biblical imperative of the "church for others." But this emphasis has also robbed the church of the centripetal dimension of mission—mission is, after all, always a two-way street, a coming-and-going, inner-and-outer reality. The church can be *inside out* only if it is *outside in.* In order to minister, it must be ministered to; in order to call others to conversion, it must be converted itself. We have seen how sin and evil are a constant threat to the church. Whenever the church falls into this trap, it enters into a situation of (functional) disbelief—its life and mission become corrupted, it becomes deaf to God's Word, and it loses touch with the Holy Spirit. In such situations, the call to conversion inside the church becomes an evangelistic priority. For, as I have said elsewhere,

> a church which loses touch with its source of strength (the Word and the Spirit), a community which loses sight of the object of its mission (the world and, particularly, the poor); a people that are unresponsive to the demands of the gospel, "cannot be the salt of the earth . . . [and] the light of the world. . . ." Indeed, such a church "*is* trapped in its own blindness, its own captivity . . . [and therefore], has to be liberated in order to be a liberating agent in the world."[13]

In all of this, we should not forget that although the church might be unfaithful, God remains faithful, and that although conversion involves our human responsibility, it is made possible because of the sovereignty of God's grace. "Turning" and "returning" are thus gifts that God invites us to accept in Jesus Christ and enables us to appropriate by the liberating action of his Spirit.

Conversion as a Life Journey

Spirituality as Praxis of the Faith

It follows that conversion is rooted in the work of the Holy Spirit. It is synonymous with the expression "new life in the Spirit." This expression refers to the inner life of human beings, or to their existence as embodied spirits, as well as to their ability to transcend material existence and enter into relation with the absolute spiritual reality of the universe. This spiritual existence, says Michael Collins Reilly, S.J., enables people both to grasp reality and to express themselves in "the complexity of form and symbols which make up human cultures." Moreover, it enables them to articulate the meaning of reality in a worldview "determined by a relationship with a deity or an ultimate concern."[14]

For Christians, life in the Spirit is that existence which is lived in accordance with the Spirit of the Triune God. To live in the Spirit is to live thirsty and hungry for God. This is why Gustavo Gutiérrez states that "the search for God is the ultimate meaning of any and every spirituality."[15] Such a search is inspired, motivated, and spearheaded by the Holy Spirit. Life in the Spirit is, therefore, a Spirit-led journey.

The Converter: The Holy Spirit, Giver of Life

From a Christian perspective, no human being is capable of converting someone else. Only the Holy Spirit can convert individuals and communities.

The Holy Spirit is the wellspring, the energy, and the ground of spiritual life. This assertion proceeds from the conviction of biblical faith that the Divine Spirit is the "Breath" *(ruach)* that gives life, generates energy, and fills the needs of the world.

When we speak of the Holy Spirit, we are referring to God in action. Indeed, the Spirit is more than the presence of transcendence; it is transcendence making one aware of its presence. The Spirit is more than the "numinous"[16]; it is the holy overshadowing the human and enabling it to become aware of the "other." The Spirit is the intermediary between what Martin Buber called "I and Thou," or between that aspect of transcendence which can be known and that which makes one know. In short, the Spirit is (to borrow the title of a book about the Holy Spirit and Christian mission) "the go-between God."

As we noted in Chapter V, in Christian theology the person of the Holy Spirit, the third member of the Trinity, appears in connection with the saving work of the Godhead. This is rooted in the way Scripture links the concept of "spirit" with that of "power." The Holy Spirit is the mediating force of the Godhead. Every aspect of God's economy —from creation to consummation—is associated with the Spirit. This implies that the personal identity of the Spirit is revealed in concrete events and deeds. Given this fact of biblical faith and Christian theology, I propose to describe the Holy Spirit as the giver of new life in terms of God's power in creation and redemption.

In any discourse concerning the Holy Spirit, one has to bear in mind its primal reality. The Spirit is the Creator in action. According to the Book of Genesis, the Spirit of God is the Breath that moved over the face of the waters, shaping the formless earth and filling its void

(1:2). It was by the Spirit that God created the world out of nothing. "By the word of the Lord the heavens were made, and all their host by the breath of his mouth" (Ps. 33:6). In this text, the Word of God is empowered by the creative force of God's Breath. The Spirit is the energy of the Word; the Word acts by the Spirit.

The creative power of the Spirit is particularly demonstrated in human life. The human spirit is dependent upon the Spirit of God, as the Book of Job vividly makes clear: "The Spirit of God has made me, and the breath of the Almighty gives me life. . . . As long as my breath is in me, and the spirit of God is in my nostrils; my lips will not speak falsehood" (Job 33:4; 27:3-4). These two texts, taken from two different passages, bear witness to the Spirit as the source of human life. Humankind not only has been brought into being by the Spirit, but also receives its spiritual energy through the Breath of God. The Spirit of God gives more than lifeblood to humankind. Indeed, humankind receives from the Spirit awareness of "others" and the ability to communicate, or establish community, with them. This relatedness to others is what makes human life spiritual. "Spirit," says John V. Taylor, "is that which lies between, making both separateness and conjunction real. It generates a certain quality of charged intensity which from time to time marks every [human being's] relationship with the [surrounding] world . . . and with whatever reality lies within and behind that world."[17]

To speak of the Holy Spirit as the giver of life is also to recognize an ongoing creative process. The Spirit not only brings God's creatures into being (creation) but renews "the face of the ground"—that is, the created order (Ps. 104:30). The Creator Spirit makes all things new. Thus Taylor argues that the Spirit in its creative activity (1) enhances awareness of "otherness," (2) stimulates "initiative and choice," and (3) promotes the "principle of life-through-death, of individual self-immolation in the interests of a larger claim, which is at variance with the principle of self-preservation."[18] These emphases in the Spirit's work disclose the Spirit as "the unceasing, dynamic communicator and Go-Between operating upon every element and process of the material universe, the imminent and anonymous presence of God."[19]

This primal reality of the Spirit is critically important for the church's adequate participation in evangelization. For if the Spirit is "the elemental force beyond all other forces," then the starting point of Christian mission must be "the earthly ground of God's primary activity as creator and sustainer of life."[20] This means, first of all, that we need to take the whole of life as the sphere of evangelization. No space of life should be left out of the province of evangelization. Furthermore, this means that what distinguishes our life in the Spirit is our sensitivity to others and communication with them. Neither superiority nor compartmentalization should be tolerated. "We must relinquish our missionary presuppositions and begin in the beginning with the Holy Spirit," says Taylor, "humbly watching in any situation in which we find ourselves in order to learn what God is trying to do there, and then doing it with" the Spirit.[21]

We know from biblical faith and scientific observation, however, that creation is not only dynamic and continuous but also prone to death and decay. Scripture teaches us that our planet is not solely the sphere of the Spirit. Indeed, God's creation has been contaminated by evil and sin. Nevertheless, the Spirit continues to breathe life into the nostrils of the cosmos. Accordingly, Scripture gives witness to the Spirit as the creator *and restorer* of the world. The Spirit is God's redeeming power.

In the historical books of the Hebrew Scriptures, the Spirit is mentioned in connection with the salvation of Israel in specific circumstances through charismatic leaders. In the Prophets and the five books of Moses (the Pentateuch), the Spirit of God acquires an eschatological-redemptive dimension. The Spirit is the liberating power of God revealed in the Exodus event and the restoration from exile. The Spirit is also the power of the future, revealing the *shalom* of the messianic kingdom and the concomitant transformation of the earth. One sign of the messianic age is the outpouring of God's Spirit on all as a permanent redemptive power in their hearts.

It is against this background that we noted in Chapter V the New Testament references to the role of the Spirit in redemption. This role, it was pointed out, is intimately related to the person and work of Jesus the Messiah. Indeed, Jesus begins his ministry with a claim to the messianic Spirit (Luke 4:18-19), a claim that he steadfastly holds to until the end of his life and ministry. By the same token, the Epistles speak of his death, resurrection, and continuing presence in history in connection with the Spirit. Thus the New Testament distinguishes between the Spirit *in* Jesus and the Spirit *of* the risen Christ. Hendrikus Berkhof explains why: "On the one hand the Spirit creatively precedes; he is greater than Jesus and controls him. Jesus is the work of the Spirit. On the other hand the Spirit is the work of (the risen) Jesus, interpreting Jesus and being ruled by him. Jesus is the fruit of the Spirit and the Spirit is the fruit of Jesus."[22]

The Spirit in Jesus implies, on the one hand, that he was a human person full of God (Acts 10:38). His life and ministry were a living witness to the presence of God in human history. On the other hand, the Spirit in Jesus implies that, in his obedience to the Spirit, Jesus demonstrated his faithfulness to God and became the authentic covenant partner through whom at last a new humanity could be created. Jesus was thus the bearer of the Spirit, and as such he became the "go-between" for God and humanity, the mediator of salvation.

This new relationship between Jesus and the Spirit is what led the Apostle Paul in particular to speak of the Spirit *of* Christ. Through his resurrection by the power of the Spirit, Jesus became not only the exalted Messiah, the Lord, but especially a life-giving Spirit—that is, he was made one with the Spirit. He became the Pneumatic Christ and the evangelist par excellence. The Spirit uses the prophetic and apostolic Word, the good news, to impart new life to the world by calling and empowering it to be converted to Christ.

The Converted Existence: Creative and Liberating Life

Creative liberation and redemptive liberation are complementary sides of the work of the Holy Spirit. Therefore, the new life that is imparted by the Holy Spirit in conversion should be thought of as creative and liberating—"creative" in the sense of bearing witness to the Spirit's activity in history and the created order, and "liberating" in the sense of collaborating with the Spirit's reconciling work in the world. Since I have already described the Spirit's work in reconciling the world to God (see Chapter V), here I will give a few examples of work and life in the Spirit in the created order.

John V. Taylor, author of *The Go-Between God,* has noted that the mission of the Creator Spirit has an enormous range. To illustrate, he points to

> the plant-geneticist breeding a new strain of wheat, the World Health Organization team combatting bilharzia, the reconstruc-

> tion company throwing a bridge across a river barrier, the political group campaigning for the downfall of a corrupt city council, the amateur dramatic group in the new cultural centre, the team on the new oil-rig, the parents' committee fighting for desegregated schools in the inner city.[23]

To these examples we could add many more—of a social, economic, political, biological, ecological, cultural, and even religious nature. In fact, following Taylor, everything that enhances sensitivity to others and therefore builds community, struggling for a more just and peaceful society; everything that enables people to live in freedom and, consequently, make responsible choices; and everything that compels people to make sacrifices for the common good and the ecological well-being of the earth can be identified with the creative work of the Spirit. To live in the Spirit is to glorify God by recognizing these deeds and events as "sacraments of life" (Leonardo Boff), bearing witness to them as signs of the Spirit's continuing work in creation.

The Praxis of a Converted Journey: Discipleship, Dialogue, and Discernment

The converted existence, or the new life in the Spirit, should be understood as a creative and liberating journey. It is a lifelong pilgrimage of faith in the God who makes all things new, expressed in concrete engagement. Spirituality is the practical expression of the journey, the praxis—or reflective engagement—of the faith. As such, it has at least three dimensions.

One dimension of this journey is *discipleship.* The life in the Spirit is, above all, a following of the Pneumatic Christ. Everyone who comes to the faith comes as a learner or a follower of Christ as he or she marches toward the consummation of God's kingdom. The pattern of this pilgrimage is given to us in the Gospels. The call to discipleship comes to us in the aftermath of the Resurrection; it is mediated by the call and training of the apostles prior to Easter. Only by following the pattern established in the New Testament can we understand what it means to be disciples in our lifetime.

As we noted in Chapter IV, following Jesus implies at least three things: (1) commitment to him and his ways, (2) obedience to his

Word, and (3) participation in his mission. These are the three main ingredients of the life of discipleship everywhere and at all times.

To follow the risen Christ requires an unconditional trust in him and a rejection of all earthly lords. Faith in him is not a matter of one's own choosing. It is the Spirit who takes the initiative and makes one aware of Christ's claim and commitment to our well-being. To follow him, therefore, is to accept the Spirit's invitation to enter into fellowship with him and thus to give one's loyalty to his cause.

Commitment to Christ implies obedience to his Word. Christ's Word comes to us through the gospel, appropriated in the community of faith. Scripture is to be read not only with common sense, critically and canonically, but especially in context (a point Gabriel Fackre makes). Scripture is to be heard prayerfully in the community of faith. It is to be taken as the authoritative source for all matters pertaining to Christian faith and practice.

Commitment and obedience are tested in evangelization. Hearing Christ's word and following him involve undertaking a pilgrimage through the wilderness of life — "outside the camp" (Heb. 13:13), where Christ died. Discipleship involves sacrifice, a witness unto suffering and death. It implies personal identification with Christ's suffering and solidarity with the suffering of women and men everywhere; it implies death to personal ambition and a disposition to bear others' burdens for Christ's sake. It is an undertaking, however, that is energized by the risen Lord. Therefore, believers are not to be overwhelmed by the cost of evangelization or by the many frontiers they must cross, because Christ has set them free to participate in his ongoing mission of transforming the world and liberating it from the power of sin and death.

In the Two Thirds World today—that two-thirds of the world's population living in situations of poverty, powerlessness, and oppression—Christian discipleship is being tested on the altar of life. This historical space has suddenly become a Golgotha. As Christians are coming face to face with the harsh reality of poverty, injustice, oppression, repression, and persecution, they are being forced either to stand firm on their commitment and obey God's Word or to deny their faith. In Latin America, for example, a fairly large company of believers—including pastors, priests, religious, and laity—have been prepared to suffer persecution and death for the cause of justice rather than survive through accommodation and retraction. The authenticity of faith has been measured against the standard of martyrdom that Jesus established for his disciples: "If any man would come after me, let him deny himself and take up his cross and follow me. For whoever would save his life will lose it, and whoever loses his life for my sake will find it" (Matt. 16:24-25).

To live in the Spirit of Christ in the Two Thirds World today is to run the risk of harassment, persecution, and death. Whether it be in countries like Nepal (where to be a confessing believer is to be regarded as a non-person without any status, identity, or voice), or in situations like those of South Korea, South Africa, and Central America (where the Christian leaders who have identified with the sufferings of thousands whose basic human rights have been brutally denied have faced imprisonment, exile, and even death), discipleship in these lands is a difficult, hazardous, and costly enterprise.

However, life in the Spirit is not only a costly following but an open walk. Believers have been set free to live for others. This means living as part of the human community and sharing in its common struggles, fears, and hopes. Not least, this implies being open to dialogue with people of other religious traditions.

Dialogue is another dimension of the journey of the converted life. It is an attitude of respect and sensitivity to others who may think differently and have other convictions. It is a sharing and a listening to one another from the depth of one's commitment. It is a participation in an interreligious communication based on the experiences of our common humanity, and the awareness of the holy in and through our planetary existence. Since as Christians we live by the power of the Creator as well as the Redeemer Spirit, we ought not to fear exposing ourselves to the witness of all people of goodwill, to the gifts and challenges of life and to its source and dynamic as various people express it. Indeed, we recognize that the eternal life uniquely revealed in Jesus proceeds from the Creator-God (James 1:17), who has made it available in many and sundry ways to all humanity (Rom. 1:19-21; 2:12-16).

Dialogue is, therefore, an exercise in two-way witness. From the Christian perspective, *it begins in silence,* with a willingness to listen to others and the Great Other, who often speaks through our neighbor. Only by listening can we speak; only by becoming vulnerable can we share; only by serving can we bear witness to Jesus Christ as the life and light of the world (John 1:4). We do not fear the witness of our neighbors concerning their experience of God because we serve the God who from of old has been "working salvation in the midst of the earth" (Ps. 74:12). Indeed, Scripture bears witness to the fact that what we know of God is but the bare minimum for our salvation and that there is still much more for us to learn. Isaiah of Jerusalem looks to the day when

> there will be a highway from Egypt to Assyria, and the Assyrian will come into Egypt, and the Egyptian into Assyria, and the Egyptians will worship with the Assyrians. In that day Israel will be the third with Egypt and Assyria, a blessing in the midst of the earth, whom the Lord of hosts has blessed, saying, "Blessed be Egypt my people, and Assyria the work of my hands, and Israel my heritage." (Isa. 19:23-25)

Whether this is a vision of the conversion of all the nations to the God of Israel, or, more likely, the conversion of Israel and the other nations to the living God who is the ground of all being (Tillich), is witnessed to by the religious conscience, and is both the judge of all religions and the fulfillment of their deepest aspirations, the fact remains that salvation is in the hands of God and the church is but a witness to that portion of God's truth that it has received. Our own knowledge of Christ is still in fragments, for (as we have noted) we read in the Book of Revelation that "he has a name inscribed which no one knows but himself" (19:12). Our knowledge of Christ is not a private possession but a foretaste of his ultimate identity. This means that we need to be humble and open because it may just be that there are things about him that we can learn from the witness of others. Therefore, I concur with Michael Collins Reilly when he says that a spirituality based upon the mission of the Triune God "cannot fail to be mindful of the truth that the church is not greater than God and that the mission of the church, although it is the historical community of explicit participation in the Mission of God, is not co-extensive with God's mission."[24]

Thus life in the Spirit involves an open walk and dialogue with people of goodwill and other religious traditions everywhere. But it also requires spiritual *discernment.* Indeed, we should not forget the admonition of Scripture: "Beloved, do not believe every spirit, but test the spirits to see whether they are of God" (1 John 4:1). There are good and bad spirits, creative and destructive forces, life-affirming and life-denying movements. In the context of interreligious dialogue, this means that at the very least we need to evaluate all religious truths in the light of the revelation we have received in Christ. We witness to the fact that God in Jesus the Messiah acted decisively once and for all by the power of the Holy Spirit to redeem the world from sin and death. Whatever saving truth there may be in a religious tradition, it cannot contradict—let alone substitute for—the saving significance of the event of Christ. Thus the Apostle John tells us that "every spirit which confesses that Jesus Christ has come in the flesh is of God, and every spirit which does not confess Jesus is not of God. This is the spirit of antichrist" (1 John 4:2-3). The fundamental reality of the Incarnation is that the Son of God took upon himself the identity of every human being but especially that of the lowest of us—of the poor, the powerless, and the oppressed. The Son of God appears unquestionably identified as the God of the poor and the disenfranchised who came to liberate, heal, and reconcile an alienated and death-prone world. Any spirit that does not affirm this truth is not the Spirit of Christ.

As we noted earlier in Chapter IV, the fundamental theological question for people who live on the fringes of society is this: Does religion, as a human phenomenon and as particular systems of faith, have a liberating word for them in their specific situation? From the perspective of the Christian faith, the answer is yes, but the church in mission has not always lived up to and affirmed that central fact of the faith. The result has been an alienating and life-denying spirituality rather than a liberating and life-affirming one. Frequently it has been a betrayal of the gospel and its transforming mission. A discerning spirituality enables the church to discriminate between the Spirit of truth and the spirit of deceit, between the living God and the idols of death, between the Christ and the Antichrist, between the saving power of the gospel and the illusory claims of all human strategies of salvation. Indeed, spiritual discernment is necessary for an authentic discipleship and a mature dialogic relationship with our neighbors. Discernment is a gift for those who walk according to the Spirit in both contemplation and apostolicity, in both silence and prayer, in both the solitude of the soul and the community of the faithful.

To live in the Spirit is to experience joy when all around seems sad, to hope even where there seems to be so little to be hoped for, to be childlike in a sophisticated and anxious world. It is above all to be able to sing new songs to the Lord even if one is living in a strange land. I learned one such song, written by Christians in Cuba, while visiting Nicaragua a few years ago. My wife and I offer this translation of it:

> Sent by the Lord am I.
> My hands are ready now
> to help construct a just
> and peaceful loving world.
> The angels cannot change
> a world of pain and hurt
> into a world of love,
> of justice and of peace.
> The task is mine to do.
> Make it reality—
> O help me, God, obey,
> help me to do your will.

CHAPTER VIII

The Basic Evangelizing Community

Contextual Evangelization in the Life and Mission of the Church

In the course of this book we have explored the contextual nature of evangelization from a theological perspective. We have noted that the evangelistic context involves people situated in specific sociohistorical locations who have been transformed by the gospel and consequently are committed to the transformation of the world. In evangelization we share ourselves and our circumstances as people in whose lives and social situations the gospel has become the good news of salvation. We bear witness to what God has done for us in Christ both as sinners and as the victims of sin.

We have also considered the biblical roots of contextual evangelization, underscoring its prophetic character and apostolic legacy. We examined the epic of Esther, exploring her prophetic act on behalf of the liberation of the Jewish people in the Persian Dispersion during the reign of Xerxes I (known in biblical literature as King Ahasuerus). We noted how in this gesture Esther fulfilled the mission of the evangelist as described by Deutero-Isaiah (Isa. 52:7) and further elaborated by Trito-Isaiah (Isa. 61:1-3). Esther and the Isaianic prophets proclaimed peace, bore public witness to salvation, and declared that God reigns. This model of prophetic evangelization posits the challenge of evangelization as a living witness in a context of vulnerability wherein hope in the transforming power of God becomes the salient characteristic. In this perspective, evangelization implies living in obedience to God's kingdom in such a way that one becomes a herald of good news and an agent of transformation in any human situation, but particularly in those situations in which there is a threat against life, and injustice and oppression are suffered.

Next we reflected on the apostolic legacy of Jesus the Galilean Messiah in the light of the missional Christology of the Gospel of Mark. This model describes evangelization as a ministry that is carried out from the periphery or margin of one's societal context. Jesus established his evangelistic base on the periphery, proclaiming the kingdom of God amid the alienated multitudes, and from there confronting the powers of Jerusalem with the good news of the kingdom, the eruption of a new order of life characterized by liberating love, peace, and justice. This model emerges as a radical critique of our evangelistic practice. It reminds us of the fact that "God is at the base" and that "the great theophanic space is the poor, the hungry, the oppressed, the humiliated."[1] This model questions the base of our evangelistic work, our audience (or interlocutor), and the scope of our action. At the same time, it provides us with new insights for a contextual evangelization open to the multitudes at the ends of the earth.

We proceeded to reflect on the God of the gospel as an evangelizing presence. We noted how evangelization is carried out in the active presence of a communal God known in the Christian tradition as Father, Son, and Holy Spirit. In this communitarian vision of the God of the gospel, evangelization appears as the loving story of an eternal community. In this vision we see God sending his Son for the eternal community. We witness the Son giving himself freely for the love of humanity. We also acknowledge the action of the Holy Spirit seeking to liberate the world from sin and death by faith in the crucified and risen Son of God, to transform it into a radically new world and reconcile it with the eternal communion of Father, Son, and Spirit.

In this perspective we have underscored the fact that God is *mission* (sending) and *unity* (reconciliation). We have access to the intimacy of God's being (the imminent Trinity or God in God's self) only through the revelation of God's mystery in salvation (the "economic" Trinity, or God in the work of salvation).

Evangelization appears, therefore, as a communal event that demands a base community founded upon the Trinitarian God. This implies not only that God is "at the base," stimulating, inspiring, motivating, supporting, and guiding the evangelistic process. This definition also implies that evangelization is the work of the base, the kerygmatic or transforming witness that the people of God render in concrete historical situations. Thus it is necessary to reflect (as we have done in the last two chapters) on the message of the cross and the call to conversion as essential aspects of the communication of the gospel—but also to recognize the importance of the church as the base of evangelization. Accordingly, in this chapter we shall consider the place of evangelization in the life and mission of the church as a basic evangelizing community.

The Base of Evangelization

Every transforming action—praxis—needs a base. The base is the bottom, the infrastructure, the pivot, or the sector that guarantees (because it makes possible) the activating of an organism. It is the most specific reality of that organism. Without the base, reality is distorted, an edifice collapses, or a movement is paralyzed.

It has been said that to evangelize is to participate in a transforming action—that is, the transmission of the good news of salvation. In this sense, evangelization is not a concept but rather a dynamic task, incarnated first in the life and saving action of Jesus Christ. Therefore, it cannot be reduced to a verbal formula. To evangelize is to reproduce, by the power of the Holy Spirit, the salvation that has been revealed in Jesus Christ.[2] This reproductive activity is carried out by means of testimonies and signs that point to the transforming action of the kingdom of God proclaimed and embodied by Jesus, anticipated in the experience of the Spirit, and consummated "eschatologically" in the new creation that has begun with the resurrection of Christ.

The fundamental elements in evangelization are love, faith, and hope incarnated in a ministry dedicated to the transformation of the world. It is to this imperative that the Apostle Paul referred when he wrote to the church in Corinth about visiting them to discover not their "talk" but the "power" behind it. "For the kingdom of God does not consist in talk but in power" (1 Cor. 4:20).

The base of evangelization is the congregation. As a community of love, faith, and hope, the congregation is God's instrument for the transmission of the gospel. Its life should be a continuous perpetual proclamation, "a fifth gospel," the incarnation of love, faith, and hope, the reproduction of the good news of salvation in its social context.

Evangelization is not a task that belongs to isolated believers. Rather, it is a mission that has been committed to the fellowship of faith. As we have noted previously, we see the representative character of evangelization already in the Hebrew Scriptures. Deutero-Isaiah, for example, sees Zion, the Holy City, as the evangelizer of the captives of Babylon (Isa. 40:9; 52:7). Likewise, Esther acted as a representative of her condemned people when she interceded in an attempt to liberate them, knowing quite well that she could lose her life. When the death sentence of her people was canceled, she became a symbol of God's deliverance in the Jewish tradition. The beggar, the one who tells a companion in misery where to find bread, is not a simple individual but a representative of the church as an assembly of women and men called and liberated by the Lord, and sent to bear witness in the world to Jesus, the bread of life. Finally, we have seen how the Gospel of Mark presents the Galilean Christ as the authentic representative of Israel, proclaiming to the scattered and harassed multitudes the good news of the kingdom of God.

The early church interpreted the ministry of evangelization as a communal mission. The traditions of the New Testament, which interpret both Jesus' evangelizing ministry and the various apostolic missions of the early church, affirm categorically that evangelization is not the private property of gifted individuals but rather the responsibility of the whole people of God. The very worship of the church is seen as its most significant corporate act, being a celebration and proclamation of the gospel. It is thus understood as a great witnessing event.

This conviction has been transmitted in one form or another in the history of the church. The great monastic movements, for example, have an eminently communitarian and evangelistic character. Similarly, the great modern missionary endeavors, despite the individualistic baggage that some may have carried along, reflect a strong communal undercurrent: they are voluntary associations of women and men dedicated to the collective tasks of proclaiming the good news of God in the world.

Evangelization is neither a mission that belongs to individual believers nor the private property of the ecclesiastical institution represented by a clerical elite. The gospel has been committed to a community, is transmitted by that community, and demands a community experience. Without community there cannot be a living representation of the gospel. It is the community of believers that announces the kingdom of God as a reality, which proclaims a new order of life under the sovereign action of God, which relativizes all human authority, including that of institutions. To be sure, evangelization is nourished and facilitated by individuals. It takes place, practically speaking, through individuals. But it is a witness that cannot be offered without the ecclesiastical community. It is by and through local communities of faith that Christians can share with others what God has done and is doing in their lives. This witness has no meaning, however, if it is not backed by a community whose love is translated into works of mercy, a community whose faith is manifested in a commitment to social justice and whose hope is reflected in the struggle for a just peace.

Furthermore, the gospel is a message transmitted from generation to generation. Evangelization depends, therefore, on a community with a long tradition, and this is impossible to sustain without the institutional church. The trajectory and resources of the institution are indispensable for the realization of the mission. It is no less true, however, that the ecclesiastical institution lives by the congregation or local community of faith. Without community, the apostolic tradition loses its dynamic transmission and the institutional church loses its vitality. The church then becomes a bureaucratic organization or, at worst, a relic of the past.

To speak of the community of faith (or the congregation) as an evangelizing base is to refer to the place where the gospel is manifested and lived in its most concrete reality.[3] This is the starting point for the diffusion of the gospel in the world, the location where the good news becomes *communion,* is transformed into an *apostolate,* and gives *identity* to the new world promised in the gospel. The church is the sign by which the gospel is expressed and anticipated as a "sacrament of salvation" in the world.

The word *sacrament,* the etymological root of which means "commitment," is the Latin term used to translate the Greek word *mysterion,* the word used to describe the gospel in the New Testament: the gospel is "the mystery hidden for ages and generations but now made manifest" (Col. 1:26; cf. 1:27; 2:2; 4:3; Rom. 16:25-26; Eph. 3:3; 1 Tim. 3:16). Tertullian (160-220 C.E.) is the first to refer to baptism and the Eucharist as sacraments. Vatican II described the church as a "visible sacrament of all salvific unity."[4] Leaving aside the density that such an expression may have in contemporary Roman Catholic theology, [5] I hold that the ecclesial community, as people of God and as a communication base of the gospel, is the visible sign of salvation that God offers the world in the name of Christ by the Holy Spirit. As such, the church is the divine anticipation of that promise through the communal experience of forgiveness and the solidaristic commitment to justice and peace. Evangelization is, according to the church community, good news. The church is the gospel working in efficacious and transforming action for the salvation of the world.

The Evangelistic Cutting Edge in the Church

Not everything that the church does is evangelization. The church is called to undertake several missional tasks. However, everything that the church *is* and everything that the church has been sent *to do* has an evangelistic dimension. In this section I would like to consider the evangelistic cutting edge of the life and mission of the congregation (the base of evangelization) by focusing on various ministries.

Worship and Evangelization

The church has been called to worship God; it is a liturgical community. The Greek noun *leitourgia* means "service" or "ministration." It was used in classical Greek, together with the verb *leitourgein,* to describe various services the citizen rendered to the state. This was the term used in the Septuagint to translate the Hebrew term *aboda,* which is employed in the Hebrew Scriptures to describe the priestly rites of the covenant. In the New Testament the word appears in connection with Israel's worship rendered by the church to God and the service it offers the neighbor (2 Cor. 9:12; Phil. 2:30). According to J.-J. von Allmen, the extrabiblical background of this word and the use of it in the Hebrew Scriptures and the New Testament indicate two interesting things about the nature of Christian worship. First, the word refers to an action of the people rather than of the clergy — it revindicates a declericalization of worship. Second, von Allmen notes, "In non-religious usage in antiquity it denotes a political or civil action in which the wealthy take the place of the poor who are unable to pay. Hence the suggestion is that in its liturgy the Church acts on behalf of the world, which is totally incapable of adoring and glorifying the true

God, and that the Church in its cult represents the world before God and protects it."[6]

The church exists to celebrate and call the world to honor and revere God in the freedom of the Holy Spirit in response to Christ's great redemptive work. The New Testament views the entire Christian life as a great act of worship to God (Rom. 12:1-2). Without the daily worship offered by Christians through their lives, Sunday worship lacks meaning. This is why the Apostle Paul interpreted his evangelizing mission as a great liturgical event. He saw the fruit of his apostolic mission as a great offering to God (Rom. 15:16). In Sunday worship the evangelistic work of the community of faith is celebrated. This is the moment when the church declares publicly to the world everything that it communicates to its own members—namely, that the good news of salvation that God has offered in Christ is now available for all to hear and believe.

Christian worship occurs in a kerygmatic environment because it takes place in the context of the church's evangelizing work and has the gospel as its central theme. This explains why the evangelistic ministry of Jesus, "the Galilean moment," is recapitulated during the first part of the liturgy, the service of the Word. This also explains why Christ's redemptive work is proclaimed in the celebration of baptism and the Eucharist. Through its formal worship the church becomes conscious of itself as an evangelistic community, proclaims corporately before the world the grace of the gospel, and offers thanks to God for the Spirit's power manifested in the daily witness of its members. In worship the congregation also renews its apostolic commission and receives the confirmation of the promise of the gift of the Spirit to continue to labor in the different situations of daily life.

It is a fact, however, that in too many instances in many churches the liturgy is so complex, lengthy, and obscure that only the clergy, theologians, and well-informed laity can fully appreciate its kerygmatic significance. Sadly, "hearing and knowing" do not always go together in Christian worship. Therefore, if worship is to fulfill its evangelistic potential, the faithful have to be taught the meaning of the liturgy. This point has been made in *Go Forth in Peace,* a recent Orthodox study on mission:

> In order to become a really powerful expression of the church's mission in the world, worship must be meaningfully understood

> by its participants (1 Cor. 14:6-15). It is through a full participation in the liturgy that the people realize both the teaching and then the life, death and resurrection of Jesus Christ, which is the very reality of what we are attempting to proclaim. In other words, the liturgy itself is the proclamation of the gospel in an existential and experiential manner.[7]

This implies, first of all, that the pastoral leadership must take seriously the role of the sermon or homily in the liturgy. Preaching "should never be omitted, whatever the number of those present at every occasion."[8] Indeed, preaching should be clear and relevant, should make explicit the meaning of the gospel being celebrated and its invitation to a life of discipleship. The preceding statement also implies what the study explicitly urges: "The parish members must be educated to understand what it is that is happening in the divine liturgy, and in this way to comprehend the proclamation in the liturgy."[9] Education for worship takes place not just through formal teaching but especially through congregational participation in and planning for worship.

Therefore, to be faithful to its evangelistic cutting edge, worship has to be contextualized in the language and symbols of the celebrating community—without, of course, becoming so relative that it loses its theological depth and breadth. This is the extraordinary value of liturgical creations like the Nicaraguan Peasants' Mass and the Brazilian Quilombos Mass that we referred to in Chapter II. Similarly, black American worship has traditionally been able to tell and celebrate the gospel story in the rhythms and symbols of the Afro-American cultural experience. The evangelistic cutting edge of these liturgical expressions becomes evident to the world when they are understood and lived by the liturgical communities themselves. Faithfulness to the content of the gospel goes hand in hand with commitment to and awareness of the sociohistorical reality of the worshiping community. Singing, praying, and confessing the faith in the language of the people enable congregations to have an outreach ministry even while they are praising and praying to God.

Communion and Evangelization

The church is also a *communion* (Gr. *koinonia*) created by God from the discordant, dismembered, alienated, and scattered human elements of creation. It has been graciously constituted into the body of Christ by the power of God's Spirit. Its community life—that is, the fellowship among its members — is a foretaste of the reconciliation proclaimed in the gospel. If worship is a great kerygmatic event in which the good news of salvation in Christ is proclaimed publicly and corporately, then the communion of the faithful followers of Christ *demonstrates* its firstfruits. This became one of the leading characteristics of the early church in Jerusalem, as the first chapters of the Book of Acts clearly affirm (cf. Acts 2:44).

The fellowship of the true followers of Christ is a sign of the promise and presence of the kingdom of God. It celebrates forgiveness and affirms solidarity. Through its communion the church declares before the world that in the gospel there is proclaimed a new order of life and a new mode of human existence. In *koinonia* the church bears witness to the fundamental unity that exists between God and the people of God, between the members of God's community and the Trinitarian community. This is the meaning of the Eucharist.[10]

Christian communion is not simply an act of congregational encounter, much less a mere participation in a liturgical assembly. Neither is it the undertaking of a common task. Rather, "the communion of the saints" is a fundamental attitude of openness toward each other; it is the experience of life as a gift, and the exercise of gratitude without expecting anything in return. This is why *koinonia* is manifested in concrete acts or deeds. It is demonstrated, we know, in the active presence of the Holy Spirit, with "signs and wonders," just as we are told occurred in the upper room on Pentecost (Acts 2:43). We cannot forget that according to the Book of Acts, the state of communion among believers was the sine qua non for the outpouring of the Spirit (Acts 2:1). And it is this communion by which the world evaluates believers. As it was said in the early centuries of Christian history, "Behold, how they love one another." That judgment of the world regarding Christians' life in communion corresponds to the principle of verification established by Jesus himself, according to the Gospel of John: "By this all . . . will know that you are my disciples, if you have love for one another" (13:35). Without communion among Christians, there cannot be unity in the church, and without unity, the world cannot know that Jesus is indeed the Savior and Lord sent by God (John 17:21).

The communion of the church also has an evangelistic cutting edge. It gives credibility to the message of love that is proclaimed by the community of faith, it offers a model of life that overcomes the barriers that make social peace impossible (selfishness, greed, and alienation), and it prophetically denounces human society for its classist, racist, and sexist divisions. When the church fails to live in communion, it not only destroys its credibility in the proclamation of its message but also deprives society of a wholesome and constructive vision of a far better future and of an honest and sincere criticism of its fundamental problems—namely, social and personal sin.

Service and Evangelization

The church is a liturgical community and a communion of believers. It is also a diaconate—that is, an agency at the service of humanity. Christian service, or *diakonia,* is a consequence of the new life in Christ. If in communion the church demonstrates the firstfruits of the gospel, in service it *incarnates* its message. Of course, the church offers diverse types of services. Worship and communion are ways of serving God, church members, and the world. *Diakonia,* however, is a distinct type of service in the sense that it is related to providing material help to the needy. The foundational model of *diakonia* is to be found among "the Seven" in the Book of Acts, who were set apart "to serve tables," taking care of "the daily distribution" of food to the widows (6:1-2).

Following the tradition of the law and the prophets, the New Testament describes the diaconal mission of the church as that of serving the poor, the dispossessed, and the oppressed. These are widows, orphans, children, prisoners, strangers, the thirsty and the hungry—in short, those who lack materially what is essential for life. The evangelistic cutting edge of *diakonia* lies above all at the level of motivation. The church distinguishes itself from social and philanthropic agencies by the fact that it is motivated to serve by the love revealed in the gospel, proclaimed in mission, celebrated in worship, and experienced in communion. What the church does for the social and material well-being of its members and the world is accomplished by the power of the Spirit of Christ. The church does not serve the world in order to have the opportunity to preach the gospel. Rather, its service is complete in itself, the proclaimed message of concrete deeds. *Diakonia* does not need any justification other than that of offering a gift of love for the sake of God's love.

Nevertheless, it is a fact that service opens opportunities for dialogue about the most profound aspects of the faith. In such circumstances the church has the opportunity to name Christ as the foundation of its work. Still, one must acknowledge that *diakonia,* like *koinonia,* is an indirect form of naming Jesus Christ. In many instances Christ may be received indirectly through the acceptance of Christian service, the expressions of sympathy with Christian communion, or the manifestation of an attitude and a silent devotion paid to Christian worship. The church and its "delegates of the Word" need to be sensitive to such circumstances, discerning the presence of the Spirit in them and establishing the necessary bridges for open communication about such incipient or implicit faith. Evangelization incorporates the ministry of service without taking away its authenticity or undermining its evangelical legitimacy. Service complements the process of communication and reception of the gospel until implicit faith becomes explicit and incipient faith is transformed into a mature faith.

Justice, Peace, and Evangelization

A ministry that runs parallel with *diakonia* is the church's activity as *advocate for justice and peace.* It is what the New Testament calls *dikaioma,* which literally means "a just action" (cf. 2 Cor. 9:8-15; 1 John 3:10; Rev. 22:11). According to the prophetic tradition, this is the kind of endeavor that is the guarantee of *shalom* (cf. Isa. 32:15-18; Ps. 72:1-4).

In the explicit proclamation of the gospel, the church announces the justice of the kingdom of God and transmits the good news of peace. It is not possible to celebrate worship or participate in the "communion of the saints" without making a reference to the ministry of justice and peace. The liturgical community prays and works for a just peace. The love that it lives and expresses in its fellowship becomes enfleshed in solidarity with those who suffer, struggle, and look forward to a new world of *shalom.*

When I refer to the ministry of justice and peace, however, I am indicating more explicit actions than those that are expressed indirectly in worship, communion, and service. In worship the church proclaims the gospel of justice and peace, in communion it demonstrates its first-fruits, and in *diakonia* it incarnates its love. In the ministry of justice and peace the church bears witness to the power and grace of the kingdom of God as a new order of justice and peace in the public realm.

The cry for justice and the promotion of peace are testimonies to God's love for the world. Both in the Hebrew Scriptures and in the New Testament God sends the people of faith to bear witness to his sovereign love, living for and advocating a new order of just peace. To live in the freedom of God's love is to struggle for, demand, and enjoy the space and the blessing of being agents of justice and makers of peace.[11] This implies nothing less than the protection of the right of every individual and every people to have access to the blessings of creation, to live in harmony with one another and the rest of creation. This right is protected when the church prays for, advocates, and struggles for a project of "communal well-being where God's creation is governed justly,"[12] especially in situations where people live under the threat of death and extermination. In our time this implies what is called the Two Thirds World—Africa, Latin America, Asia, and the islands of the Caribbean and the Pacific—as well as the impoverished, oppressed, and dispossessed minorities that live in the other one-third of the world.

To be sure, we live in an era in which the great majority of women, men, and children are the victims of egotistical interests, male chauvinist actions, political hegemonies, and the arms race. Consequently, they suffer malnutrition and physical ailments, inadequate housing and education, unemployment, social marginalization, and political powerlessness. Many have been thrown into prison, tortured, exiled, or simply assassinated. Their lives are worth little or nothing, caged in social systems and projects that have been designed and manufactured for a few, and imposed by local oligarchies and unscrupulous international power-brokers operating in their own economic and political interests.

As we noted earlier, these multitudes are not only sinners in need of the gospel but victims of sin. They challenge the people of God to bear witness to God's love by advocating, struggling for, and praying for their social well-being. "If the church would only say to the poor people of the world that they deserve to live, it would be making a powerful evangelistic pronouncement," says Chilean theologian Pablo

Richard.[13] By this he means that if the church worldwide would openly criticize and denounce with words and deeds those who oppress and mistreat the multitudes of the world; if the church would affirm the multitudes' right to projects and programs that promote their social, cultural, economic, and political well-being, it would be stating publicly that God is their defender, that those who work against these people are opposed to God and that in the kingdom of God there is space to live in justice and peace. This space is both a *promise* (cf. Isa. 65:17; Rev. 21:1ff.; 22:1-5) and a *reality* that becomes ever more clear and concrete through sociopolitical praxis. The church has the great privilege of participating prophetically in that praxis and discerning the presence of the Spirit in its midst, of opening small but effective spaces of justice and peace through secular agents.

The evangelistic dimension of the ministry of justice and peace is manifested both in what the church does and in what it says. All public events on behalf of a just peace have an evangelistic cutting edge, because they create a positive atmosphere for dialogue about the faith. All historical events and secular processes that open the door for a more just and fulfilling life offer the church the opportunity to make an evangelical interpretation of history, affirming justice and peace as a gift and a task of the kingdom of God. The ministry of *dikaioma* (justice and peace), like that of *diakonia* (service), liberates evangelization from the danger of sectarian proselytism, which reduces the gospel to an ideological slogan that seeks nothing more than a cheap increase in the number of adherents in a community that is already alienated from history and God's purpose for it. The ministry of justice and peace enables the church to make a historical witness open to the transformation of the world. It is true that the evangelistic invitation that proceeds from such a ministry has the goal of "more adherents," but not in any superficial sense—the goal is to increase the number of witnesses for justice and peace. I fully agree with Harvie Conn's assertion that when the church participates in such acts, it lets "people know that by giving their allegiance to Christ, they will be embarking on a great campaign to banish war and poverty and injustice, to set up a life where love and service and justice have taken the place of selfishness and power. [People will know then] that the church that sends out this manifesto plans to be an advanced copy of the new world order it preaches."[14]

Christian Education and Evangelization

We must add the ministry of teaching *(didache)* to the other ministries we have discussed—worship *(leitourgia),* communion *(koinonia),* service *(diakonia),* and justice and peace *(dikaioma).* The church, as a community of disciples, has been sent to teach the nations to observe all things that the Lord has commanded (Matt. 28:19-20). This is an educational task by which the church is to interpret the faith, equip for its practice, and motivate and instruct for its communication. It is through the ministries of *diakonia* and *dikaioma* that evangelization gains credibility; similarly, it is through the ministry of Christian education that the church's content is taught, its practice is critically evaluated, its agents are equipped, and its base of support is encouraged.

As an educational agency, the church seeks to accomplish three general objectives: (1) to *form* (character, abilities, and thought), (2) to *inform* (the mind, contemplation, and praxis), and (3) to *transform* (values, individuals, institutions, and communities) for the kingdom of God by the grace and power of the Holy Spirit.[15] The church's teaching ministry involves not only exploring the mystery of faith but also leading to the obedience that is faith (Rom. 1:5). This ministry is expressed in following Jesus to the consummation of the kingdom (Matt. 28:16-20) and is verified in the creative and renovating action of the people of God (Rom. 12:1-2; 1 Cor. 4:20; 2 Cor. 5:17). The church finds its educational model par excellence in the teaching ministry of Jesus. To teach the faith is to do what Jesus did with his disciples—namely, to invite them to follow in his steps, enabling them to hear and understand God's Word, equipping them to obey him in all things, and empowering them, by the Spirit, to communicate the gospel effectively.

It is interesting to note that at the same time Jesus educated he also evangelized—he preached the gospel of the kingdom and healed "every disease and every infirmity" (Matt. 9:35). His evangelistic ministry was accompanied, supported, and stimulated by his educational ministry. This same thing is evident in the apostolate of the early church. Peter, Paul, and the other apostles evangelized through their teaching and educated through their evangelistic proclamation.

The common denominator shared by Christian education and evangelization is the *gospel.* The church has no other message to teach or proclaim. Christian education serves evangelization by clarifying the content of the gospel and facilitating the development of skills for its communication. Accordingly, there cannot be a serious evangelistic effort without the parallel existence of a dynamic program of Christian education. The Sunday school or church school, instruction of new and young believers in the faith, Bible studies, vacation Bible school, courses in church leadership, courses and workshops of Christian formation for children, young people, and adults—these and other educational activities are essential not only for instructing new believers in the faith but also for motivating, stimulating, and preparing the church for the daily communication of the faith to its neighbors. In fact, in many cases such activities may be direct vehicles for evangelization because they attract those who have not yet made a responsible, well-thought-out decision for the gospel. For them, Christian education is evangelistic instruction.

All the ministries of the church have, therefore, an evangelistic cutting edge. To be sure, one ought not to confuse evangelization with the multiple missional tasks of the church. Nevertheless, one ought to recognize the evangelistic potential of all of these tasks. The evangelizing congregation (that is, the church at its base) is not simply one that keeps itself "busy" with special evangelistic activities but rather one that discovers the evangelistic cutting edge in everything that it is and has been called to do, and does not hesitate to put this "edge" to use. This is something of what the Apostle Paul might have had in mind when he exhorted Timothy to "preach the word . . . in season and out of season" (2 Tim. 4:2).

When the church takes seriously the fact that it has been called to be "good news" and that every aspect of its life and mission can contribute, directly or indirectly, to evangelization, when it takes advantage of the evangelistic potential of everything that it is and does, then the church experiences an extraordinary renewal and makes a permanent impact on its sociocultural context.

The Story of the Church in Evangelization

If evangelization is an ecclesial endeavor, and if everything that the church is has an evangelistic dimension, it follows that in communicating the gospel one tells the story of the church as an assembly called by the Holy Spirit, a community of Christian faith, and God's covenantal people. This proceeds from the fact that the story of the church is transmitted through its apostolic legacy (the gospel) in time and space. To transmit the gospel is to tell the story of the community that was born and is sustained by the gospel.

The Story of "the Saints"

Evangelization tells the story of the "assembly of the saints" called by the Holy Spirit through faith in Christ. To proclaim the gospel is for generations and peoples to share the words of love of those who have been called from darkness into God's "marvelous light" (1 Pet. 2:9). It means bearing witness to the great "cloud of witnesses" (Heb. 12:1) that the community of faith represents, from Abraham to the present and "the spirits of just men made perfect" (Heb. 12:23)—that is, those who have died in the Lord and await the Resurrection.

When the gospel invites us to become part of such a distinguished assembly, it also extends an invitation to participate in that history of communion through time and space. It offers to make us sisters and brothers in solidarity.

For this reason evangelization cannot be solitary or ahistorical. To tell the story of "the saints" and extend an invitation to its communion is an ecumenical activity that applies to the whole church and all of its parts. To promote divisions or isolation in the name of evangelization is a contradiction. Evangelization is not meant to be a competitive activity of congregations competing for members but rather the affirmation of the mutuality and solidarity among the members of the household of faith. Of course, evangelization makes possible the quantitative as well as the qualitative growth of the church. However, such growth should not function as a justification for separation; it should not occur at the expense of fellowship and communion. Every divisionist or isolationist act is a negation of the story of the communion of the saints and therefore a negation of the spirit and content of the gospel.

The Story of the Company of Faith

In evangelization we also share the story of the company of faith. That is to say, one represents a body of believers confessing their faith in the God of the gospel. The church evangelizes because it believes in the gospel and reflects on its content and significance. The church is characterized by its theological integrity.

We have to acknowledge that the confessing church is not homogeneous. It is a complex community of multiple structures, cultural backgrounds, and theological expressions. Its confession of faith is equally complex. The story of its profession is mediated by churches or denominations with their respective congregations or local churches. The story of the faith reflects not only the complex reality of the churches but also their intellectual and spiritual resources.

Evangelization does not present an "ideal" church. Rather, it tells the story of a very real church. Indeed, it narrates the story of a community of forgiven sinners, created by the grace of God out of the dismembered pieces and discordant elements of human society to be first-fruits of a new creation. In evangelization the church's cultural particularity, social fragmentation, and theological limitations are affirmed. Its understanding and articulation of the mystery of the faith are always subject to the judgment of the cross, because the church has yet to reach its fullness. Thus it is provisional and in constant need of critical evaluation, revision, and renewal. Even so, the church is a community of hope, confident of its future in God. Despite its historical limitations, the church confesses to be a universal community, set apart (sanctified) by the Holy Spirit for the glory of God and the well-being of humanity. Its theological story is, therefore, the narrative of faith in the God of love and hope.

The Story of a Covenant People

Evangelization also implies the story of a covenant people. The covenant is the symbol of the relationship that God has established with the people of Israel and the church (cf. Rom. 11:1-16).[16] It points to God's steadfast love and the faithfulness and obedience that is expected of God's people. As the Gentile component of God's covenant people, grafted onto that body by the mystery of the grace revealed in Christ

(Rom. 9:25), the church in its pilgrimage of faith is to bear witness to God's covenantal mercy, wisdom, and steadfast love. From this perspective, the history of the church is the narrative of its covenantal walk with God.

Evangelization announces God's faithfulness in the everyday life of the church and affirms the commitment of its members to God. This is a communitarian pilgrimage: the people of God are accompanied by the Lord of history en route to the consummation of the kingdom. Accordingly, we are dealing not with a static history but a dynamic history, not with a perfect and finished people but with a company of pilgrims who are being changed and shaped. We are dealing with an eschatological history, the narrative of the fulfillment of God's promises in the obedience of a covenant people.

Evangelization is, therefore, a universal invitation to all women and men to become part of the pilgrim people of God in the march toward the new order of life that is the kingdom of God. It is an invitation to become part of a new humanity.

To be God's instrument in the formation of a new humanity is the extraordinary privilege of the evangelizing church. But as we have noted, the church evangelizes not in a vacuum but in concrete situations. Its evangelistic witness is always a contextual task.

Toward a Contextual Evangelistic Practice

Unfortunately, the evangelistic practice of many churches, both in the Americas and elsewhere, has suffered from the absence of a clear vision of their sociohistorical contexts. Consequently, their evangelistic practice has been contextually shallow. Recognizing this, we have been arguing not so much for a new type of evangelization as for a new way of understanding and practicing contextual evangelization. This implies a sociohistorical approach to the biblical roots of evangelization, a communal theological ground, and an ecclesial vision informed by the theological and social base of the church.

With this in mind, we have considered two biblical models of contextual evangelization, both "on the periphery" of their respective contexts. Such examples necessitate the acknowledgment that contextual evangelization is not simply the application of the gospel to a given situation but rather the communication of the good news from the "base" or "margin" where we find the absentees of history, the most vulnerable and needy people of society. This perspective implies returning the evangelistic ministry to the grass roots of the church and establishing a preferential option for the marginalized of society.

To ground contextual evangelization in a Trinitarian theology is to see God as the spiritual base for the communication of the gospel. It is to understand God as an eternal community of love, God as mission and unity who seeks and reconciles, sends and calls. The spirituality that proceeds from such an understanding is liberating and transforming. Conversion, justification, and sanctification are equally dynamic. Instead of separating the evangelized from the world and alienating them from its transformation, such spiritual experience will liberate them for it. To be converted to Christ, therefore, will be to experience a change of mind, to re-orient one's life in the direction of God's kingdom and its justice. To be justified by faith will be to appropriate the justice of God revealed in Christ, to be declared just before God and set free to do the works of justice. And sanctification will be understood as the process by which the Holy Spirit makes ever more efficacious the consecration of believers for the service of God's kingdom in history.

The fundamental task of the church as an evangelizing community is bearing witness to the kingdom of God under the sign of the cross, not searching for its own triumph. In evangelization, as in other ministries, the church ought to say of the kingdom of God and itself what John the Baptist said of Christ and himself: "He must increase, but I must decrease" (John 3:30). Contextual evangelization relativizes ecclesiastical triumphalism and at the same time deepens the growth of the church.[17] It enables the evangelizing church to focus on the cross of Christ and look forward to the kingdom of God, investing its energies in the message of the cross and the service of the kingdom. This produces a holistic growth, gratuitous but not superfluous, in which available energies are multiplied for the well-being of humanity and for the glorification of the God whose kingdom we await in faith and hope.

Endnotes

Notes to Chapter I

1. Cf. Paul Tillich, *Systematic Theology,* vol. 1 (London: James Nisbet & Co., 1968), pp. 21-25.

2. Here I depart from the fourfold formula advocated by John Wesley and the Methodist tradition—namely, Scripture, tradition, experience, and reason. For me, reason is a medium of theological knowledge but not a source of inquiry into the faith. As a *logos* theology cannot exist without the mediation of reason. Reason is a means by which we process the content of revelation, but it is not in itself a source of theological knowledge.

I also differ from Paul Tillich, who argued that the sources of theology are Scripture, tradition (or church history), the history of religion, and culture. He limited experience, however, to "the medium through which the objective sources are received" (*Systematic Theology,* p. 52). *Tillich believed experience to be linked with existential awareness rooted in the mystical Augustinian principle of "immediate awareness" of being-itself, which is at the same time "truth-itself." Therefore, he saw the value of experience in theology but did not see experience as a source by which new revelatory material could be added to the other sources. Curiously, he assigned to the history of religion and to culture*—but not to experience—roles as sources of theological knowledge, as if religion and culture were less susceptible to the danger of "intentional subjectivity" than experience.

James Cone describes experience as the history and culture of a people, their awareness of the event of revelation (the Word) and the appropriation of its truth. He thus associates the Christian experience of black Americans with the content of Scripture. He considers the former a source of knowledge for black theology because it revolves around the message of Scripture. He looks to Jesus Christ as the norm of theological truth and, therefore, the criterion by which Scripture and experience are to be interpreted and evaluated. These two sources bear witness to Jesus as the liberator of the oppressed. In the light of this witness, black theology makes use of tradition. The latter might be described as a resource that is useful for black theology insofar as it conforms to the aforementioned Christological norm in accordance with Scripture and the Christian experience of black Americans. (See *God of the Oppressed* [New York: Seabury Press, 1975], pp. 30ff.)

Still another approach is that of my colleague Gabriel Fackre. In *A Narrative Interpretation of Basic Christian Doctrine* (rev. ed., vol. 1 of *The Christian Story* [Grand Rapids: Eerdmans, 1984]), he claimed that Scripture is the source of Christian knowledge, the church (tradition) the resource, and experience the setting in which the knowledge of the faith is explored and appropriated (p. 17). In *Authority: Scripture in the Church for the World* (vol. 2 of *The Christian Story* [Grand Rapids: Eerdmans, 1987]), he corrects this earlier model, placing experience in the category of "aid" to the discernment of truth. He argues that "human experience as such is distorted by the Fall, but [it is] an *aid* in discerning [truth], by a common (and Christic) grace." (See also Fackre, *Theology and Culture Newsletter,* no. 25 [Advent 1986], p. 4.)

I appreciate Tillich's fear of subjectivism, Cone's broader understanding of experience, and Fackre's care to avoid confusing the foundational source of Christian knowledge (Scripture) with experience and tradition. I have sought to take these various views into account in my proposal of a primary source (Scripture) and two secondary sources (tradition and experience). Incorporating religious practice and culture into the notion of experience and understanding experience socially rather than individually establishes an internal corrective against "intentional subjectivity." Likewise, the fact that Scripture is viewed as a primary witness to the faith gives an objective referent to tradition and experience even as all three sources are subjected to the norm of Jesus Christ, and the sociohistorical context provides the perspective from which theology is done.

There is a basic difference between Fackre's concept of experience and mine. Whereas he locates experience in the realm of fallen humanity, I deal with experience in the sphere of a redeemed people. Thus he speaks of human experience aided by common (or Christic) grace, whereas I speak of Christian experience saturated by the witness of the Holy Spirit, which is the common denominator of my three sources of theology.

3. The Hebrew Scriptures consist of 39 sacred books that were definitively fixed as the Jewish canon at the Council of Jamnia (ca. 100 C.E.). In the Hebrew they appear as 24 books divided into three major parts: *Torah* (the Law, the Pentateuch, or the Five Books of Moses); *Nebi'im* (the Prophets), and *Ketubim* (the Writings). The Prophets are subdivided into the Former Prophets, containing the four historical works (Joshua, Judges, Samuel, and Kings), and the Latter Prophets (Isaiah, Jeremiah, Ezekiel, and the Twelve [Minor] Prophets: Hosea, Joel, Amos, Obadiah, Jonah, Micah, Nahum, Habakkuk,

Zephaniah, Haggai, Zechariah, and Malachi). The Twelve were formerly written in a single scroll and thus appear as one book. The Writings consists of poetry and wisdom literature (Psalms, Proverbs, and Job); a collection known as the five scrolls (Song of Songs, Ruth, Lamentations, Ecclesiastes, and Esther, which have been grouped together according to the annual cycle of their public reading in the synagogue); and the books of Daniel, Ezra-Nehemiah, and Chronicles.

A Greek canon, developed among Jews in Alexandria, includes an additional list of 14 books. To Roman Catholics, 8 of these are known as deuterocanonical (that is, added later to the canon); the other 6 are known as apocryphal. To Protestants, all 14 are known as aprocryphal. It was the Alexandrian canon that was declared binding for the Old Testament at the Council of Florence (706 C.E.) and again at Trent (1546). However, the Hebrew Bible remained bound to the Jamnian canon. The Protestant Reformation denied canonical status to all books that were not in the Hebrew Bible.

To the 39 books of the Hebrew Bible the Christian church added 27 additional writings revolving around the life, ministry, death, and resurrection of Jesus, and the experience of early Christians under the guidance of the Spirit of Jesus. These writings can be grouped into three major collections in accordance with the order by which they gradually became accepted as authorized writings between the years 150-200 C.E.: (1) the Pauline Epistles, (2) the four Gospels, and (3) the General Epistles, Acts of the Apostles, Revelation, and Hebrews. It was not until the fifth century, however, that the 27 books of the New Testament became confirmed as a canon of Christian authorized writings. Although in 367 Athanasius had designated the 27 books of the New Testament as constituting a firmly established canon with the Old Testament books (cf. *Festal Letter 39*), it was the *Decree of Gelasius* (Synod of Rome, 382 C.E.) which defined the New Testament canon. This was confirmed in 405 by a letter of Pope Innocent I and the African Synods of Hippo Regius (393) and Carthage (297, 419). The New Testament canon was determined by the use of the books in the life and worship of the churches, the material consent of the Christian community, and the principle of apostolicity (i.e., the fact that they were apostolic in origin, though not all of them were written by apostles). Cf. Paul Neuenzeit, "Canon or Scripture," in *Sacramentum Mundi,* 6 vols., ed. Karl Rahner et al. (New York: Herder & Herder, 1969), 1: 252-57; *Encyclopedia Britannica, Micropaedia,* s.v. "Biblical Literature"; R. H. Pfeiffer, "Canon of the OT," in *Interpreter's Dictionary of the Bible,* vol. 1 (Nashville: Abingdon Press, 1962), pp. 498-520; F. W. Beare, "Canon of the NT," in *Interpreter's Dictionary of the Bible,* vol. 1, pp. 520-32.

While the canonical books of the New Testament have been accepted by all the Christian churches, it is readily acknowledged that there are critical problems related to the "necessity and limit of the NT canon" (W. G. Kümmel). Nevertheless, the fact remains that the Scriptures of the Old and New Testament not only provide primary knowledge of the Christian faith but have functioned over the centuries as a body of authorized writings in the church, thereby giving common ground and continuity to the faith. (This is especially crucial in the church's relation with Israel; the Hebrew canon provides common ground for the theological conversation between Christianity and Judaism.) A church without a canon would cease to represent and speak for "one universal and apostolic" faith. Indeed, it would end up lost in a sea of multicultural expressions, without an objective link with its origins and, consequently, unable to test the theological validity of its faith.

For further discussion on the question of canon and biblical authority, see, in addition to the preceding sources, the following: Brevard S. Childs, *Introduction to the Old Testament as Scripture* (Philadelphia: Fortress Press, 1979), and *The New Testament as Canon* (Philadelphia: Fortress Press, 1984); James A. Sanders, *Torah and Canon* (Philadelphia: Fortress Press, 1972), and *Canon and Community: A Guide to Canonical Criticism* (Philadelphia: Fortress Press, 1984); Joseph Blenkinsopp, *Prophecy and Canon: A Contribution to the Study of Jewish Origins* (Notre Dame: University of Notre Dame Press, 1977); Gabriel Fackre, *Authority: Scripture in the Church for the World;* Leonard J. Swidler, *Scripture and Ecumenism* (Pittsburgh: Duquesne University Press, 1965); *The Bible: Its Authority and Interpretation in the Ecumenical Movement,* ed. Ellen Fleeseman-Van Leer (Geneva: WCC, 1980); Gerald T. Sheppard, "Canon Criticism: The Proposal of Brevard Childs and an Assessment for Evangelical Hermeneutics," *Studia Biblica et Theologica* 4 (1974): 3-17; and *Wisdom as a Hermeneutical Construct* (New York: Walter de Gruyter, 1980); Walter Brueggemann, *The Creative Word: Canon as a Model for Biblical Education* (Philadelphia: Fortress Press, 1982); Stephen Reid, "The Book of Exodus: A Laboratory for Hermeneutics," in *Conflict and Context: Hermeneutics in the Americas,* ed. Mark Lau Branson and C. René Padilla (Grand Rapids: Eerdmans, 1986), pp. 155-70; J. Rogers and D. McKim, *The Authority and Interpretation of the Bible* (San Francisco: Harper & Row, 1979); *The Authoritative Word,* ed. Donald McKim (Grand Rapids: Eerdmans, 1983); G. C. Berkouwer, *Holy Scripture,* trans. Jack Rogers, Studies in Dogmatics series (Grand Rapids: Eerdmans, 1975); Robert Johnson, *The Use of the Bible in Recent Theology: Evangelical Options* (Atlanta: John Knox Press, 1985); Robert Schreiter, *Constructing Local Theologies* (Maryknoll, N.Y.: Orbis Books, 1985); George Lindbeck, *The Nature of Doctrine* (Philadelphia: Fortress Press, 1984); James Barr, *Beyond Fundamentalism* (Philadelphia: Westminster Press, 1984); *Feminist Interpretation of the Bible,* ed. Letty Russell (Philadelphia: Westminster Press, 1985); *El debate contemporáneo sobre la Biblia,* ed. Pedro Savage (Barcelona: Ediciones Evangélicas Europeas, 1972); Luis Alonso Schökel, *La palabra inspirada,* 2nd ed. (Barcelona: Herder, 1969); J. Alfaro, *Revelación cristiana, fe y teología* (Salamanca: Ediciones Sígueme, 1985); Pierre Grelot, *Biblia y teología* (Barcelona: Herder, 1969).

4. Commenting on the report of the Faith and Order study of the WCC

entitled *Tradition and Traditions,* Letty Russell notes the latter's distinction between tradition, traditions, and the Tradition: "In this report, 'tradition' refers to the total traditioning process that operates in human history and society; 'traditions' refer to the patterns of church life, such as confessions, liturgies, polities, etc., that have developed in each confessional church group; the Tradition refers to Christ as the content of the traditioning process by which God hands that over to men and women." (See *Human Liberation in a Feminist Perspective: A Theology* [Philadelphia: Westminster Press, 1974], p. 75. See also *Faith and Order Findings,* ed. Paul S. Minear [London: SCM Press, 1963], pp. 1-63; Yves Congar, *Tradition and Traditions* [London: Burns & Oates, Ltd., 1966], pp. 135-36.)

For Russell, Tradition and God's mission "belong to the same theological spectrum" (p. 76). In fact, "*Tradition is Mission* because its very description is that of God's missionary activity in handing Christ over into the hands of men and women in order that all people may come to the truth (I Tim. 2:4)." The traditioning process is the "means by which people participate in the . . . sharing . . . receiving and passing on of Christ" (p. 77). The traditioning process has a built-in critical and liberating dynamic, according to Russell. Indeed, it makes it possible to overcome the distortions of the various traditions, because God's mission is "constantly breaking through oppressive human traditions" (p. 78). Although the traditioning process can be distorted by particular traditions, it can also be set free by God's Tradition: the "dynamic of God's Tradition transcends and judges all human traditions and actions" (p. 79). (See also Letty M. Russell, "Tradition as Mission: Study of a New Current in Theology and Its Implications for Theological Education," Ph.D. diss., Union Theological Seminary, 1969; "Tradition as Mission," *Study Encounter* 6:2 [1970]: 1-63.)

What in the text I call "apostolicity," "the apostolic rule of faith," or "the apostolic tradition" corresponds to what Russell and the WCC study refer to as "the Tradition." Likewise, I use "tradition" to refer to the traditioning process. I also use the term "tradition" when referring to a concrete pattern of ecclesial life, be it a confessional church group or a theological or spiritual movement.

5. On the context of theology as a global web "comprehending every particular local context," see Max L. Stackhouse, "Contextualization and Theological Education," *ATS Theological Education: Global Challenges and Perspectives in Theological Education* 22 (Autumn 1986): 67-84.

6. Segundo, *The Liberation of Theology,* trans. John Drury (Maryknoll, N.Y.: Orbis Books, 1975), p. 8.

7. *Ibid.*

8. I call Segundo's hermeneutical process a "circulation" because ultimately his theory of interpretation leads in the direction of a spiral rather than a circle. This process might be summarized as follows: (1) Ideological suspicion arises out of one's historical insertion. (Why are our conceptions of real-

ity so different from the *real* world?) (2) One applies that ideological suspicion to culture in general and to theology in particular. (Could it be that our culture and theology have hidden away reality?) (3) One develops a new way of experiencing theological reality, which leads to exegetical suspicion. (If culture and theology have been ideologically conditioned, then most probably biblical exegesis has also been ideologically conditioned.) (4) One develops a new way of interpreting the faith. (This becomes the basis for a new hope—namely, the transformation of the world and the church.)

The difference between Segundo and Padilla lies in their respective styles and emphases. They both start with the situation. For Segundo, however, what sets the hermeneutical process in motion is a new experience of reality leading to an ideological suspicion. Padilla starts simply with the kinds of questions the situation poses to Scripture. These questions, however, are informed by the interpreter's world-and-life view. Segundo applies the ideological suspicion to culture in general and to exegesis in particular. Padilla, on the other hand, goes to Scripture with questions from the situation and then back to the situation with questions from Scripture. In the process the interpreter's world-and-life-view is challenged and the questions he or she asks are refined. Padilla fails to take into account from the beginning the interpreter's new experience and hermeneutical suspicion as the forces that generate the hermeneutical process. Segundo fails to take into account the possibility of Scripture questioning the situation and the interpreter's perceptions.

9. Padilla, "Hermeneutics and Culture: A Theological Perspective," in *Down to Earth: Studies in Christianity and Culture,* ed. John R. W. Stott and Robert Coote (Grand Rapids: Eerdmans, 1980), pp. 75-76.

10. Cf. Padilla's comment that "the grammatico-historical approach to Scripture—in which every effort is made to let Scripture speak for itself—is seen to be the logical consequence of the view in which Scripture is regarded as authoritative for faith and practice" ("Hermeneutics and Culture," p. 76). See, however, the discussion in *Conflict and Context,* pp. 3-36, 155-280. Gabriel Fackre proposes four movements in the process of biblical exegesis. He argues that to do justice to Scripture, the interpreter must discern the *common, critical, canonical,* and *contextual* senses of a text. He describes these senses as follows:

> The common sense of a text is pursued by reading it as we would the daily newspaper, the office memo, the mystery story. . . . (Word in sentence, sentence in paragraph, paragraph in next unit, etc., according to language conventions and simple laws of logic.) If the Bible is the people's charter, the people ought to be able to understand it. . . . Therefore, "common sense" is just what it says: a *commonality* of sense, a community reading, an inclusive reading that invites a variety of perspectives into the conversation. . . .
>
> The critical sense of the text is the welcome of the scholar into the textual inquiry. If the *being* of the text's meaning is given by common sense, then its critical sense constitutes its *well-being.* This entails . . . contextual, historical,

grammatical, literary, form, tradition, redaction criticism. But the critical sense *also* means facing . . . the captivity of traditional and critical exegesis, and even the text itself, to sex, race, class and condition biases. . . . However, the genetic fallacy applies here as anywhere. The humanity of biblical origins *does not disqualify* Scripture as authoritative. A vulnerable God uses the way of vulnerability, "the weak things of the world and the despised."

The *canonical sense* is the *full* meaning and therefore the theological truth of a text. Canonical meaning is determined by a) the reading of the text within the *whole* of the Christian canon, b) the construal of it in relationship to the *substance* of Scripture, [and] c) the discernment of its meaning according to the *Center* [that is, Christ]. . . . How that textual meaning is understood is established by the christological norm at the center of the Christian story.

A crucial step remains in exegesis: the movement from the *meaning* of the text ascertained by common, critical and canonical approaches, to its *significance.* The contextual sense of a text is its significance in *social* and *personal* settings. The quest for it entails a movement . . . from the center to the circumference. Such a movement includes the discernment of the nature of the context and its perspectival appropriation from within the biblical center, and with the help of ecclesial perceptions. But the purpose of the movement itself is to relate the meaning of the text to the cultural context of the interpreter, its idiom and issues. The truth of the text comes home when it is *truth for us* in historical context and *truth for me* in personal context. (*Theology and Culture Newsletter,* pp. 3-4; see also vol. 2 of *The Christian Story,* pp. 158-253)

The value of Fackre's exegetical approach is its methodological thoroughness and ecumenical inclusiveness. However, the detailed outline of the hermeneutical scheme of which this exegetical approach is a part seems too precise for a narrative theological approach. The detailed identification and naming of every aspect of the hermeneutical process makes one ask if the very result may not be already predicted, in which case the process becomes a circle rather than a circulation, as Fackre proposes it to be. Even so, Fackre's proposal is instructive for contextual and liberating theologies.

11. By "Two Thirds World" I mean that zone of contemporary life which represents a religious and cultural mosaic and is home to most of the poor, powerless, and oppressed people on earth: Africa, Asia, the Caribbean, continental Latin America, the Middle East, and Oceania.

12. See my book entitled *Christ Outside the Gate: Mission beyond Christendom* (Maryknoll, N.Y.: Orbis Books, 1982), pp. 33-36, 86-88, 103-4, 123-26, 174-86.

13. An expression borrowed from Nicholas Wolterstorff, *Until Justice and Peace Embrace* (Grand Rapids: Eerdmans, 1983), pp. 3ff. He refers to the pattern of social and spiritual reformation found in early Calvinism as "world-formative Christianity."

14. See Bernard Semmel, *The Methodist Revolution* (New York: Basic

Books, 1973); J. Taylor Hamilton and Kenneth G. Taylor, *History of the Moravian Church: The Renewed Unitas Fratrum,* 1722-1957 (Bethlehem, Pa. and Winston-Salem, N.C.: Interprovincial Board of Christian Education, Moravian Church in America, 1967); *The Story of Serampore and Its College,* ed. William S. Stewart (Serampore: The Council of Serampore College, n.d.); Donald W. Dayton, *Discovering an Evangelical Heritage* (San Francisco: Harper & Row, 1976); R. Pierce Beaver, *American Protestant Women in World Mission: A History of the First Feminist Movement in North America,* rev. ed. (Grand Rapids: Eerdmans, 1980); J. van den Berg, *Constrained by Jesus' Love: An Inquiry into the Motives of the Missionary Awakening in Great Britain in the Period Between 1698 and 1815* (Kampen: J. H. Kok, 1956); David Moberg, *The Great Reversal: Evangelism Versus Social Concern,* rev. ed. (Philadelphia: Lippincott, 1977); Joan Jacobs-Brumberg, *Mission for Life: The Story of the Family of Adoniram Judson* (New York: Free Press, 1980); Timothy Smith, *Revivalism and Social Reform: American Protestantism on the Eve of the Civil War* (Baltimore: Johns Hopkins, 1980); James Washington, *A Testament of Hope: The Essential Writings of Martin Luther King, Jr.* (San Francisco: Harper & Row, 1986); John Perkins, *Let Justice Roll Down* (Glendale, Calif.: Regal Books, 1976).

15. See my essay entitled "Evangelical Theology in the Two Thirds World," *Conflict and Context,* pp. 311-23.

16. See Wolterstorff, *Until Justice and Peace Embrace,* pp. 21-22.

17. A good example of the Anabaptist combination of the gospel (the evangel) and ethics is the following hymn of Menno Simons (ca. 1496-1561):

> True evangelical faith cannot lie sleeping
> for it clothes the naked,
> it comforts the sorrowful;
> it gives to the hungry food,
> and it shelters the destitute.
> It cares for the blind and lame
> the widow and orphan child;
> that's True evangelical faith
> It binds up the wounded man;
> it offers a gentle hand.
> We must become ev'rything to everyone.
> Abundantly we have received
> and gratefully we will respond
> with True evangelical faith.
> So over come evil with good;
> return someone's hatred with love.
> We must become ev'rything to everyone.

(This hymn was translated by Larry Nichol and made available to the Mennonite Central Committee, Canada.) See also John Driver, *Understanding the*

Atonement for the Mission of the Church (Scottdale, Penn.: Herald Press, 1986), for an explicitly radical evangelical study in an Anabaptist perspective.

18. See Ernest F. Stoeffler, *The Rise of Evangelical Pietism* (Leiden: Brill, 1971), and *German Pietism in the Eighteenth Century* (Leiden: Brill, 1973).

19. See Smith, *Revivalism and Social Reform;* Dayton, *Discovering an Evangelical Heritage;* Gayraud S. Wilmore, *Black Religion and Black Radicalism* (Garden City, N.Y.: Doubleday-Anchor Books, 1972).

20. Cone, *God of the Oppressed,* p. 1.

21. Quoted in Piri Thomas, *Savior, Savior, Hold My Hand* (New York: Bantam Books, 1972), p. 18.

22. *Ibid.,* p. 68.

23. Virgilio Elizondo, *Galilean Journey: The Mexican-American Promise* (Maryknoll, N.Y.: Orbis Books, 1983), p. 32.

24. On the evangelization of culture and the inculturation of the gospel, see the materials from the International Congress of Theology held in San Miguel, Argentina, from 2-6 September 1985 in *Stromata* 41 (July-Dec. 1985). This issue includes an impressive number of articles analyzing the theme from a historical, theological, pastoral, and sociocultural perspective, with special reference to the contemporary situation of the Catholic Church in Latin America.

25. Arias, *The Cry of My People: Out of Captivity in Latin America* (New York: Friendship Press, 1980), p. 101.

26. Puebla Documents, Nos. 1130, 1142, 1143-65, quoted in *Ibid.,* pp. 118-19. Cf. *Puebla and Beyond: Documentation and Commentary,* ed. John Eagleson and Philip Sharper, trans. John Drury (Maryknoll, N.Y.: Orbis Books, 1979).

27. "Letter to Christian Churches and the Interdenominational Bodies of Latin America," cited in Arias, *The Cry of My People,* pp. 121-22.

28. This does not mean, of course, that all Catholics and Protestants share this common experience. In fact, there is resistance on both sides. But resistance, even from a majority, cannot overcome the power of the Spirit as Puebla, Oaxtepec, the base community movement, and a growing number of hymns, poems, and theological-spiritual publications continue to demonstrate.

29. For a lucid Catholic theological exposition of the spiritual journey of the Latin American peoples, see Gustavo Gutiérrez, *We Drink from Our Own Wells: The Spiritual Journey of a People* (Maryknoll, N.Y.: Orbis Books, 1984).

30. See my *Christ Outside the Gate,* p. 186.

31. Berkouwer, *Holy Scripture,* p. 146.

32. Barth, *Church Dogmatics,* I/1, trans. G. T. Thomson (Edinburgh: T. & T. Clark, 1936), pp. 117-18.

33. For further discussion and various perspectives on the questions of revelation, inspiration, and hermeneutics, see, in addition to the works cited in notes 3, 5, 8, and 9, the following: Barth, *Church Dogmatics* I/1, pp. 51-283; *Church*

Dogmatics, I/2, trans. G. T. Thomson and Harold Knight, ed. G. W. Bromiley and T. F. Torrance (Edinburgh: T. & T. Clark, 1956), pp. 457-740; Carl F. H. Henry, *God, Revelation and Authority: The God Who Speaks and Shows,* vols. 1-4 (Waco, Tex.: Word Books, 1976-1979), *passim;* James Barr, *The Bible in the Modern World* (London: SCM Press, 1973); Gabriel Fackre, *The Christian Story,* 2 vols.; J. Severino Croatto, *Liberacion y libertad* (Buenos Aires: Ediciones Mundo Nuevo, 1973), pp. 11-146 (English edition published by Orbis Books, Maryknoll, N.Y.); José Míguez Bonino, *Doing Theology in a Revolutionary Situation* (Philadelphia: Fortress Press, 1975), pp. 86-105.

34. On the problem of proselytism, see *The Evangelical–Roman Catholic Dialogue on Mission, 1977-1984: A Report,* ed. Basil Meeking and John Stott (Grand Rapids: Eerdmans, 1986). This report emphasizes three aspects of the World Council of Churches–Roman Catholic document entitled *Common Witness and Proselytism* (1970):

> First, proselytism takes place when our *motive* is unworthy, for example when our real concern in witness is not the glory of God through the salvation of human beings but rather the prestige of our own Christian community, or indeed our personal prestige.
>
> Secondly, we are guilty of proselytism whenever our *methods* are unworthy, especially when we resort to any kind of "physical coercion, moral constraint or psychological pressure," when we seek to induce conversion by the offer of material or political benefits, or when we exploit other people's need, weakness or lack of education. These practices are an affront both to the freedom and dignity of human beings and to the Holy Spirit whose witness is gentle and not coercive.
>
> Thirdly, we are guilty of proselytism whenever our *message* includes "unjust or uncharitable reference to the beliefs or practices of other religious communities in the hope of winning adherents." If we find it necessary to make comparisons, we should compare the strengths and weaknesses of one church with those of the other, and not set what is best in the one against what is worst in the other. To descend to deliberate misrepresentation is incompatible with both truth and love. (Pp. 90-91)

Notes to Chapter II

1. See Mortimer Arias, "In Search of a New Evangelism," *The Perkins School of Theology Journal* 32 (Winter 1979): 3-4.

2. On the context as "the psychosocial foundation of communication," see my book entitled *Christ Outside the Gate: Mission beyond Christendom* (Maryknoll, N.Y.: Orbis Books, 1982), pp. 4-5.

3. Fung, "Good News to the Poor — A Case for a Missionary Move-

ment," *Your Kingdom Come: Mission Perspectives—Report on the World Conference on Mission and Evangelism* (Geneva: WCC, 1980), pp. 84-85. See also Matthew Lamb, *Solidarity with Victims* (New York: Crossroad, 1982), pp. 2-7. Lamb describes the anguish of the world as the historical perversity of humanity: "The terrors of nature have tended to take a back seat to the horrors of history" (p. 3). Thus humanity itself is largely responsible for human misery. Lamb identifies as "social sin" the suffering of "innocent victims" who suffer without cause at the hands of others. He rightly states that "the social sins . . . of economic oppression, racism, ecological pollution, and sexism stain human history with their all too evident horrors. Indeed, the very means which previously were cultivated to promote human emancipation — science and technology—are increasingly seen as permeated by a necrophilic bias" (p. 4).

4. Fung, "Good News to the Poor," p. 88.

5. *Ibid.*

6. See Leonardo Boff, *Jesucristo el liberador* (Buenos Aires: Latinoamerica Libros, JRL, 1975), p. 196. The English translation from the original Portuguese is entitled *Jesus Christ the Liberator: A Critical Christology for Our Times* (Maryknoll, N.Y.: Orbis Books, 1978).

7. Cf. James D. G. Dunn, *Christology in the Making: A New Testament Inquiry into the Origins of the Doctrine of the Incarnation* (Philadelphia: Westminster Press, 1980), *passim.*

8. On the Incarnation as the point of departure for the communication of the gospel, see my *Christ Outside the Gate,* pp. 3-20.

9. Obatala, Olorum, and Oio are African deities whose memory the slaves carried with them to Brazil and the Americas.

10. "En nome de Deus," on *Misa dos Quilombos,* LP recorded in Caraca, M.G., Brazil, March 1982, by Ariola Discos Fonograficos; words and music by Milton Nascimento, Pedro Casaldaliga, and Pedro Tierra.

11. Brian Wren, "God of Many Names," in *Praising a Mystery: Thirty New Hymns* (Carol Stream, Ill.: Hope Publishing Co., 1986), no. 8.

12. "Vos sos el Dios de los pobres," *La misa campesina nicaragüense,* por Carlos Mejía Godoy.

13. Barth, *Against the Stream: Shorter Post-War Writings, 1946-52* (New York: Philosophical Library, 1954), p. 165.

14. Cf. Victorio Araya, *El Dios de los pobres* (San José, Costa Rica: DEI Sebila, 1984).

15. Castro, *Sent Free: Mission and Unity in the Perspective of the Kingdom* (Grand Rapids: Eerdmans, 1985), p. 102.

16. Pagura, "Because He Came into Our World," in *Jesus Christ—The Life of the World: A Worship Book for the Sixth Assembly of the World Council of Churches* (Geneva: WCC, 1983), pp. 140-41.

17. Oduyoye, *Hearing and Knowing: Theological Reflections on Christianity in Africa* (Maryknoll, N.Y.: Orbis Books, 1986), p. 9.

Notes to Chapter III

1. *New Encyclopedia Britannica, Micropedia,* s.v. "Model, scientific."

2. Dulles, *Models of the Church* (Garden City, N.J.: Doubleday-Image Books, 1974), pp. 16-37. For a further discussion of the use of models in religious studies, see Andrew Greeley, *Religion: A Secular Theory* (New York: Free Press, 1982), *passim.*

3. See J. Alberto Soggin, *Introduction to the Old Testament: From Its Origins to the Closing of the Alexandria Canon,* rev. ed., trans. John Bowden, Old Testament Library (Philadelphia: Westminster Press, 1982), pp. 310ff.; William L. Holladay, *Isaiah: Scroll of a Prophetic Heritage* (Grand Rapids: Eerdmans, 1978), pp. 15ff.; 177f.; "Ester," in *Introduction to the Old Testament,* 2 vols., ed. A. Robert and A. Feuillet, trans. Patrick W. Skehan et al. (Garden City, N.Y.: Doubleday, 1970), 2: 156-62; John Bright, *A History of Israel,* 2nd ed. (Philadelphia: Westminster Press, 1972), p. 355.

4. Holladay, *Isaiah,* p. 127.

5. *Ibid.,* p. 121; cf. Bright, *A History of Israel,* p. 348.

6. The plot of the Book of Esther has been identified with the period of Xerxes I (485-465 B.C.E.), who is believed to be King Ahasuerus, though the date of the book is much later (probably in the third or the second century B.C.E.). For a detailed discussion of the date with a much wider *terminus a quo* and *terminus ad quem* (400-114 B.C.E.), see *Esther: A New Translation with Introduction and Commentary,* by Carey A. Moore, Anchor Bible series (Garden City, N.Y.: Doubleday, 1984), pp. LVII-LX. The book presupposes an audience of Jews from the eastern diaspora, in the Hellenistic period, though it is more probable that some elements of the story had been preserved and transmitted by oral tradition. On the critical-literary aspects related to the Book of Esther, see the following sources: *Esther,* pp. XVI-LXXII; Brevard S. Childs, *Introduction to the Old Testament as Scripture* (Philadelphia: Fortress Press, 1979), pp. 598-607; Norman K. Gottwald, *The Hebrew Bible: A Socio-Literary Introduction* (Philadelphia: Fortress Press, 1985), pp. 561-67; Soggin, *Introduction to the Old Testament,* pp. 401-5, 439-41; *La Nueva Biblia Española,* trans. Luis Alonso Schökel and Juan Mateos (Madrid: Cristiandad, 1975), pp. 839-50; *The New Jerusalem Bible* (Garden City, N.Y.: Doubleday, 1985), pp. 621, 659-73; *La nueva Biblia Latinoamericana,* translation and commentary by Ramon Riccardi and Bernardo Huralt (Madrid: Ediciones Paulinas, 1972), pp. 839-50; *The New English Bible,* Oxford Study Edition with the Apocrypha, ed. Samuel Sandmel (New York: Oxford University

Press, 1976), pp. 84-96; Bernhard W. Anderson, "Esther: Introduction," in *The Interpreter's Bible,* vol. 3 (Nashville: Abingdon Press, 1954), pp. 823-32; and "The Place of the Book of Esther in the Christian Bible," *Journal of Religion* 30 (1950): 32-43; Demetrius R. Dumm, "Esther," in *The Jerome Biblical Commentary,* ed. Raymond E. Brown, Joseph A. Fitzmyer, and Roland E. Murphy (Englewood Cliffs, N.J.: Prentice-Hall, 1968), pp. 628-32; J. Alonzo Dias, "Ester," in *La Sagrada Escritura, texto y comentario, Antiguo Testamento,* vol. 3, *Biblioteca de Autores Cristianos* (Madrid: Editorial Católica, 1968), pp. 211-49; H. Lusseau, "Esther," in *Introduction to the Old Testament,* vol. 2, pp. 155-62, 263-65; Tomas D. Hanks, "El libro de Ester," in *Diccionario ilustrado de la Biblia,* ed. Wilton M. Nelson (San José, Costa Rica: Editorial Caribe, 1974), p. 212; Werner H. Schmidt, *Introducción al Antiguo Testamento,* trans. Manuel Olusagarti (Salamanca: Ediciones Sígueme, 1983), pp. 388-91.

7. A good example of the theological importance of the story of Esther among North American ethnic and racial minorities is the article of the Asian-American theologian Roy I. Sano entitled "Ethnic Liberation Theology: Neo-Orthodoxy Reshaped—or Replaced?" in *Mission Trends,* No. 4: *Liberation Theologies in North America and Europe,* ed. Gerald H. Anderson and Thomas F. Stransky (Grand Rapids: Eerdmans, 1979), pp. 247-58. See also my article entitled "The Subversiveness of Faith: Esther as a Paradigm for a Liberating Theology" in the *Ecumenical Review* 40 (Jan. 1988): 66-78.

8. It should come as no surprise, however, that exegetes and preachers traditionally choose Mordecai over Esther as the greater hero of the story. Carey A. Moore, for example, states, "Between Mordecai and Esther the greater hero in the Hebrew is Mordecai, who supplied the brains while Esther simply followed his directions" (*Esther,* p. LII). Yet it is Esther who called for a fast on her own initiative, risked her life and political future to intercede for the Jews, and set up the trap for Haman. This reflects leadership and cleverness rather than passiveness and dependence.

9. The Essene community at Qumran (second century B.C.E. to first century C.E.) did not regard the Book of Esther as canonical, and there has been other Jewish opposition to the book. For a summary account of this opposition, see Moore, *Esther,* pp. XXI-XXV. Notwithstanding the initial lack of unanimity regarding the book's canonical status (which has its parallel in similar opposition to the book among Christians), the fact remains that the Book of Esther has come to play an important role in Jewish religious life since then, as evidenced by the celebration of Purim and by the history of oppression of Jews following the Council of Jamnia (ca. 100 C.E.), including the Middle Ages and the Holocaust of this century. For a note on Esther's popularity among Jews, see Moore, *Esther,* pp. LVI-LVII. See also Albert I. Baumgartner, "The Scroll of Esther," in *Encyclopaedia Judaica,* 16 vols. (Jerusalem: Keter Publishing House, Ltd., 1971), 14: 1048-58; Lois Jacobs, "Purim," in *Encyclope-*

dia Judaica, vol. 13, pp. 1389-96; Andre Hajdu and Yaacov Mazor, "Hasidim," in *Encyclopedia Judaica,* vol. 7, pp. 1404-20.

10. There are 107 additional verses (four and one-half chapters) in Greek versions, including the Septuagint (LXX), which do not appear in the Hebrew text. This additional material is located before 1:1; after 3:13; 4:17; 8:12; 10:3; and at the end of the book. For Jerome, the canonical authority of these verses was controversial; accordingly, he placed them in an appendix in the Vulgate. Contemporary Catholic versions tend to follow the order of the Septuagint and the numbering of the Masoretic Text. (See, for example, *La nueva Biblia Española,* pp. 771-85; *The New Jerusalem Bible,* pp. 659-73; and *La nueva Biblia Latinoamericana,* pp. 839-50, for three samples of contemporary Catholic translations.) The revised (in 1960) Protestant-Spanish version, *Casiodoro de Reina* (1569), follows the Hebrew text and leaves out the additional verses in the Greek versions. (The same thing is true of the King James Version and the Revised Standard Version.)

The additions give the book a greater theological justification and supply elements that are not found in the main text. For example, they speak of God directly, include prayers, and give a direct theological focus to particular problems. Without this material, several scholars argue, the book lacks theological content, and its canonical justification is endangered. J. Alberto Soggin observes, very perceptively, that the additional material, notwithstanding its theological explicitness, makes the book a sort of anti-Gentile manifesto on account of its excessive nationalistic language. It seems to me that the main text may be justified theologically by itself, given the twofold references to fasting and providence. These two references point indirectly to God, which coincides with the tradition of avoiding pronouncing God's name. The additional material, however, demonstrates an excessive zeal to preserve the identity of a sector of the Diaspora in light of the Gentile threat, and takes to the extreme the festival of Purim as a symbol of nationalist authenticity. Moreover, it eliminates the universal value of the original story. (See also Moore, *Esther,* pp. LXI-LXIV, 103-13.)

11. Holladay, *Isaiah,* p. 180.

12. A similar claim can be made with regard to contemporary Judaism and especially the State of Israel as a representative of the Jewish tradition. See the challenging analysis of Marc H. Ellis, *Toward a Jewish Theology of Liberation* (Maryknoll, N.Y.: Orbis Books, 1987). See also Jacobo Timerman, *The Longest War: Israel in Lebanon,* trans. Miguel Acoca (New York: Vintage Books, 1982).

Notes to Chapter IV

1. See, for example, Michael Green, *Evangelism in the Early Church* (Grand Rapids: Eerdmans, 1970), *passim;* Donald Senior and Caroll

Stuhlmueller, *The Biblical Foundations for Mission* (Maryknoll, N.Y.: Orbis Books, 1983), pp. 141ff., 318-21.

2. One notable exception is that of C. S. Mann. In *Mark: A New Translation with Introduction and Commentary,* Anchor Bible series (Garden City, N.Y.: Doubleday, 1986), he argues that Mark was not the first Gospel.

3. See E. Lohmeyer, *Galiläa und Jerusalem* (Göttingen: Vandenhoeck & Ruprecht, 1936); Willi Marxsen, *Mark the Evangelist: Studies on the Redaction History of the Gospel,* trans. James Boyce, Donald Juel, and William Poehlmann, with Roy A. Harrisville (Nashville: Abingdon Press, 1969); R. H. Lightfoot, *Locality and Doctrine in the Gospel* (New York: Harper, 1937); L. E. Elliot-Binns, *Galilean Christianity* (London: SCM, 1956); W. D. Davies, *The Gospel and the Land* (Berkeley: University of California Press, 1974), pp. 221-43; Günter Stemberger, "Galilee—Land of Salvation?" in *The Gospel and the Land,* pp. 409-38; Seán Freyne, *Galilee from Alexander the Great to Hadrian, 323 B.C.E.–135 C.E.* (Notre Dame: University of Notre Dame Press, 1980), pp. 3-21, 259-304, 344-94. These authors do not necessarily agree about the importance of Galilee in Mark's Gospel. They are the best-known representatives of an ongoing debate. Lohmeyer, Marxsen, Elliot-Binns, and Lightfoot all underscore the importance of Galilee as a locality, while Davies and Stemberger challenge their arguments. Freyne, who among them has written the latest and most complete study of Galilee, concludes that Galilee was significant for Mark "as the place of the first ministry of Jesus, which was an integral part of the gospel story, and had to be included in any authentic proclamation by the later church. Yet the Galilean happenings had to be properly understood and that explains why it is necessary to return there to discover their true meaning as Mark has presented it, illumined by the Easter experience" (p. 359).

Similarly, Stemberger — notwithstanding his criticism of theories of Markan Galilean Christianity, with which Freyne is in general agreement — acknowledges "a certain emphasis on Galilee in the gospels." He states, "The strongest single influence is . . . the tradition of the life of Jesus, the knowledge that most of his ministry was dedicated to this region. Many of the followers of Jesus were Galileans. . . . The Galileans were the official witnesses to Jesus because they had been with him from the beginning. This makes it understandable that a certain emphasis was laid upon Galilean traditions; the first disciples were proud that it was in their own region, the despised Galilee, that the Lord had proclaimed the good news" (p. 435). Further on, Stemberger notes, "The Galilean tradition may have encouraged the young Church to take up the mission. The Church sees in Christ's life a paradigm for her own activity. In Christ's Galilean ministry she recognizes that her mission, too, is to the lowly, the despised, the sinners" (p. 436).

Following this perspective, I shall argue that Galilee is important in Mark precisely as an evangelistic landmark and, therefore, as the point of departure for the church's universal mission of evangelization.

4. Mateos, *Los "Doce" y otros seguidores de Jesús en el Evangelio de Marcos* (Madrid: Ediciones Cristiandad, 1982), pp. 247ff.

5. *Ibid.*, p. 247.

6. *Ibid.*

7. *Ibid.*, pp. 249, 251.

8. *Ibid.*, p. 252.

9. Virgilio Elizondo, *Mestizaje: The Dialectics of Cultural Birth and the Gospel* (San Antonio: Mexican-American Cultural Center, 1978), pp. 427ff. On the historical background of Galilee, see Freyne, *Galilee from Alexander the Great to Hadrian;* E. Meyers and J. Strange, *Archeology: The Rabbis and Early Christianity* (Nashville: Abingdon Press, 1981), pp. 31-47; and *Explore: A Journal of Theology* 3 (Winter 1977), dedicated to the region of Galilee.

10. Elizondo, *Mestizaje,* p. 595. See also S. Zeitlin, "Who were the Galileans? New Light on Josephus' Activities in Galilee," *Jewish Quarterly Review* 64 (1974): 189-203.

11. Lane, *The Gospel of Mark,* NICNT series (Grand Rapids: Eerdmans, 1974), p. 55.

12. Berkhof, *Christian Faith,* trans. Sierd Woudstra (Grand Rapids: Eerdmans, 1979), p. 297.

13. As a symbol of the cultural, social, political, and theological periphery, Galilee has enormous importance for the peoples of Latin America in general and for the Hispanic community in the United States in particular. The bilingualism of Galilean Jews and the fact that they were the object of ridicule among southern Jews is not without significance, especially for Hispanics in North America, whose peculiar accent and linguistic limitations (in Spanish or English or both) have frequently been the objects of patronizing ethnic jokes and denigrating comments. This is a reality that is typical of every cross-cultural situation, including that of Spanish-speaking countries and multicultural societies like Canada and Australia.

More significant, however, is the hostility that prevails in the dominant Anglo/white community toward Hispanics because of their uncompromising commitment to the use of Spanish as a primary means of communication. Ninety percent of the approximately 25 million Hispanics in the United States speak Spanish, and nearly fifty percent either know no English or know barely enough to get by. This is why a reporter for the *Dallas Morning News* stated recently that "much of the hostility aimed at Hispanics . . . is aimed at the language they continue to speak" (Allen Pusey, "Battling A Bilingual Voice," *Dallas Morning News,* 1982, p. 29).

There is such resistance to Spanish—and other foreign languages—as a principal means of communication that in the state of California a voter referendum in November 1986 made English the official language of the state. This new state law has been seen as a prelude for the "English only amendment" to the U.S. Constitution being advocated by a number of people who fear that the United States might become a bilingual or multilingual society. Such reactionary activity is in fact a hostile move against Hispanics, who are already the largest ethnic/ racial minority in the country.

The hostility and fear is not limited to language, however. People in the mainstream reject Hispanics as bona-fide members of North American society because of their cultural identity, their persistent affirmation of their traditions, and their historical link with Latin America. They are seen as a threat to the traditional "American way of life" and, therefore, as people not to be trusted. It does not matter how much their forebears contributed to the development of the Southwest. It is of little significance that they have fought courageously for the defense of the United States and that they work tirelessly on farms and in steel mills, textile shops, and the food-producing industry of the nation. It is of little value that they have made great contributions to North American sports and entertainment, or that U.S. businesses have profited greatly from the raw materials that Latin American countries produce and the cheap labor they provide. In certain circles Hispanics are considered despicable foreign intruders who threaten the traditional "American way of life." They can never be "true Americans" and are to be treated as perpetual outsiders.

In view of the coincidence of historical situations, it is interesting to note that many Hispanic Christians in the United States are increasingly discovering their identity and mission in Jesus the Galilean. This is evident in a passage in the final document produced by the First Hispanic Ecumenical Theological Conference held in San Antonio, Texas, during October 24-29, 1978: "From the perspective of Hispanics, seeking to follow Jesus we discover our identity and our evangelizing mission. Rejected and scorned by the powers of this country, we, like the Galileans, are chosen by God to live out and to proclaim the good news of liberation for all" ("Mensaje a la comunidad hispana de los Estados Unidos y de Puerto Rico y el pueblo cristiano estadounidense del Proyecto Ecuménico Teológico Hispano," p. 5).

The Hispanic presence in the continental United States is not a recent phenomenon. Many Hispanics are descendants of the first settlers. Others are the sons and daughters of established immigrants. The rest are the direct product of the migratory wave that has flowed from Latin America and the Caribbean in recent years as a result of the precarious economic situation, social injustice, and political oppression that has increasingly characterized the countries of the region. The Hispanic presence across the length and breadth of the United States has implications not only for the evangelization of Hispanics but also for the entire evangelizing mission of the church on the Northern American subcontinent. Indeed, Hispanics and other oppressed minorities constitute an evangelizing potential in the United States, as noted in Chapter I. See my article entitled "Evangelizing an Awakening Giant: Hispanics in the U.S.," in *Signs of the Kingdom in the Secular City,* comp. David J. Frenchak and Clinton E. Stockwell, ed. Helen Ujuarosy (Chicago: Covenant Press, 1984), pp. 55-64.

14. On the place of Galilee in the Fourth Gospel, see L. Diez-Merino, "Galilea en el Cuarto Evangelio," *Estudios Bíblicos* 31 (July-Sept. 1982): 253ff.

15. Elizondo, *Galilean Journey: The Mexican-American Promise* (Maryknoll, N.Y.: Orbis Books, 1983), p. 49.

16. Von Allmen, *Worship: Its Theology and Practice,* trans. Harold Knight and W. Fletcher Fleet (New York: Oxford University Press, 1965), p. 23.

17. See Norman Perrin, *Jesus and the Language of the Kingdom: Symbol and Metaphor in New Testament Interpretation* (Philadelphia: Fortress Press, 1976), pp. 29-32. For a contemporary Latin American study of evangelization based on Jesus' proclamation of the kingdom, see Mortimer Arias, *Announcing the Reign of God: Evangelization and the Subversive Memory of Jesus* (Philadelphia: Fortress Press, 1984). The kingdom is a key theme in Latin American theology. See, among others, the following: Jorge Pantelis, "Reino de Dios e iglesia en el proceso historico de liberacion" (Ph.D. diss., Union Theological Seminary, 1975); A. Christopher Smith, "The Essentials of Missiology from the Perspective of the 'Fraternidad Teológica Latinoamericana'" (Ph.D. diss., Southern Baptist Theological Seminary, 1983); Julio de Santa Ana, *Por las sendas del mundo caminando hacia el reino* (San José, Costa Rica: Departamento Ecuménico de Investigaciones y Ediciones SEBILA, 1984); Emilio Castro, *Freedom in Mission—An Ecumenical Inquiry: The Perspective of the Kingdom* (Geneva: WCC, 1985); two books of mine: *The Integrity of Mission* (San Francisco: Harper & Row, 1979) and *Christ Outside the Gate: Mission beyond Christendom* (Maryknoll, N.Y.: Orbis Books, 1982); *El reino de Dios y America Latina,* ed. C. René Padilla (El Paso, Tex.: Casa Bautista de Publicaciones, 1975); C. René Padilla, *Mission between the Times: Essays on the Kingdom* (Grand Rapids: Eerdmans, 1985); George Pixley, *God's Kingdom: A Guide for Biblical Study,* trans. Donald Walsh (Maryknoll, N.Y.: Orbis Books, 1981).

18. Elizondo sees in Galilee and Jerusalem a double hermeneutical principle: (l) "What human beings reject, God chooses as his very own" (the Galilean principle); and (2) "God chooses an oppressed people not to bring them comfort in their oppression, but to enable them to confront, transcend, and transform whatever in the oppressor society diminishes and destroys the fundamental dignity of human nature." See his *Galilean Journey,* pp. 91, 103; cf. pp. 91-114. R. H. Lightfoot, in *Locality and Doctrine in the Gospel,* makes a similar point. He refers to Galilee as the sphere of revelation and Jerusalem as that of judgment.

19. Cf. Joachim Jeremias, *Jerusalem in the Times of Jesus,* trans. F. H. Cave and C. H. Cave (Philadelphia: Fortress Press, 1969), p. 51.

20. *Ibid.,* p. 138.

21. Cf. *ibid.,* p. 74.

22. *Ibid.,* p. 223.

23. *Ibid.*, pp. 232, 241.

24. *Ibid.*, p. 242.

25. *Ibid.*, p. 148.

26. *Ibid.*, p. 196.

27. Mateos, *Los "Doce,"* p. 254.

28. *Ibid.*, p. 255.

29. *Ibid.*, p. 178.

30. Cf. Robert Meye, *Jesus and the Twelve: Discipleship and Revelation in Mark's Gospel* (Grand Rapids: Eerdmans, 1968), pp. 80ff.; Mateos, *Los "Doce,"* pp. 191-92.

31. *Ibid.*, p. 193.

32. B. Metzger et al., *A Textual Commentary on the Greek New Testament* (New York: United Bible Societies, 1970), pp. 122-26. Cf. W. Farmer, *The Last Twelve Verses of Mark* (Cambridge: Cambridge University Press, 1974).

33. Mateos, *Los "Doce,"* p. 193.

34. Schüssler Fiorenza, *In Memory of Her: A Feminist Theological Reconstruction of Christian Origins* (New York: Crossroad, 1984), p. 322.

35. *Ibid.*

36. Meye, *Jesus and the Twelve*, p. 85.

37. For my view on the privileged position of the poor in Scripture, see my book entitled *The Integrity of Mission*, pp. 76-83.

38. Cf. José Marins, "Basic Ecclesial Community," *The Community of Believers UISG Bulletin*, no. 55, p. 293. See also Guillermo Cook, *The Expectation of the Poor: Latin American Basic Ecclesial Communities in Protestant Perspective* (Maryknoll, N.Y.: Orbis Books, 1986), pp. 6, 7, 61ff.; the April 1975 issue of *Concilium*, which features articles by Enrique Dussel, José Marins, José Comblin, and Gabriel Garaudy; Alvaro Barreiro, *Basic Ecclesial Communities: The Evangelization of the Poor*, trans. Barbara Campbell (Maryknoll, N.Y.: Orbis Books, 1982); Leonardo Boff, *Ecclesiogenesis: The Base Communities Reinvent the Church*, trans. Robert Barr (Maryknoll, N.Y.: Orbis Books, 1986); Jao Batista Libanio, *Evangelizacão e Libertacão* (Petrópolis: Editora Vozes, 1976); José Marins et al., *Missão Evangelizadora da Comunidade Eclesial* (São Paulo: Editora Paulinas, 1977); *Modelos de Igreja: Comunidad Eclesial na America Latina* (São Paulo: Editora Paulinas, 1977); José María González Ruiz, *Dios está en la base* (Barcelona: Editorial LAIA, 1973).

39. Here I am obliged to enter a critical note on contextual evangelistic models that concentrate on cultural, linguistic, or psychological adaptation without probing or questioning in depth the larger problem of social, economic, and political relations. (See Charles Kraft, *Christianity in Culture: A Study in Dynamic Biblical Theologizing in Cross-Cultural Perspective* [Maryknoll, N.Y.: Orbis Books, 1979]; Edward Dayton and David Fraser, *Planning Strategies for World Evangelization* [Grand Rapids: Eerdmans, 1980]; David J. Hes-

selgrave, *Communicating Christ Cross-Culturally: An Interpretation of Missionary Communication* [Grand Rapids: Zondervan, 1978].)

These models may offer some cultural-anthropological help, but they are socially and theologically deficient. For the kingdom of God is a comprehensive and transforming reality; it is nothing less than the power of the new creation (see 1 Cor. 4:20; 2 Cor. 5:17). An evangelization that is interested only in discovering the formal equivalences of a given culture or only in discovering the felt needs of a people in order to make the gospel culturally, linguistically, or psychologically relevant is contextually superficial and prophetically acritical. In fact, it reflects a theological escapism in light of the reality of our evil planet, under the leadership of demonic principalities and powers present in practically every human situation. It seems to me that only a prophetically critical and evangelically radical contextual evangelistic approach can do justice to the cutting edge of the gospel, which is its transforming and liberating message for the poor, the dispossessed and the oppressed. For this reason, its demand of conversion to the cause of the kingdom makes necessary a social base on the periphery of every historical situation.

40. See Penny Lernoux, *Cry of the People* (Garden City, N.Y.: Doubleday, 1980), pp. 3ff.

41. On the concept of the "massification" of the faith, see Juan Luis Segundo, *Masas y minorías en la dialéctica divina de la liberación* (Buenos Aires: Editorial la Aurora, 1973), and *The Liberation of Theology* (Maryknoll, N.Y.: Orbis Books, 1975), pp. 208-40.

42. In Latin America these phenomena can be observed especially during the age of colonial Christendom—thus the denunciation and prophetic evangelistic postulate reflected in the works of Bartolomé de las Casas. See Enrique Dussel, *A History of the Church in Latin America: Colonialism to Liberation,* trans. Alan Neely (Grand Rapids: Eerdmans, 1981).

43. See Rudolf Bultmann et al., *Kerygma and Myth,* trans. Reginald H. Fuller (London: SPCK, 1953). For Bultmann it was necessary to free the presentation of the biblical message of all mythical elements. That required rejecting the biblical worldview because it was part of a prescientific cosmology and thus unacceptable to contemporary humanity. Bultmann called this project of extirpation "demythologization." The problem with the approach that Bultmann and many of his students took was their assumption that all of contemporary humanity shared a scientific worldview; they forgot that the majority of human beings in the twentieth century have been on the margins of the scientific and technological advancement of modernity. Bultmann did not take into account the fact that biblical cosmology was quite comprehensible to two-thirds of humanity. Moreover, he did not take into account the sociohistorical correspondence between a great part of the biblical world and the multitudes who live on the periphery of the contemporary world. This flaw proceeds from Bultmann's "existentialist" viewpoint. He ended up accentuating individual

existence over the social reality within which humans exist. Accordingly, he failed to see that "no man is an island, entire of itself; every man is a piece of the continent, a part of the main" (John Donne). Or, as José Ortega y Gasset put it, "I am myself and what is around me."

44. For a full discussion of the biblical concept of "principalities and powers," see Walter Wink, *Unmasking the Powers* (Philadelphia: Fortress Press, 1985), and *Discerning the Powers* (Philadelphia: Fortress Press, 1986). See also H. Berkhof, *Christ and the Powers,* trans. John Howard Yoder (Scottdale, Penn.: Mennonite Publishing House, 1962), *passim;* Richard J. Mouw, *Politics and the Biblical Drama* (Grand Rapids: Eerdmans, 1976), p. 86; Albert H. van den Heuvel, *Those Rebellious Powers* (London: SCM Press, 1966), *passim;* James Wallis, *Agenda for Biblical People* (New York: Harper & Row, 1976), pp. 56ff.; Ronald J. Sider, *Christ and Violence* (Scottdale, Penn.: Herald Press, 1978), pp. 43ff.

Notes to Chapter V

1. Juan Luis Segundo, in his *Theology for Artisans of a New Humanity,* vol. 3: *Our Idea of God* [Maryknoll, N.Y.: Orbis Books, 1974], pp. 21-31), uses Paul's sermon to describe three constitutive elements of human history that correspond to successive stages of God's Trinitarian revelation: (1) "God before us" (pp. 30-37); (2) "God with us" (pp. 37-42); and (3) "God amongst us" (pp. 42-46). The first stage corresponds to Yahweh, the revelation of God in the history and Scriptures of Israel. The second—anticipated in the prophetic literature where Yahweh "truly becomes, up to a certain point, *Emmanuel,* that is, 'God with us'" (Isa. 7:14; 8:8-10; Ps. 46:7, 11)—corresponds to the revelation of the Word of God in Jesus. The third corresponds to the revelation of the Spirit, who, "attuned to the rhythm of history, ensures the continuing presence of Jesus in a creative way" (pp. 44-45). Segundo concludes,

> Precisely because the revelation of the Christian God brings us face to face with history, God willed to dole it out gradually as history made it feasible and necessary. Saint Gregory [of Nazianzus] describes the unfolding development of this revelation in these terms: "The real situation is this. The Old Testament spoke openly of the Father, and more obscurely of the Son. The New Testament pointed plainly and clearly to the Son, and obscurely to the divinity of the Spirit. Now the Spirit dwells with us and openly presents [him/herself] to us. In and for history, the Spirit leads us toward the full truth." (P. 46)

2. The reference to God as Father has been strongly debated by feminist theology. See, among others, Mary Daly, *Beyond God the Father* (Boston: Beacon Press, 1973), and Rosemary Radford Ruether, *Sexism and God-Talk*

(Boston: Beacon Press, 1983). These and other feminist theologians question the traditional, exclusively male Trinitarian language. Ruether acknowledges that both in the biblical traditions and in the varied history of Christianity one finds multiple feminine references to God. Nevertheless, she questions whether the fact that God "has both mothering or feminine as well as masculine characteristics" or that the Holy Spirit is to be identified with the feminine aspect of the Trinity "resolves the problem of an exclusive male image of God." She states, "It is doubtful . . . that we should settle for a concept of the Trinity that consists of two male and one female 'persons.' Such a concept falls easily in an androcentric or male-dominant perspective. The female side of God then becomes a subordinate principle underneath the dominant image of male divine sovereignty" (p. 60).

Ruether insists that all language about God as father and mother "reinforces patriarchal power rather than liberates us from it" (p. 70). She proposes, therefore, a language that begins with "the Divine as redeemer, as liberator, as one who fosters full personhood," and further proposes, "in that context, to speak of God/ess as creator and source of being" (p. 70).

The problem of exclusive male language both in biblical literature and in the theological trajectory of the Christian church must be readily acknowledged. Likewise, we need to recognize, with Ruether and many other theologians (male and female), that in the tradition one finds not only that there are alternatives to the exclusively male imagery which acknowledge the female side of God but also that the God of the Exodus, whom Jesus called *"Abba"* (an Aramaic term that expresses intimacy), cannot be limited to any one sex because such a God overcomes both patriarchy and paternalism.

Even so, we need to bear in mind that in the Christian tradition the designation of God as Father, Son, and Holy Spirit expresses, above all else, the communal identity of God—that is, God as eternal community. It is not so much the images of patriarchy or paternalism or of the family as the central principle of the doctrine of God that are at stake but rather the affirmation of God as "being-in-relation." The unity of God and the organizing principle of the three persons of the Trinity is located in their interrelational mutuality. This is also the basis of Christian existence. As Segundo has noted, "Christian existence as a whole is conceived in relation to the Father, the Son, and the Spirit. And this holds true from the very earliest writings in the New Testament" (*Our Idea of God*, p. 20).

We need also to take into account the fact that the Christian notion of God is particularly derived from Jesus. It is on the basis of his teaching and practice that we address God as Father. To cease to speak of God as Father would be to break with the foundational source of Christian tradition as well as to reject the very example of Jesus and his teachings. It would imply losing sight of the teachings of the New Testament on the God and Father of our Lord Jesus Christ, which, as noted, has nothing to do with the sexuality of God but, on the contrary, with the overcoming of all sexism. (See W. A. Visser 't Hooft, *The Fatherhood of God in an Age of Emancipation* [Geneva: WCC, 1982], p. 33.) As a study group of the Church of Scotland has declared, "Instead of repudiating belief in and language about God our Father, . . . we should on the contrary emphasize . . . the Fatherhood of God all the more, since all that Christ reveals of the Father stands in such clear contradiction of masculine domination" (*The Motherhood of God,* ed. Alan C. Lewis [Edinburgh: St. Andrews Press, 1984], p. 24).

Susan Brooks Thistlethwaite, while acknowledging the importance of the Trinity for an adequate understanding of God-in-relation-to-the-world, has nevertheless questioned the exclusive use of "Father" and "Son" to refer to the first and second persons of the Trinity. She notes, "That Jesus called God 'Father' is the basis for our thinking about Jesus Christ as one of the three persons of the Trinity. As the words of the Nicene Creed state, Jesus Christ is 'begotten, not made, being of one substance with the Father.' This is a relationship which cannot be claimed by any created being. The relationship which the Father/Son imagery of the New Testament seeks to evoke is that Jesus is of the same substance as God" ("God Language and the Trinity," *EKUCC Newsletter,* Feb. 1984, pp. 21-23).

However, she goes on to argue that "if God the Son proceeded from God the Father alone, this procession is both a male and female action, a begetting *and* a birth. God is the motherly father of the child who comes forth." She further points out that "it was the Orthodox dogmatic tradition which most dramatically defended Trinitarian language about God, and it is this tradition which speaks most boldly of God's bisexuality. According to the Third Council of Toledo, 'it must be held that the Son was created, neither out of nothingness nor yet out of any substance, but that He was begotten or born out of the Father's womb *(de utero Patria),* that is, out of His very essence' " ("God Language and the Trinity," pp. 21-23).

Seeking to express "the same intimacy, caring, and freedom, of Jesus' identification of God as Abba," Thistlethwaite proposes, as does *The Inclusive Language Lectionary,* the adoption of the more inclusive metaphors "Father" and "Mother." She further suggests the use of "Child of God" as "a metaphor which equally expresses both the exclusivity of Jesus' unique relationship to God and the inclusivity of the participation of all humanity in this relationship." This, she adds, "proceeds from the conviction that 'Sonship' has no essential relationship to Jesus as male" but is rather related to his uniqueness, which "is exclusive in order to bring about inclusivity" ("God Language and the Trinity," pp. 21-23).

Thistlethwaite's article is a lucid exploration of the social Trinity. She correctly points out that when "God is understood as fundamentally and inseparably social," this concept offers tremendous potential for understanding the relationship of God with the world. It is in this context that she is critical of any Trinitarian formula that does not provide for "the inter-Trinitarian relationship" between the members of the Trinity, such as "Creator, Christ and Holy Spirit." Her alternative formula, however ("God, the Mother and Father, Jesus, the Child of God, and God the Holy Spirit"), is not fully satisfactory. It is wanting, first of all, because it is doubtful whether it is historically and linguistically acceptable to translate the term *Abba,* which Jesus used to express his relationship to God, as "Father and Mother." We do not need to force a translation to have a socially inclusive understanding of the Trinity. The formula "Father, Son, and Holy Spirit" belongs to the history of the ecumenical church. Our task is not to rephrase it but to *re-interpret* it in its fullest significance. A second criticism of Thistlethwaite's formulation is that, while it is true that the metaphor "Child of God" is one of several that can be used to describe Jesus' relationship with God, the fact remains that the title of "Son" is so intrinsically connected with the person of Jesus that it would be difficult to substitute "Child" for "Son" without affecting the very inclusiveness for which the historical Jesus stood for. (See Joachim Jeremias, *New Testament Theology,* vol. 1, trans. John Bowden [New York: Scribner's, 1971], pp. 257ff.) The two come as part and parcel of the "exclusive/inclusive" significance of the person of Jesus as the revelation of the second member of the Trinity.

For a further discussion on the matter, see the following sources, among many others: Hendrikus Berkhof, *Christian Faith,* rev. ed. (Grand Rapids: Eerdmans, 1986), p. 120; Gabriel Fackre, *The Christian Story,* vol. I, rev. ed. (Grand Rapids: Eerdmans, 1984), pp. 62-66; Yves Congar, *I Believe in the Holy Spirit,* vol. 3 (New York: Seabury Press, 1983), pp. 155-64; Letty M. Russell, *Human Liberation in a Feminist Perspective: A Theology* (Philadelphia: Westminster Press, 1974), pp. 93-103; Donald L. Gelpi, *The Divine Mother: A Trinitarian Theology of the Holy Spirit* (Lanham, Md.: University Press of America, 1984), *passim.*

3. I am indebted to Jürgen Moltmann for this insight and perspective on the Trinity; see *The Crucified God,* trans. R. A. Wilson and John Bowden (London: SCM Press, 1974), pp. 235ff.; *The Church in the Power of the Spirit,* trans. Margaret Kohl (New York: Harper & Row, 1977), pp. 50ff.; and *The Trinity and the Kingdom: The Doctrine of God,* trans. Margaret Kohl (New York: Harper & Row, 1980), *passim.* For another relational model of the Trinity, one stressing "relations of opposition" among the members of the Godhead yet underscoring the divine missions, see Karl Rahner, "Trinity, Divine," in vol. 6 of *Sacramentum Mundi,* 6 vols., ed. K. Rahner et al. (New York: Herder & Herder, 1970). In a privately circulated working paper entitled "Reciprocal Relations in Trinitarian Theology," Vincent Martin, of the Tantur Ecumenical Institute for Theological Research in Jerusalem, proposes replacing the classical Western concept of "oppositional relationships" for the Trinity with one of "reciprocal relationships." Building upon Rahner's model, he locates the unity of the Godhead in the notion of the "Living God" wherein the "three persons are

one consciousness, one freedom, one creativity" (p. 23). The Trinity is thus described as the self-communication of the Living God "through complementarity between uttering and receiving" (p. 23).

Such an approach comes close to the model I follow in the stress of the divine missions ("uttering" = Word, and "receiving" = Spirit). Building upon Moltmann, I speak of God as mission (the sending of the Son by the Father in the power of the Spirit for the salvation of the world) and as unity (the reconciliation of the world by the Spirit through the Son for the glory of the Father). The difference between my approach and that of Rahner and Martin lies in the fact that these two work within the framework (though modified) of the Augustinian psychological metaphor for the Trinity, whereas I follow Moltmann's use of the social metaphor, which he derives from the Eastern tradition. Thus Rahner and Martin locate the oneness of God in the Father, whereas I (with Moltmann) locate God's oneness in the eternal Trinitarian community of love, or the communal event of Father, Son, and Spirit. This preserves the medieval notion of God as "pure act" without falling into either the trap of a tritheism (three gods) or the trap of a theistic monarchy (monothe*ism*). Yet it must be admitted that Martin's model of reciprocal relations, in its proposal of "one consciousness, one freedom, one creativity," also allows for the notion of "one in community," especially in relation to the world. Thus, Martin states, "we are always faced with the perfect unity of a triune act, the one act of three subjects. . . . The imminent relations among them are based on the correlative expression of the Infinite Self of God into Giving and Receiving" (p. 31). In this formulation the Living God appears not as an eternal monarch but as an eternal "tri-subjectivity in one act"—or, as I would say, an eternal "communal event."

4. Forsyth, *Positive Preaching and the Modern Mind* (London: Independent Press, 1954), p. 242.

5. John H. Rodgers, *The Theology of P. T. Forsyth: The Cross of Christ and the Revelation of God* (London: Independent Press, 1965), p. 37.

6. P. T. Forsyth, *This Life and the Next: The Effect on This Life of Faith in Another* (London: Independent Press, 1953), p. 29.

7. Sobrino, *Christology at the Crossroads: A Latin American Approach,* trans. John Drury (Maryknoll, N.Y.: Orbis Books, 1978), p. 71.

8. The allusion to the story of Isaac's sacrifice is a constituent part of early Christian understanding of the atonement. Likewise, in the Jewish tradition the Akedah, or the binding of Isaac, stands as a symbol of the vicarious suffering of faithful Jews and God's provision of an adequate reward for their suffering. In his instructive essay entitled "The Atonement—An Adequate Reward for the Akedah?" Nils Alstrup Dahl explores the Judeo-Christian roots of the role of the Akedah in the Christian doctrine of the Atonement and its parallels and differences with the Jewish tradition. He concludes that there may have "existed a specifically Jewish-Christian 'doctrine of the atonement,'"

which stands in the distant background of the Pauline texts (see Rom. 8:32; Gal. 3:13-14) that directly allude to the Akedah.

Dahl adds, however, that "the fragments surmised to be contained in Paul's letters . . . cannot belong to the very beginnings of Christian doctrine," since their interpretation of Genesis 22 presupposes the identification of Jesus as Messiah and Son of God, which appears to be a later development. Yet "the interpretation of the Pauline texts must be early, because it would seem to have been germinal to the phrase 'God gave his Son' and possibly to the designation of Jesus as 'the only Son' and 'the lamb of God.'" In this specifically Jewish-Christian tradition of the Atonement, says Dahl,

> The death of Jesus upon the cross was interpreted as fulfilling what God had promised Abraham by oath: As Abraham had not withheld his son, so God did not spare his own Son, but gave him up for Isaac's descendants. As the sacrifice, provided by God, he expiated their former sins. Vicariously he was made a curse to redeem them from the curse covered by their transgressions of the law, so that even the Gentile nations sought to be blessed in the offspring of Abraham, the crucified Messiah Jesus. That God in his great mercy rewarded Abraham by acting as the patriarch did at the Akedah would thus seem to be part of fairly coherent early Christian theology in which the crucifixion of Jesus was interpreted in the light of Genesis 22.

This early Christian interpretation, says Dahl, is "an independent parallel" rather than a derivative of "Jewish Akedah traditions." Thus, even though the interpretation of Genesis became, in later Christian history, a bone of contention between Christians and Jews, "the earliest Christian interpretation antedates the controversy. Not any competition, but the close correspondence between the Akedah and the atonement was stressed, quite possibly to the extent that the redemption by Christ was seen as an adequate reward for the binding of Isaac" (Dahl, *The Crucified Messiah and Other Essays* [Minneapolis: Augsburg Publishing House, 1974], pp. 158-60).

9. Moltmann, *The Crucified God,* p. 241.

10. This is a process that takes place within the Triunity, as Moltmann has well noted:

> The goal of the subordination of the Son to the Father and the significance of the transference of the kingdom to the Father is not simply the sole rule of God, but the consummation of the Fatherhood of the Father. . . . The goal of the consummation does not lie in the dissolution by Christ of his rule so that it is taken up in the rule of God, but in the consummation of the obedience of the Son and thus in the consummation of the brotherhood of believers. In respect of the world, . . . one can see the consummation of salvation in the transition from the rule of Christ to the sole rule of God. But in respect of the inner relationship of the Son to the Father, the consummation of the salvation of the world lies in the consummation of the history of God within the Trinity. In the first respect it is possible to speak of the provisional functions of God's Christ as representative and mediator be-

> coming superfluous. In the second respect, however, one must speak of the abiding significance of the Son who is delivered up and then raised. It follows from this that the crucified Christ does not disappear when the fulfillment comes, but rather becomes the ground for redeemed existence in God and the indwelling of God in all. In that event the crucified Christ in fact no longer has representative functions. But new existence is indebted to him forever. The functional and soteriological representative-christology then becomes a doxological Son-christology. And as the end brings about this universal, so too it is present in the confession of the Christian believer from the beginning. Historical christology, too, must . . . itself be an expression of the brotherhood of the believer with the Son and express that doxologically in thanksgiving and praise. Thus the necessity of representation "for us" becomes the freedom of thankfulness "from us." (*The Crucified God,* p. 266)

11. Thus, for example, Rahner postulates as a methodological principle for the doctrine of the Trinity "the identity of the Trinity of the economy of salvation and imminent Trinity" ("Trinity, Divine," p. 298). He proposes that "the economic Trinity is (already) the imminent Trinity, because the basic event of the whole economy of salvation is the self-communication of God to the world, and because all that God (the Father) is to us in Jesus Christ the Son and the Holy Spirit would not really be the *self*-communication of God, if the twofold missions were not intrinsic to him, as processions, bringing with them the distinction of the three persons" ("Trinity in Theology," *Sacramentum Mundi,* vol. 6, p. 301).

While I agree with Rahner that our knowledge of the Trinity comes by way of the economic Trinity, I object to the way in which he identifies the economic and imminent Trinity on the grounds that it replaces God's inner existence as a Trinitarian event with a unitarian concept of God.

12. Moltmann, *The Church in the Power of the Spirit,* p. 150.

13. Moltmann, *The Trinity and the Kingdom,* p. 212.

14. For a study of the relationship of the Holy Spirit to the world within a similar Trinitarian approach, see M. Douglas Meeks, "The Holy Spirit and Human Needs: Toward a Trinitarian Economics," *Christianity and Crisis* (10 *Nov. 1980), pp. 307-16, and his forthcoming volume on the Trinity and economics, to be published by Fortress Press.*

15. Moltmann, *The Crucified God,* p. 240.

16. Cf. my book entitled *Christ Outside the Gate: Mission beyond Christendom* (Maryknoll, N.Y.: Orbis Books, 1982), pp. 188-94.

17. Newbigin, *The Open Secret* (Grand Rapids: Eerdmans, 1978), pp. 44ff.

18. Cf. Moltmann, *The Crucified God,* p. 246.

19. Cf. Xavier Pikaza, *Los hermanos más pequeños de Jesús* (Salamanca: Ediciones Sígueme, 1984).

Notes to Chapter VI

1. See John R. Stott, *The Cross of Christ* (Leicester, Eng.: Inter-Varsity Press, 1986), pp. 32-40; Leon Morris, *The Apostolic Preaching of the Cross* (Grand Rapids: Eerdmans, 1955), *passim;* Martin Hengel, *The Atonement,* trans. John Bowden (Philadelphia: Fortress Press, 1981), pp. 34ff.

2. See C. L. Mitton, "Atonement," in *The Interpreter's Dictionary of the Bible,* vol. 1 (Nashville: Abingdon Press, 1962), p. 309.

3. *Ibid.,* p. 310.

4. See Louis Jacobs, "Halakhah," in *Encyclopaedia Judaica,* vol. 7 (Jerusalem: Keter Publishing House, Ltd., 1971), pp. 1155ff.

5. See Rabbi I. Epstein's foreword to *Midrash Rabbah,* vol. 1: *Genesis,* trans. Rabbi Dr. H. Freedman (New York: Soncino Press, 1983), p. IX.

6. See Ernst Daniel Goldschmidt, "Haggadah, Passover," in *Encyclopaedia Judaica,* vol. 7, pp. 1079ff.

7. See Robert J. Daly, *The Origin of the Christian Doctrine of Sacrifice* (Philadelphia: Fortress Press, 1978), pp. 56-57.

8. Jeremias, *The Eucharistic Words of Jesus,* trans. Norman Perin (London: SCM Press, 1966), p. 228.

9. Stott, *The Cross of Christ,* p. 145.

10. Hengel, *The Atonement,* p. 60.

11. See E. Schüssler Fiorenza, *In Memory of Her: A Feminist Theological Reconstruction of Christian Origins* (New York: Crossroad, 1983); and Leonardo Boff, *Passion of Christ, Passion of the World,* trans. Robert R. Gass (Maryknoll, N.Y.: Orbis Books, 1987)—along with their respective sources—as examples of the former view. For the other view, see Jeremias, *The Eucharistic Words of Jesus,* p. 231; *The Central Message of the New Testament* (London: SCM Press, 1965), p. 46; J. Jeremias and W. Zimmerli, *The Servant of God* (London: SCM Press, 1957); J. Jeremias, "pais theou," in *Theological Dictionary of the New Testament,* vol. 5, ed. Gerhard Friedrich, trans. Geoffrey Bromiley (Grand Rapids: Eerdmans, 1967), pp. 654-717; Hengel, *The Atonement,* pp. 53-75. See also O. Cullmann, *Baptism in the New Testament,* trans. J. K. L. Reid (London: SCM Press, 1951), p. 18; *Christology in the New Testament,* trans. S. C. Guthrie and C. A. M. Hall (London: SCM Press, 1959), chap. 3; Vincent Taylor, *The Atonement in the New Testament Teaching* (London: Epworth Press, 1940), p. 18.

12. Stott, *The Cross of Christ,* p. 14c.

13. Jeremias and Zimmerli, *The Servant of God,* p. 45.

14. William L. Holladay, *Isaiah: Scroll of a Prophetic Heritage* (Grand Rapids: Eerdmans, 1978), p. 180.

15. *Ibid.,* p. 168.

16. Douglas Rawlinson Jones, *Isaiah 56–66 and Joel: Introduction and Commentary* (London: SCM Press, 1964), p. 25.

17. Sanders, "From Isaiah 61 to Luke 4," in *Christianity, Judaism and*

Other Greco-Roman Cults: Studies for Morton Smith at Sixty, ed. Jacob Neusner (London: E. J. Brill, 1975), p. 88.

18. Cf. 11QMelch, one of the documents found at Qumran.

19. Sanders, "From Isaiah 61 to Luke 4," pp. 91-92.

20. *Ibid.,* p. 104.

21. *Ibid.,* p. 94.

22. *Ibid.,* p. 95.

23. *Ibid.*

24. *Ibid.,* p. 97.

25. *Ibid.*

26. *Ibid.*

27. *Ibid.,* p. 104.

28. Cf. Stott, *The Cross of Christ,* p. 135.

29. *Ibid.,* p. 139 n. 9.

30. It is in this framework that we need to locate the various theories of the Atonement. Rather than seeing them as individual, self-contained units, we should interpret them in terms of the inclusivity of Christ's work on the cross. Therefore, the various theories of the Atonement (subjective, objective, redemptive, substitutionary, and regenerative) should be seen in their unity in light of the kerygmatic Christ, as P. T. Forsyth suggested early in the twentieth century. See John H. Rodgers, *The Theology of P. T. Forsyth: The Cross of Christ and the Revelation of God* (London: Independent Press, 1965), pp. 286-88. See also John Driver, *Understanding the Atonement for the Mission of the Church* (Scottdale, Penn.: Herald Press, 1986), in which the various theories of the Atonement are critically analyzed in relation to the overall mission of the church. Driver tries to see the unity of these theories and their relevance as well as their limitations for mission.

31. Kenneth Bailey, interview with author, Jerusalem, Israel, 23 Apr. 1987. I am indebted to Bailey for this insight into the Koran.

32. Stott, *The Cross of Christ,* p. 40.

33. Zwemer, *The Glory of the Cross* (London: Marshall, Morgan & Scott, 1928), p. 6.

34. P. T. Forsyth, *Positive Preaching and the Modern Mind* (London: Independent Press, Ltd., 1957), pp. 242-43.

35. *Ibid.*

36. Forsyth, *The Work of Christ* (London: Independent Press, Ltd., 1957), p. 136.

37. Gandhi, quoted in Stott, *The Cross of Christ,* p. 42.

38. Hengel, *The Atonement,* pp. 28-29.

39. *Ibid.,* p. 31.

40. Nietzsche, *The Anti-Christ* (1895; rpt. New York: Penguin Books, 1968), pp. 128, 168.

41. See "Paradidomi," in *A Greek-English Lexicon of the New Testa-*

ment and Other Early Christian Literature, comp. Walter Bauer, trans. and ed. William F. Arndt and F. Wilbur Gingrich (Chicago: University of Chicago Press, 1957), pp. 616-17.

42. Driver, *Understanding the Atonement for the Mission of the Church,* p. 29.

43. *Encyclopaedia Britannica, Macropaedia,* s.v. "Constantine the Great."

44. *Ibid.*

45. *Encyclopedia Britannica, Macropaedia,* s.v. "Crusades."

46. See my book entitled *Christ Outside the Gate: Mission beyond Christendom* (Maryknoll, N.Y.: Orbis Books, 1982), p. 34.

47. See Marc H. Ellis, *Toward a Jewish Theology of Liberation* (Maryknoll, N.Y.: Orbis Books, 1987), pp. 7-24. In this section Ellis reviews the perspectives of the leading Jewish figures who view the Holocaust as a "universal crisis"—Elie Wiesel, Richard Rubenstein, Emil Fackenheim, and Irving Greenberg. Ellis concludes with this observation:

> Unfortunately, few Christians have contemplated the haunting difficulty raised by the Jewish Holocaust: What does it mean to be a Christian when Christian understandings and actions issued in the death camps of Nazi Germany? The first response of those who have authentically confronted this evil is to ask forgiveness of the Jewish people and seek forgiveness from Jesus, himself a Jew, whose essential message of love was betrayed. The second response is to remain in dialogue with the experience of the Holocaust as a formative event for Christians as well. For to recognize the reality of the death camps and of Christian complicity involves a questioning of the authenticity of Christian faith and activity. Only by realizing and admitting how their conduct denied true Christianity can Christians both salvage and reconstruct their faith. Only by entering into the nothingness of the death camps can a contemporary Christian way of life become authentic. (p. 23)

48. Benson, *Discretion and Valor: Religious Conditions in Russia and Eastern Europe* (London: Collins, 1974), p. 139.

49. Justo L. González, "The Two Faces of Hispanic Christianity," *The Judson Bulletin,* vol. 6, no. 1 (new series), p. 20.

50. *Ibid.*

51. *Ibid.*

52. *Ibid.*

Notes to Chapter VII

1. William L. Holladay, *A Concise Hebrew and Aramaic Lexicon of the Old Testament* (Grand Rapids: Eerdmans, 1971), pp. 362-69. See also his book

entitled *The Root Šûbh in the Old Testament* (Leiden: E. J. Brill, 1958), pp. 51ff.

2. Barth, "Notes on 'Return' in the Old Testament," *Ecumenical Review* 19 (July 1967): 310-11.

3. George Bertram, "Epistrepho," in *Theological Dictionary of the New Testament,* vol. 7, ed. Gerhard Friedrich, trans. G. W. Bromiley (Grand Rapids: Eerdmans, 1971), p. 727.

4. William Barclay, *Turning to God: A Study of Conversion in the Book of Acts and Today* (Grand Rapids: Baker Book House, 1964), pp. 21-22.

5. Bertram, "Epistrepho," p. 727.

6. J. Behm, "Noeo: Metanoeo, Metanoia," in *Theological Dictionary of the New Testament,* vol. 4, ed. G. Kittel, trans. G. W. Bromiley (Grand Rapids: Eerdmans, 1967), pp. 976-77.

7. Míguez Bonino, "Notes on Conversion—For a Critical Rethinking of the Wesleyan Doctrine," unpublished paper prepared for a Roman Catholic–Methodist dialogue, n.d.

8. Cf. Jim Wallis, *The Call to Conversion: Recovering the Gospel for These Times* (San Francisco: Harper & Row, 1981), *passim.*

9. Míguez Bonino, "Notes on Conversion," p. 6.

10. This process is qualified by the *eschaton,* the consummation of history, in which God's glorious kingdom shall be revealed in its fullness.

11. This perspective does overlap somewhat with the concept of sanctification. But there does not seem to be any hard biblical or theological evidence for the neat, clear-cut distinction between conversion and sanctification that has been made in the formulation of the *Ordo salutis* (order of salvation) in traditional Protestant theologies. On the contrary, sanctification seems to be implicit in conversion and vice versa. The term *Ordo salutis* describes the process by which salvation is realized in the life of women and men. The exact order varies according to the various traditions. Traditional Reformed dogmatics, for example, includes seven stages (calling, regeneration, faith [conversion], justification, adoption, sanctification, and glorification); traditional Lutheran dogmatics has six (illumination, faith, confession, justification, mystical union, sanctification, and glorification). Most theologies that prefer to use this kind of language do insist on separate stages for conversion and sanctification. They all agree, however, that this is more of a logical way of describing the process of salvation than an exact chronology of it, even though it is a fact that they have often given the impression that the description is a chronological one.

12. Míguez Bonino, "Notes on Conversion," p. 6.

13. See my book entitled *Theology of the Crossroads in Contemporary Latin America* (Amsterdam: Editions Rodopi, 1976), p. 350.

14. Reilly, *Spirituality for Mission* (Maryknoll, N.Y.: Orbis Books, 1984), pp. 22, 24.

15. Gutiérrez, *We Drink from Our Own Wells: The Spiritual Journey of a People,* trans. Matthew J. O'Connell (Maryknoll, N.Y.: Orbis Books, 1984), p. 34.

16. Rudolf Otto, *The Idea of the Holy,* trans. John K. Harvey (London: Oxford University Press, 1923).

17. Taylor, *The Go-Between God: The Holy Spirit and the Christian Mission* (Philadelphia: Fortress Press, 1972), p. 8.

18. *Ibid.,* pp. 28, 35.

19. *Ibid.,* p. 64.

20. *Ibid.,* pp. 45, 39.

21. *Ibid.*

22. Berkhof, *Christian Faith,* trans. Sierd Woudstra (Grand Rapids: Eerdmans, 1979), p. 324. See also Berkhof's *Doctrine of the Holy Spirit* (Atlanta: John Knox Press, 1976).

23. Taylor, *The Go-Between God,* p. 38.

24. Reilly, *Spirituality for Mission,* p. 200.

Notes to Chapter VIII

1. See José María Gonzalez Ruiz, *Dios esta en la base,* 2nd ed. (Barcelona: Editorial LAIA, 1975).

2. See Sergio Arce Martínez, "Evangelization and Politics from the Cuban Point of View," in *Evangelization and Politics,* ed. Sergio Arce Martínez and Oden Marichal (New York: New York Circus Publications, Inc., 1982), p. 38; Mortimer Arias, *Announcing the Reign of God: Evangelization and the Subversive Memory of Jesus* (Philadelphia: Fortress Press, 1984), p. 1; Mortimer Arias, the "Fondren Lectures," *Perkins Journal,* Winter 1979, pp. 11-17.

3. See Charles Olsen, *The Base Church* (Atlanta: Forum House Publishers, 1973), pp. xiv-xvi.

4. *Lumen Gentium,* par. 9, in *The Documents of Vatican II* (New York: America Press, 1966). See also the following points of Vatican II documents in this volume: *Lumen Gentium,* pars. 1, 48, 59; *Gaudium et spes,* no. 45; *Sacrosanctum concilium,* nos. 5, 26; and *Ad gentes,* no. 9.

5. See Gustavo Gutiérrez, *Theology of Liberation* (Maryknoll, N.Y.: Orbis Books, 1972); E. Ruffini, "Sacramentos," in *Diccionario teológico interdisciplinar,* vol. 4 (Salamanca: Ediciones Sígueme, 1983), pp. 247-68.

6. Von Allmen, *Worship: Its Theology and Practice,* trans. Harold Knight and W. Fletcher Fleet (New York: Oxford University Press, 1965), p. 16.

7. *Go Forth in Peace: Orthodox Perspectives on Mission,* ed. Ion Bria (Geneva: WCC, 1986), p. 20.

8. *Ibid.*

9. *Ibid.*

10. Julio De Santa Ana underscores and expands the meaning of this fact in his study of the Eucharist entitled *Pan, vino y amistad* (San José, Costa Rica: Departamento Ecuménico de Investigaciones, 1985).

11. See, for instance, the following texts: Gen. 18:19; Deut. 10:12-19; Amos 5:12; 6:12; Isa. 32:16-17; 61:1-4; Mic. 6:8; Matt. 5:6; 6:33; 2 Cor. 9:8-10; James 2:14-17, 24.

12. Cf. Ann Ahles, Mitzi Hill, Judy McCullough, "A Just Peace: A Study Guide for the Local Church," course paper submitted at Andover Newton Theological School, 13 Dec. 1984, p. 56.

13. Richard, lecture delivered in San José, Costa Rica, Jan. 1984.

14. Conn, *Evangelism: Doing Justice and Preaching Grace* (Grand Rapids: Zondervan, 1982), p. 56.

15. See Daniel Schipani, *El reino de Dios y el ministerio educativo,* pp. 159-61; Rolando Gutiérrez Cortés, *Educación teológica y acción pastoral en América Latina hoy* (Mexico: Iglesia Bautista Horeb, 1984), *passim*; and my essay entitled "Educación teológica y misión," in *Nuevas alternativas de educación teológica,* ed. C. René Padilla, Nueva Creación series (Grand Rapids: Eerdmans, 1986).

16. Cf. "Covenant, Guarantee, Mediator," in *The New International Dictionary of New Testament Theology,* vol. 1, ed. Colin Brown (Grand Rapids: Zondervan, 1976), pp. 365-76; "Covenant," in *Sacramentum Mundi,* 6 vols., ed. Karl Rahner et al. (New York: Herder & Herder, 1968), 2: 18-23. Both articles have ample bibliographical references. On the relation between Israel and the church, see Wesley H. Brown, "Christian Understandings of Biblical Prophecy, Israel and the Land and the Christian-Jewish Encounter," *Immanuel* 18 (Fall 1984): 79-95; Hendrikus Berkhof, "Israel as a Theological Problem in the Christian Church," *Journal of Ecumenical Studies* 6 (Summer 1969); J. Verkuyl, *Contemporary Missiology,* trans. and ed. Dale Cooper (Grand Rapids: Eerdmans, 1978), pp. 118-62.

17. For my own theory of holistic church growth, see the following: *The Church and Its Mission* (Wheaton, Ill.: Tyndale House, 1974), pp. 87-90; *The Integrity of Mission* (San Francisco: Harper & Row, 1979), pp. 37-60; *Christ Outside the Gate: Mission beyond Christendom* (Maryknoll, N.Y.: Orbis Books, 1982), pp. 43-57; "A Wholistic Concept of Church Growth," in *Exploring Church Growth,* ed. Wilbert R. Shenk (Grand Rapids: Eerdmans, 1983), pp. 95-107; "Crecimiento integral y palabra de Dios," *Misión: Revista internacional de orientación cristiana* 2 (Jan.-Mar.): 1-13.

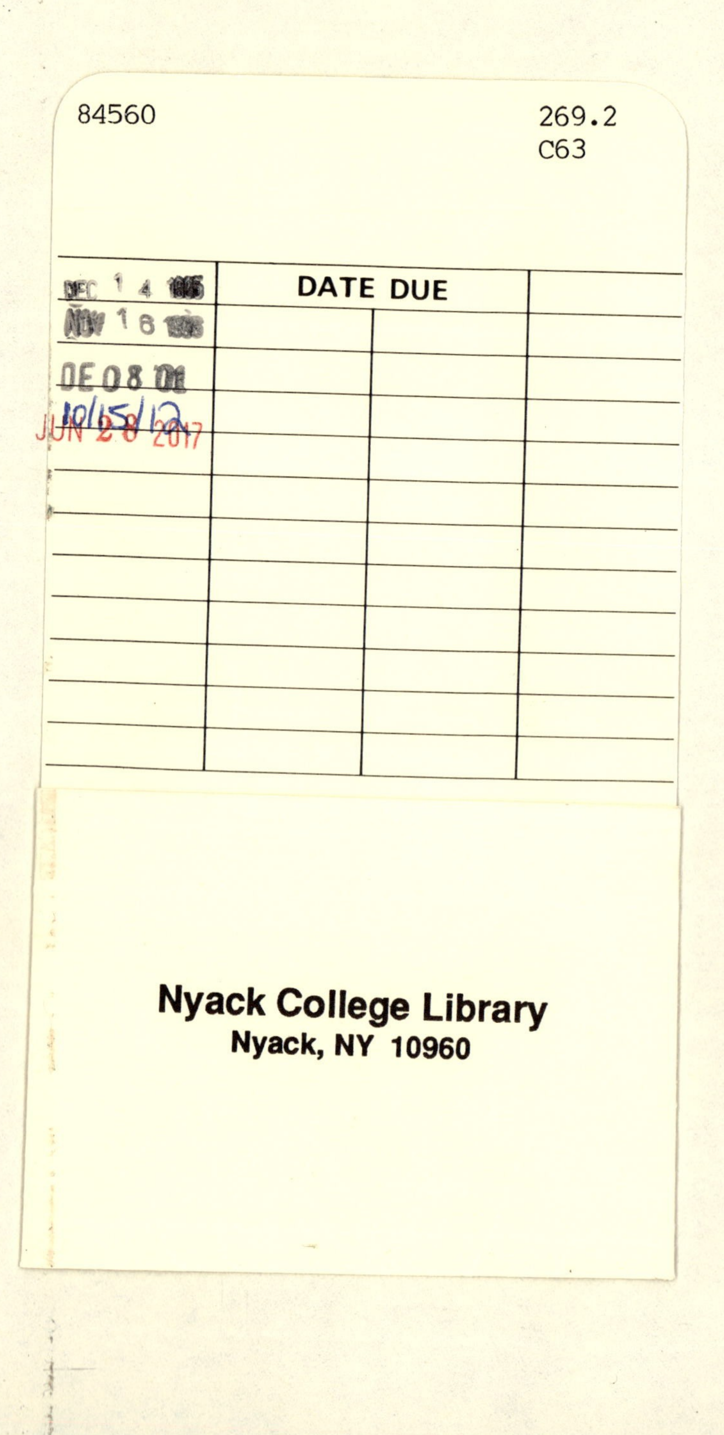